THE BOOK OF ZOPE

THE
BOOK
OF ZOPE

HOW TO BUILD
AND DELIVER
WEB APPLICATIONS

beehive

Casey Duncan, Technical Editor

An imprint of No Starch Press, Inc.

San Francisco

Printed in Canada

1 2 3 4 5 6 7 8 9 10–04 03 02 01

Co-Publishers: William Pollock and Phil Hughes
Editorial Director: Karol Jurado
Assistant Editor: Nick Hoff
Technical Editor: Casey Duncan
Cover and Interior Design: Octopod Studios

Composition: Michele O'Hagan
Copyeditor: Carol Lombardi
Proofreader: Karla Maree
Indexer: Nancy Humphreys

The Book of Zope is an English translation of *ZOPE: Content- Management- & Web-Application-Server*, the German original edition published in Germany, copyright © 2001 dpunkt.verlag GmbH. English translation prepared by Jody Byrne.

Distributed to the book trade in the United States by Publishers Group West, 1700 Fourth Street, Berkeley, CA 94710; phone: 800-788-3123 or 510-528-1444; fax: 510-528-3444.

Distributed to the book trade in Canada by Jacqueline Gross & Associates, Inc., One Atlantic Avenue, Suite 105, Toronto, Ontario M6K 3E7 Canada; phone: 416-531-6737; fax 416-531-4259.

For information on translations or book distributors outside the United States and Canada, please contact No Starch Press, Inc. directly:

No Starch Press, Inc.
555 De Haro Street, Suite 250, San Francisco, CA 94107
phone: 415-863-9900; fax: 415-863-9950; info@nostarch.com; http://www.nostarch.com

Library of Congress Cataloging-in-Publication Data

```
Zope. English.
The book of Zope / Beehive; translated by Jody Byrne.
     p. cm.
Includes index.
ISBN 1-886411-57-3 (pbk.)
1. Zope (Computer file) 2. Web site development–Computer programs. 3. Internet programming–Computer programs.
I. Beehive (Internet Service Provider)  II. Title.
TK5105.8885.Z65 Z67 2001
005.7'13769–dc21
```

                                                                                2001030347

BRIEF CONTENTS

CONTENTS IN DETAIL

PREFACE

1

ZOPE FUNDAMENTALS

2

QUICKSTART

3

NAVIGATING ZOPE

4

DTML

5

WORKING WITH ZOPE VERSIONS

6

USERS, ROLES, AND SECURITY

7

LOCAL ROLES AND PERMISSIONS

8

SOME METHODS FOR THE ROLE.PY AND USER.PY MODULES

9

ZCLASSES

10

WORKING WITH THE ZCLASS

11
THE ZCATALOG

12
ZOPE AND MYSQL

13

PROGRAMMING ZOPE: PYTHON IN A JIFFY

14

SCRIPTING ZOPE WITH PYTHON

15

ZOPE PRODUCTS

16

DEBUGGING

17

EXTERNAL DATA ACCESS

A

DTML AND BUILT-IN ATTRIBUTES

B

THE REQUEST OBJECT

C

SOURCE CODE FOR THE WEBSITE PRODUCT

PREFACE

Who Is This Book For?

We have designed this book as an introduction to Zope for beginners, and as a more complete reference for experienced users. We hope that it makes getting to know Zope much easier for you and that it will form the basis for your productive work with Zope. The following will be both beneficial and important, especially for later chapters:

- HTML knowledge is helpful.
- Python knowledge is necessary for later chapters.

This book stems from our Zope documentation (marketed as E-Books in English and German throughout the world—visit www.beehive.de for more information). The E-Books deal only with individual aspects of Zope, but this book will describe and explain all of the fundamental characteristics and technologies of the Zope system.

What Version of Zope Does It Cover?

This book deals with versions of Zope through version 2.3. As such, we recommend you start with Zope version 2.3 or earlier and use this book as your guide. You should install the latest version of Zope only after you have mastered the basics of Zope covered in this book.

As newer versions of Zope are released, we will add to and update this book by posting additional and reworked chapters at www.beehive.de/zope/books/theBookofZope.html.

(This update concept has proved to be a great success with our electronic books on Zope and an effective way of bridging the gap until the next edition is published.)

We welcome your comments or suggestions. Just mail us at zopebook@nostarch.com. We will endeavor to include your suggestions in the online updates and in future editions.

How to Use This Book

Depending on your level of experience, you can work through this book in any of the following ways.

Zope Beginners with HTML Knowledge

Once you have completed Chapters 1 through 8, be sure to have a Python book close at hand to give yourself the Python knowledge necessary for Chapter 9.

Zope Beginners with Both HTML and Python Knowledge

You can work through the book on your own from beginning to end.

Advanced Zope Users with No Prior Knowledge of Python

If you already have some experience with DTML, you can begin with Chapter 4 or 5. You will, however, need Python knowledge for Chapter 9.

Advanced Zope Users with Prior Knowledge of Python

You can start using the book from Chapter 4 or 5. Chapter 11 requires no previous knowledge and can be read at any time. Once you have worked through the book at your own pace, you can then use the individual chapters and appendices as reference material during your continued work with Zope.

Where Did Zope Come From?

The idea for Zope arose from software developer Jim Fulton, after he presented a CGI programming course. Jim, who is a huge fan of object-oriented software, found CGI programming extremely impractical because the programs were seriously lacking in their ability to build on each other. This often resulted in a lot of code being forgotten or rewritten unnecessarily.

Jim wanted to create modules that could be used over and over again, regardless of the type of web application he wanted to develop. To that end, he designed a number of software modules for his employer, Digital Creations, including "Bobo" and later "Document Template" (which is particularly well loved among Python programmers).

Digital Creations used Bobo and Document Template, together with other unreleased modules, as the basis for their consulting and development projects.

This combination of self-designed, freely available modules and commercial modules was marketed by DC as Principia.

The investment banker Hadar Pedhazur, a user of both Python and the freely available Digital Creations software Bobo, liked Digital Creations and began speaking with its chief executive, Paul Everitt, about investing in the company. He convinced the Digital Creations stockholders to market Principia as open source software to guarantee the quickest market penetration possible. Indeed, market penetration and awareness were the biggest problems for Principia, because Digital Creations had neither the marketing budget nor the high profile of other manufacturers of web application servers such as Apple (Web Objects) or Allaire (Cold Fusion).

Another reason for making Digital Creations' web application server open source was that the revenues from software licensing would be negligible compared with the revenues from providing solutions based on Principia. In other words, the more Principia users who changed to Zope as a result of the open source license, the more positive the effects on Digital Creations' main source of income: consulting and solutions development.

Once the decision was made to take Principia down the road to open source, it was time to find a new name for this open source platform. Eventually, the company chose the name Zope, which stands for "Z Object Publishing Environment."

About the Authors

Enough about Zope and this book, it's time to introduce ourselves. We all have something in common beyond our enthusiasm for Zope: We all work for the same Berlin and Washington, D.C.-based company, Beehive, L.L.C., which has been providing Zope solutions for many years. The following "bees" lent their authoring skills to this book: Katrin Kirchner, Martina Brockmann, Nico Grubert, Mark Pratt, Sebastian Luehnsdorf, and Alexander Schad.

Special reference should be made to the work of Katrin Kirchner, Martina Brockmann, and Nico Grubert. Not only did they write the vast majority of this book but, through their electronic books (E-Books) and training courses held throughout Germany, they have also helped hundreds of developers join the Zope community. These training courses are also available through our Washington, D.C., office.

We at beehive would like to thank the staff of dpunkt.verlag and especially René Schönfeldt, who was always there for us with suggestions and constructive criticism regarding how we could improve this book.

1

ZOPE FUNDAMENTALS

This chapter introduces ways of using Zope for web development and as a web application and content manager server. The second half of the chapter takes you through installing Zope under the various operating systems.

1.1 Web Applications

The World Wide Web is no longer merely a collection of static web pages, but is increasingly becoming a transport medium for many services that blur the lines between content and software. Examples include knowledge databases and Internet search engines, as well as entirely new software categories such as content management systems (for managing and publishing content to websites or intranet sites); community portal systems (which allow Internet communities to create and exchange content); and weblogs (news systems, usually featuring discussion forums, such as slashdot.org).

These software systems are referred to as *web applications* because they require only a web browser for access and no additional software. They are typically relatively easy to use.

As the demands placed on these web applications have become increasingly complex, programmers have hit the boundaries of what can be done with traditional CGI (common gateway interface) programming, thus creating a demand for suitable alternatives. And, because web programmers have no interest in using web applications that work with CGI scripts to implement recurring basic systems (such as user authentication and authorization applications for ecommerce or community portals), they are turning to systems such as Cold Fusion, PHP 3 and 4, and Zope to provide these basic services and make software development easier.

1.1.1 The Advantages of Zope for Web Application Programmers

Zope has a lot to offer web application programmers:

- Zope is entirely object-oriented.
- Zope contains an integrated object-oriented database and a webserver.
- Zope is transaction-oriented and allows users to do things like undo actions and so on.
- Thanks to database adapters (DAs), Zope can be connected to relational databases such as Oracle, Sybase, Postgres, MySQL, and Interbase.
- Zope's extremely flexible open source license allows developers to use Zope for both their own projects and customer projects without any restriction or license fees.
- The Zope community makes available hundreds of applications just for Zope (known as Zope Products), which can be easily implemented by users with no programming knowledge using Zope's integrated web management system.
- Zope's scripting language, DTML, and ZClasses let you program Zope systems via the Web using only your web browser.
- Thanks to Python's object-oriented structure, hundreds of available modules can be integrated into Zope to allow you to perform specialized tasks, such as creating reports in PDF format.

1.2 Zope As a Web Application Server

A web application server functions as the bridge (middleware) among the browser, the developer's software application, and a database.

As the boundaries between websites and web applications disappear, it is more important for integrated teams of software, database, and interface developers to establish a common basis for their work. The Zope web application provides this basis, allowing you to mix HTML, DTML, SQL, Python, and eventually even Perl Code into Zope as desired.

In addition, Zope's own scripting language, DTML, can be used to access a vast array of functions and to perform complex actions and templating with just a few lines of code. For example, to allow a group of users (subscribers, for instance) to view content different from what the "ordinary" web visitor sees, you can use Zope's integrated authentication system (see Chapter 5) to see whether the user logging in belongs to a particular user role or has any special security permissions.

1.2.1 Content-by-Role

We at Beehive call this ability to let different user types view different content *content-by-role*. This is a fundamental function of content management systems used, for example, to provide editors with different permissions or menu options than those available to freelance journalists.

1.2.2 SQL = Structured Query Language

SQL, the Structured Query Language for databases, can also be used directly in Zope (provided a suitable *database adapter* (DA) has been compiled beforehand). This feature allows database developers to decide how much program logic to store in the database and how much to store in the Zope server.

1.2.3 Python

Because Zope is mainly written using Python, it can communicate relatively easily with Python modules or programs. This feature gives Zope programmers instant access to hundreds of program modules that make it easy, for instance, to create PDF or graphics files.

1.3 Zope As a Content Management Server

Many organizations want the ability to structure the content on their websites to make it possible for a broad spectrum of users to input and maintain content. Although web design tools such as Microsoft FrontPage and Adobe GoLive can serve this purpose, they are really better suited for professional designers. People who only occasionally enter a press release or a special offer into the Web site may find them difficult to use.

In contrast to other web application servers, Zope offers a basic content management system as its web administration screen, and many of the functions of *content management systems* (CMS) are already integrated in Zope. An experienced Zope programmer can use Zope to quickly build a customized CMS that, for example, displays selected Zope functions to users. Other functionality, such as staging or workflows, can be programmed later if necessary.

1.3.1 Open Source Software

Zope differs significantly from commercial products. For one thing, nobody claims that Zope is a product that you simply unpack, press a button, and have running with a mouse click. In fact, to date there is no such thing as a ready-to-go, straight out-of-the-box CMS solution.

Two of Zope's major benefits in comparison with other content management systems are the facts that it is object-oriented and that it is open source software. As object-oriented software, knowledge developed within an organization for a CMS can be quickly used to develop a portal or extranet. Because it is open source software, Zope is free—and its source code is also available to you, for free. As such, Zope has a good chance of becoming "the people's CMS" because employees do not need to consult a purchasing department or be allocated a budget in order to use Zope. What's more, you needn't depend on a vendor or risk the chance that Zope will cease to be available because the manufacturer goes bankrupt. Zope will always be available and can be distributed by anyone, according to its open source Zope Public License (ZPL). Also, as a direct result of this license, users are free to modify or extend Zope itself to best fit their own needs.

1.4 Technical Requirements

There are virtually no barriers to installing Zope (which has contributed to the breathtaking increase in the number of Zope users). The file download for Windows is currently only 5 MB, and the Unix version, at 3 MB, is even less. Linux users, check your package index to see whether Zope is already on your distribution's CD or DVD; it's included with Red Hat and SuSE Linux and likely others.

1.4.1 Hardware Requirements

Compared to other commercial web application servers, Zope's hardware requirements are quite modest. A Pentium-II computer with 128-MB RAM is sufficient for development. Using this hardware configuration, Zope will even run under Windows 95, 98, and so on, without any problems. Also, given that Zope comes with its own webserver and object database, you don't need to install any other software. (You may, however, want to try some of the more than 250 Zope products available for Zope because they provide you with new ideas and examples to learn from.) You can also develop Zope products on a Windows computer and then install them on a Linux computer without any problems.

1.5 Installation

This section takes you through installing Zope under various operating systems.

1.5.1 Windows

To install Zope on a Windows machine, you will need the Zope installation file for Windows (for example, Zope-2.3.2-win32-x86.exe).

Once you have saved the file to your hard drive, click on it in Windows Explorer or open the Start menu and select Run... to start the setup program. The setup program is almost entirely automatic, and you will need to enter only a small amount of information.

First off, enter a name for your Zope installation, as shown in Figure 1-1.

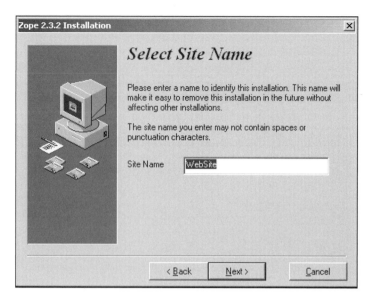

Figure 1-1: Specify a name for your Zope installation

Now select the directory where you want to install Zope (see Figure 1-2).

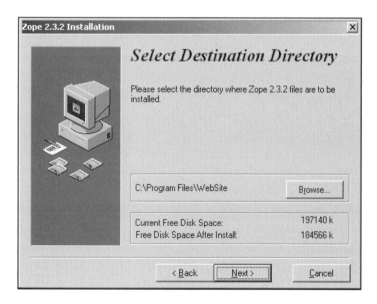

Figure 1-2: Select the destination directory

You are then asked to enter an initial manager name and password (see Figure 1-3). Write down this name and password, because you'll need them before you can work with Zope.

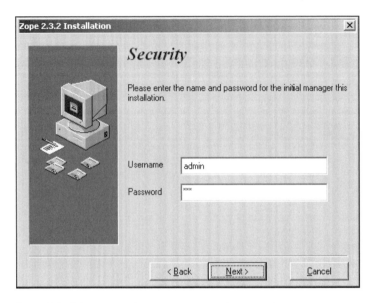

Figure 1-3: Select an initial manager name and password

1.5.2 Windows NT

Under Windows NT or 2000, you have the option of running Zope as a service, meaning that the Zope server will start up automatically when Windows starts so you don't have to start it manually. To set this option, click on Run as Win32 service.

1.5.2.1 The Zope Service

If you are not using Windows NT or 2000, or you decide not to run the Zope server as a service, you will need to start the server manually by running the start.bat file in the Zope directory. To do so, click on the file in Windows Explorer or open the Start menu, choose Run…, and type in the filename.

Once you have started the Zope server, you can begin working with Zope. To do so, simply open your web browser. By default, you access the Zope server using the following URL:

```
http://localhost:8080
```

When you go to this URL, the Start screen appears as shown in Figure 1-4.

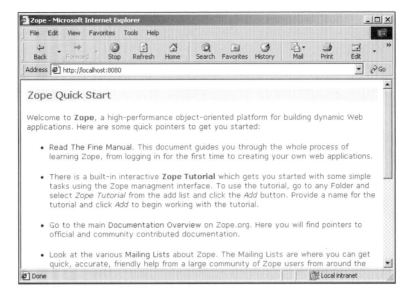

Figure 1-4: Zope welcome screen

1.5.3 Linux

Installing Zope on a machine running Linux is slightly more complicated than the Windows installation.

1.5.3.1 Python 1.5.2 or Higher

Before you begin the installation process, make sure you have Python version 1.5.2 or higher installed on your machine. If not, you must install it before you proceed.

NOTE *For the purposes of our own test installation, we used a SuSE Linux 6.4 server. The procedure for installing Zope is the same under Red Hat.*

1. Log on as root and, in the directory /usr/local/, create the directory ZopePark as shown below. (We will use this directory later to contain our Zope installation.)

```
mkdir ZopePark
```

2. Download the archive Zope-2.3.0-src.tgz (or the most current version) and copy it to the directory /usr/local/ZopePark/.

3. Change to the directory ZopePark by entering the following:

```
cd /usr/local/ZopePark/
```

4. Unpack the archive Zope-2.3.0-src.tgz as follows, using the number of the version you've downloaded:

```
tar xvzf Zope-2.3.0-src.tgz
```

This creates a directory called Zope-2.3.0-src in the directory /usr/local/
ZopePark/. The files and subdirectories contained in the archive are unpacked
into this directory.

5.   Change the name of the directory Zope-2.3.0-src to your desired webserver.
     We will call ours Testserver, and thus type:

```
mv Zope-2.3.0-src/ Testserver
```

NOTE   *Zope comes with a separate webserver called ZServer, which allows you to run the Zope server as an independent webserver. (This means you don't have to use another webserver, like Apache webserver.)*

1.5.3.2 Compiling the ZServer
Now compile the ZServer. To do so, open the directory /usr/local/ZopePark/
Testserver and enter the following at the prompt:

```
python wo_pcgi.py
```

The Python modules will now be compiled.

NOTE   *The option "wo" stands for "without" pcgi-wrapper; the compilation takes place without the pcgi-wrapper. If you are installing a version of Zope earlier than version 2.2.0, the modules are compiled with the pcgi-wrapper (python w_pcgi.py).*

Once the modules have been compiled, the following text appears:

```
creating default inituser file
Note:
        The initial user name and password are 'admin'
        and '3JTWrAVb'.

        You can change the name and password through the Web
        interface or using the 'zpasswd.py' script.

chmod 0600 /usr/local/scratch/Zope/Zope-2.3.0-src/inituser
```

Done!

1.5.3.3 Changing the Initial Manager Name and Password

Write down the initial manager name and password! To change them, enter the following:

```
python zpasswd.py access
```

Then enter your new username and password:

```
Username: admin
Password: 12345
Verify password: 12345
```

To later access the Zope server using your web browser, you will need to enter your username and password as shown in Figure 1-5.

Figure 1-5: The Zope log-in window

1.5.3.4 Password Encryption

Once you have specified a username and password, the screen will ask you to specify a format for encrypting your password, as follows:

```
Please choose a format from:
SHA - SHA-1 hashed password
CRYPT - UNIX-style crypt password
CLEARTEXT - no protection.
Encoding: SHA
```

We'll select the format "SHA," which provides the best security.

Next, the Domain Restrictions query appears. For this option, you can specify a domain from which you can have direct access to the Zope Management screen. Leave this option blank (to allow access from all domains) and press RETURN.

```
Domain restrictions:
```

Give the "root" user access to all files in the /Testserver directory.

1.5.3.5 Access Permissions
Change to the directory /usr/local/ZopePark and enter the following:

```
chown -R root.root Testserver
```

The var and access directories must be given different access permissions. Change to the Testserver directory and enter the following:

```
chown -R nobody.nogroup var
chown -R nobody.nogroup access
```

The ZServer is started and stopped using a start script called start and a stop script called stop. These scripts are located in the Testserver directory.

1.5.3.6 Assign IP Addresses
You now need to assign an IP address to the Zserver, because you will no doubt want to access your Zope server using a specific WWW address at a later stage (for example, www.mycompany.com). To do this, either you or your ISP will need to enter this WWW address and the associated IP address in the name server entries.

For example, assume our web address is www.mycompany.com and our allocated IP address is 212.11.222.333. To assign this IP address to the ZServer, you'll need to make a number of changes to the start script, as discussed below.

Start Script
The start script should look like this at present:

```
#! /bin/sh
reldir=`dirname $0`
PYTHONHOME=`cd $reldir; pwd`
Export PYTHONHOME
Exec /usr/bin/python \
    $PYTHONHOME/z2.py \
    -D "$@"
```

Change this source code as follows:

```
#! /bin/sh
reldir=`dirname $0`
PYTHONHOME=`cd $reldir; pwd`
Export PYTHONHOME
Exec /usr/bin/python \
    $PYTHONHOME/z2.py \
    -D "$@" -a 212.11.222.333 -f 8021 -u nobody -w 8080 -m -
```

The following table explains the individual options:

Option	Description
–a 212.11.222.333	IP Address = 212.11.222.333
–f 8021	FTP to Port 8021
–u nobody	Username = nobody
–w 8080	HTTP Server on Port 8080
–m	Monitor Server is switched off

(For further information on the individual options, see the file z2.py in your Zope server directory.)

Now change to the /Testserver directory and start the ZServer using the following command:

```
./start &
```

The following information should now appear on your screen:

```
[1] 3001
root@linuxserver:/usr/local/ZopePark/Testserver > ──
2001-08-30T12:46:28 INFO(0) ZServer Medusa (V1.16.4.2) started at Wed Aug 30
14:46:28 2001
        Hostname: linuxserver.mycompany.com
        Port:8080

────
2001-08-30T12:46:28 INFO(0) ZServer FTP server started at Wed Aug 30 14:46:28 2001
        Authorizer:None
        Hostname: linuxserver
        Port: 8021
```

NOTE *The name "linuxserver" is the name of your Linux server.*

You can now start your web browser and access the Zope server by entering the following URL:

```
http://linuxserver.mycompany.com:8080
```

at which point the screen shown in Figure 1-4 should appear. Click the management screen link for the log-in screen shown in Figure 1-1.

Alternatively, you can enter:

```
http://linuxserver.mycompany.com:8080/manage
```

to directly access the log-in window and bypass the "Welcome to Zope" screen.

You have now installed a Zope server on your computer and, depending on the type of installation, you can access it via the Web or only through the local network.

Summary

Now that we've introduced you to some of Zope's potential as both a content management system and as a web application server—and now that you know how to install Zope on your system—let's begin working with Zope. Chapter 2 will explore the different parts of the Zope Management screen as well as how to create, edit, and delete objects in Zope.

2

QUICKSTART

This chapter gives you the basics you need to begin developing Zope applications. We'll introduce you to Zope's management interface and components, which will familiarize you with the Zope features you'll use as you work through future chapters.

Zope is closely linked to object-oriented programming, so we'll take a brief look at the principles of object-oriented programming as they relate to Zope. At the same time, we'll introduce you to the most important Zope objects, such as DTML documents and methods, and show you how to work with them. Various examples will help you synthesize these new techniques, after which you'll have a chance to try them yourself.

By the end of this chapter, you should be familiar with the basic Zope functions and the most important Zope objects. Once you have finished this chapter's tutorials, you should be ready to put Zope to use.

2.1 Preparations

Once you've installed Zope on your server, you'll need to change a number of settings to begin working with it.

1. If the Zope server is not already started, start it with start.bat under Windows or by running the start script under Linux.

2. Open your web browser and enter the URL for the Zope server. The example in Figure 2-1 shows a local installation on a networked Windows NT machine.

Once the Zope server starts, the screen shown in Figure 2-1 appears.

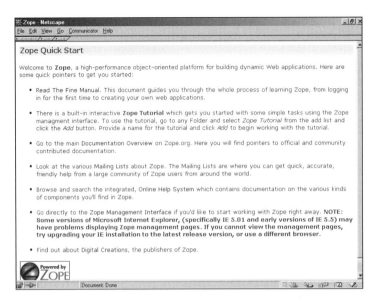

Figure 2-1: The Zope welcome screen

Begin by reading the sections below for an overview of Zope and its functions or visit the Zope Corporation support (www.digicool.com) area for up-to-date information. Or, if you prefer, go directly to the management screen to begin working by clicking on the management screen link.

NOTE *To skip this welcome screen in the future and go directly to the management screen, enter* http://localhost:8080/manage. *Enter the name and password you specified during installation (see Chapter 1 installation instructions for your system) to log on.*

You should now be in management view.

NOTE *If you are using Internet Explorer 5 (or higher) and are unable to view the management screen as shown, your version of IE may have an authentication bug. Upgrade to the latest version of IE to correct the problem.*

2.1.1 Creating a User Account

Before looking at the management screen, create a user account for yourself, as described below. (For more information on users, roles, and permissions, see Chapters 6 and 7.)

1. Click the link acl_users (User Folder); the screen in Figure 2-2 appears.

□ ⌷ acl_users (User Folder)

Figure 2-2: Click the link to open a user overview screen

2. Click Add on the next screen.

3. Enter a username for yourself; we'll use User1, so enter it now (see Figure 2-3). Enter a password and confirm it in the Confirm field.

NOTE *Both the username and password are case-sensitive in Zope, so be sure to watch your capitalization.*

4. Select Manager in the Roles field to create a user with access to all Zope functions (you can ignore the Domain field), then click Add to create the new user.

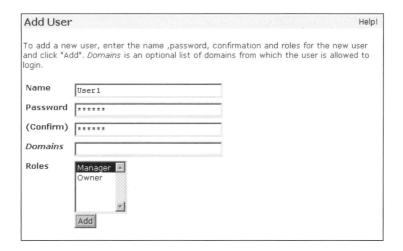

Figure 2-3: Adding a user

You have just created a new user whose name should appear in the user list as "User1."

2.2 Zope's Interface: The Management Screen

The management screen serves as Zope server's user interface. Let's have a look at how it works.

Log in as User1 by closing and restarting your browser, entering the URL for your Zope server, and logging in as User1. The management screen should appear as shown in Figure 2-4.

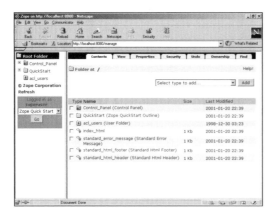

Figure 2-4: The management screen

The management screen consists of left and right frames.

2.2.1 The Left Frame of the Management Screen

The left frame of the management screen (Figure 2-5) shows a hierarchical view of all folders and other container objects on the Zope server (see section 2.3). To quickly navigate through them, click a folder to list its objects in the right-hand frame. Click the plus and minus icons next to the folders in the left frame to expand or collapse the view of the object hierarchy.

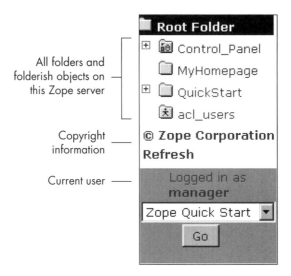

Figure 2-5: The left frame of the management screen (current user information appears in the top frame by default)

- The © Zope Corporation link takes you to the Zope copyright page, the Zope and Python licenses, and the Zope credits.

- Click Refresh at any time to update the left frame; this function is particularly useful if you've been working on the server for a while and have created or deleted objects.

- The name of the current Zope server user, User1, appears at the bottom of the left frame.

2.2.2 The Right Frame of the Management Screen

The tabs at the top of the right frame of the management window (Figure 2-6) give you access to the various management pages or views of the currently selected object. For example, from here you can edit the object's contents or properties, locate other objects with Find, or even undo certain actions (see Chapter 3).

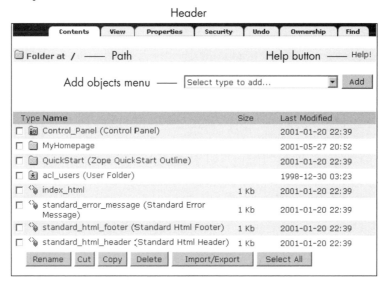

Figure 2-6: The right frame of the management window

- The complete path for the object you are working on appears directly beneath the tab bar. Click the links in the path to move up the folder hierarchy.

- The Add Objects menu, found only on the Contents View tab, lets you create various Zope objects.

- Help buttons within views link to help text, which contains additional information related to the functions in the current view.

2.3   Zope Objects

Let's take a closer look at Zope's object-oriented approach as well as individual Zope objects such as DTML methods and documents, folders, external methods, and so on. As we do, you'll become familiar with each object's functions and their relationships to each other. Then we'll show you how to create your own objects; use them to perform various tasks; and how to copy, delete, and rename folders and other objects.

2.3.1   Zope and Object-Oriented Programming

Zope's most important underpinning is *object-oriented programming.*

NOTE   *You can skip this section and still get satisfactory results. However, to take full advantage of all of Zope's benefits and gain a complete understanding of how it works, we strongly recommend that you read it.*

The object-oriented philosophy is based on the fact that the world consists of discrete objects. An object is a real-world thing, with a status and the ability to perform actions and communicate with other objects. In a programming language, we can represent any individual real-world thing—be it a table, a house, or a car— as an object with properties.

For example, imagine a spaceship called the *USS Le Chuck,* with a maximum crew of 120, 20 cargo bays, and a maximum speed of warp factor 9.6. The crew, the cargo, the speed, and the ship's name define the spaceship's state. But our spaceship must also perform actions, such as picking up crew, travelling through space, transporting freight, avoiding other spacecraft, and communicating with other spacecraft to perform avoidance maneuvers. How do we account for this information in a programming language?

2.3.1.1   Methods and Attributes

From a programming perspective, the spaceship's state corresponds to the *attributes* or *properties* of an object; the spaceship's actions are implemented in *methods.* For example, our spaceship has the attributes *name, crew, cargo,* and *speed,* which each have specific values. If the spaceship has a full crew complement, the attribute crew will have the value 120, and the value for the attribute name is *USS Le Chuck.*

Because a spacecraft must be able to carry out certain functions, the appropriate methods must be implemented for it to function properly. We might write these methods or actions as pickCrewUp, fly, transportFreight, and avoidCraft. Together, the attributes and their values, as well as the implemented methods, define the spaceship object. An object is, therefore, defined by its attributes and methods.

An object is determined by what it knows and what it can do. For example, the *USS Le Chuck* knows how many crew members are on board, its speed, and how many of its cargo bays are full. In addition, it can carry out the actions specified by its methods.

2.3.1.2 Classes

Now imagine that the real *USS Le Chuck* meets a similar spaceship, the *USS Largo*. The *Largo* is smaller, has fewer crew members, and its maximum speed is less than the *Le Chuck's*. The ships communicate with each other, and the smaller ship begins an evasive maneuver.

Despite the differences between the two crafts, both are spaceships with identical capabilities, such as the ability to perform evasive maneuvers, pick up crew, and so on; they differ only in their characteristics, namely size and maximum speed. Were you to check the attributes and implemented methods of the *USS Largo,* you would find that, apart from the specific attribute values, they match those of the *USS Le Chuck.* Because the objects can both carry out the same actions, we say that they belong to the same *class*. A class describes all objects that have the same methods and attributes.

2.3.1.3 Objects

An object is derived from a class and is built according to the properties of a class. *Deriving* is analogous to manufacturing an object in the real world according to certain specifications. Similarly, a class is the plan or specification according to which the associated objects are created. If, for example, you want to create a spaceship, you first derive an object from the spaceship class, then assign various attribute values to the objects to differentiate them from each other.

When working with Zope, you will almost exclusively be working with objects. For example, you can create folders that are like file directories by deriving a folder object from the class that defines the attributes and methods for folders. When you do so, you then assign a name to the object and any other attribute or property values it requires. The same applies to everything you create in Zope; you derive objects from classes and then change the object's attributes.

The following sections show you how to use the fundamental Zope objects and their most important functions. Step-by-step examples let you practice what you learn.

2.3.2 *Creating a Folder*

A *folder* is an object that, like a directory, can contain other objects. Objects that are not standard Zope folders but that can contain other objects are considered *folderish* objects (for example, User Folders). Folderish object classes are common components of products (discussed in Chapter 12). Although you generally need not define these folderish object classes yourself (given that they are installed automatically with a product), you can create your own custom folderish Zope objects using ZClasses (see Chapters 9 and 10 for more information) or by constructing a Python class in an external Zope product.

To create a standard folder, go to the folder where the new folder is to be located. Select Folder from the Add Objects menu and then enter the following information in the form that appears (see Figure 2-7).

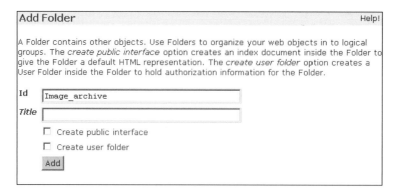

Figure 2-7: Creating a folder

Id: Objects are identified in Zope using its id or name. Each id must be unique within the folder; an error message will appear if you try to enter an id that already exists in the current folder. For the sake of this overview, we'll begin the id of a folder with an uppercase letter.

Title: This field is optional. Enter a title here to provide a more detailed description of a folder to help to distinguish it from other folders.

Create Public Interface: If you select this check box, a DTML document called index_html is created in the new folder. (DTML documents are explained in Section 2.3.4.) The object index_html is opened by default when a user enters the URL in a browser for the folder that contains the object. If the folder lacks an index_html object and its URL is viewed, Zope will attempt to find an index_html object in a higher level folder using a process called acquisition (see section 2.5 for more information). If you choose not to select this option now, you can always add an index_html object to the folder manually at a later time.

Create User Folder: Selecting this check box creates a user folder, within which you can define localized users who have access permissions only for this folder and its subordinate objects. As with the above, you can add a user folder manually later on if you choose not to select this option when the folder is created. (See Chapter 7, "Users.")

2.3.2.1 Example: Creating an Image Archive

To create an image archive, you create an empty folder for storing image files as follows:

1. Create a folder with the id Image_archive in the Zope root folder by opening the Add Objects menu and selecting Folder (Figure 2-8), then entering the appropriate information on the configuration form. Leave the check boxes blank.

Figure 2-8: The Available-Objects menu is opened, and Folder is selected

2. Enter the id in the form (see Figure 2-7).

3. Click Add to confirm the information and create the folder.

4. When you click on the new folder to open it, you will find it empty, as shown in Figure 2-9. Because we have not selected either of the check boxes on the configuration form shown in Figure 2-8, we have created a folder with no objects.

Figure 2-9: Contents of the image archive folder

2.3.2.2 Assigning Objects to Folders

All objects contained in a folder, such as images in an image archive, are assigned to that folder; and, in fact, these objects become attributes of their containing folder. If a folder contains additional folders, those folders are, in turn, assigned to the superordinate folders.

Objects that do not appear to be assigned to any other object are, in fact, assigned to the root folder. The root folder stores all Zope server objects, including all folderish and nonfolderish objects. (To find out precisely what the assignment of objects to folders means, see section 2.5, "Acquisition and Standard Objects.")

Let's have a look at how to create and use some other standard Zope objects.

2.3.3 *Creating Files*

Before you can call images or other file types from within a DTML document or method, you must first create them on the Zope server. To create image objects, open the Add Objects menu and select Image; for all other types of files, including audio, text, or video, select the File object.

You must complete the configuration form (Figure 2-10) for each object regardless of whether you want to insert a file or image. Image objects, however, have two additional properties—height and width measurements—which can be modified if necessary.

These are the basic properties of the configuration form:

Id   The Zope internal object identifier.

Title   An optional title for the object.

File   Enter the full path and filename for the file containing the data for the file or image object, or a blank object will be created.

Browse Use this button to browse to your desired file. To insert the object, click the Add button.

2.3.3.1 Example: Adding an Image

Let's insert an image object from an image file stored on your hard disk with the id image1 and a suitable title (the title is used to generate the alt tag for the image). In this example, we'll use the picture man.gif.

1. Select Image from the Add Objects menu.

2. Specify an id and title; then choose the file you want to use either by entering its full path and filename or by browsing to it, as shown in Figure 2-11.

Figure 2-10: The file configuration form

3. The image has now been added, and it appears in the Contents view for Folder 1, as shown in Figure 2-12. Click the image object in the Contents view to see the image properties, which include width and height.

Figure 2-11: Adding an image

4. Click View on the tab bar to display your image. Our image sample looks like Figure 2-13.

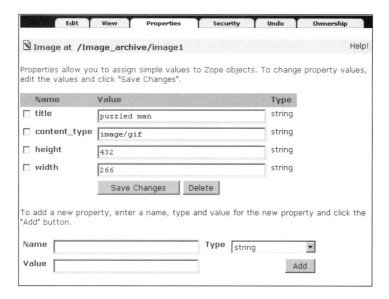

Figure 2-12: This link opens up the properties for image1

To change the size of the image, click Properties on the tab bar to get to the Properties view. To change the size of the displayed image, simply change the values for width and height and click Save.

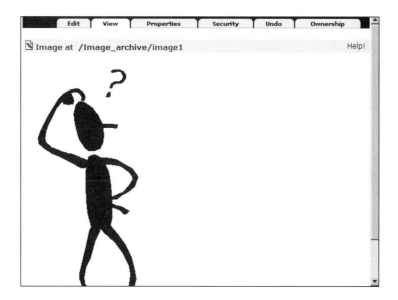

Figure 2-13: Image1 displayed at full size

2.3.4 DTML Documents and Methods

Now that you know how to insert images and other files into your Zope server, let's look at DTML methods and DTML documents, two of the most important Zope objects. Though somewhat similar, they differ greatly in the way they are used and how they work.

One drawback to HTML is that it does not work with dynamic content. DTML (the acronym for Zope's Document Template Markup Language), on the other hand, lets you dynamically program web pages and thus work around this disadvantage in HTML. You can use DTML code in both *DTML documents* and *DTML methods.*

DTML documents can be used to store text, complex documents, or any other content, such as information that you might use as content in your website. They are roughly analogous to a web page. DTML methods carry out actions on your data or content (for example, working with external methods or creating dynamic content). They can also be used to modularize complex dynamic web pages into simple components, each of which is a single DTML method; a separate DTML method or document then assembles these pieces into a web page.

The most important difference between DTML methods and documents is that DTML documents can have their own properties, whereas DTML methods cannot; DTML methods assume the properties of the superordinate folder or the object they are called from instead. For example, consider the following directory structure:

```
/Folder1/Subfolder
```

Upon opening Subfolder, you would find the DTML method method1 and the DTML document document1. To display the id for each object, enter the line

```
<dtml-var name="id">
```

into the document. This will work for the DTML document, and your browser should display the id "document" at the upper left side of its screen.

This is not quite the case with the DTML method; the id displayed on the screen reads "Subfolder." This result is unexpected, but it is nonetheless correct because method1 has no properties of its own. Instead, a DTML method uses the id of the folder in which it is located (Subfolder in our example).

2.3.5 Creating a DTML Document

To create a DTML document, navigate to the folder that will hold the new document, then select DTML Document from the Available-Objects menu. Fill in the configuration form with the following information (refer back to Figure 2-11):

Id   As with folders, the id identifies the document in the Zope database. No two objects in the same folder may have the same id.

Title   You may enter a title here to provide a more detailed description of the document.

File   To insert the contents of a file on your hard disk, enter its complete path as in c:\texts\New\record.txt.

Browse   Click this button to browse to a text file on your hard disk. The path to the file you select is displayed in the File field.

Add   Click this button to create the document, thus ending the configuration process.

Add and Edit Click this button to create the new document and call up the Edit screen to begin editing the document.

2.3.5.1 Linking to a File

Say you want to create a DTML document whose content is a quotation already contained in a separate HTML file. Rather than type the quotation again, it's easier to link to the existing document. Here's how:

1. From the Add Objects menu, select DTML Document. On the configuration form, enter the id quote_dtml and a title for the document if you wish; then browse to the file containing the text you want to use (Figure 2-14). (Select any text file to follow this example.)

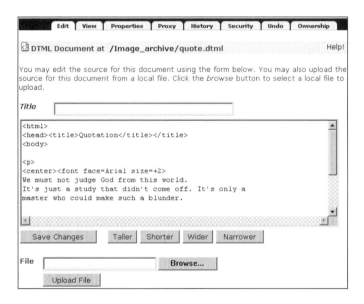

Figure 2-14: The contents of the file quote.html will be inserted into the new DTML document

2. To immediately see the Edit screen for the new document, click the Add and Edit button.

3. The Edit screen for quote_dtml now appears as shown in Figure 2-15. (The Taller, Shorter, Wider, and Narrower buttons adjust the size of your viewing area only.)

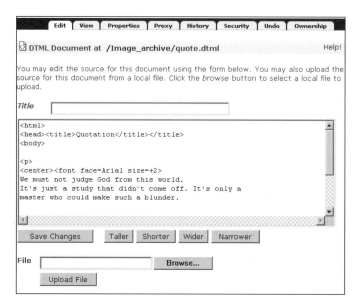

Figure 2-15: The Edit screen for quote.dtml

4. To preview the document, click View in the tab bar. The View of our sample document is shown in Figure 2-16.

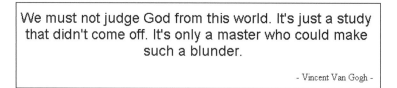

Figure 2-16: The View screen for quote.dtml

2.3.6 Creating a DTML Method

The best way to create a simple website containing your DTML document and the image object you installed earlier is to use a DTML method that defines the way in which the picture and the quote will be displayed.

Create a DTML method as follows:

1. Open the directory where you want to install the method. Select DTML Method from the Available Objects menu and fill in the configuration screen as shown in Figure 2-17; click Add and Edit.

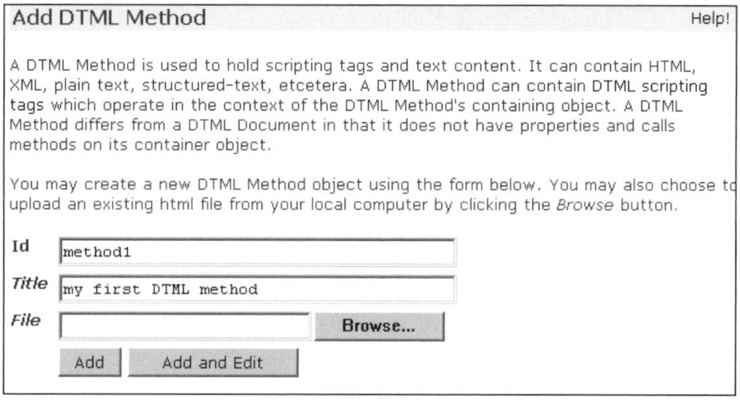

Figure 2-17: Creating a DTML method with the Id method1

2. Replace the existing source text in the Edit screen for the new method with the following, excluding the line numbers and colons:

```
1:       <dtml-var standard_html_header>
2:       <table>
3:       <tr>
4:       <td><dtml-var image1></td>
5:       <td><dtml-var quote.dtml></td>
6:       </tr>
7:       </table>
8:       <dtml-var standard_html_footer>
```

Lines 1 and 8 call two standard objects that already contain an HTML header and footer so that you do not have to enter these again. (The HTML footer ensures that the Zope logo appears at the end of the website.) Line 4 displays the image by inserting the appropriate <img> HTML tag, and line 5 retrieves the content of the DTML document and inserts it.

NOTE *The code shown above is simple DTML source code that will generate HTML when it is viewed by a web browser. (The special DTML tags are shown in boldface.) We explain this code only briefly here because DTML is fully explained in Chapter 3.*

3. Click Save Changes.

4. Click View in the tab bar to view your first Zope web page. The basic structure should match the screen shown in Figure 2-18—though, if you used your own file for this example, its appearance will differ.

We must not judge God from this world. It's just a study that didn't come off. It's only a master who could make such a blunder.

- Vincent Van Gogh -

Powered by ZOPE

Figure 2-18: Your first Zope web page

2.4 Managing Objects

Now that we've introduced you to the most important Zope objects and how to create and edit them, let's look at how to manage them by copying, moving, renaming, and so on.

2.4.1 Changing an Object Id

You can change an object id only in the Contents view of the folder containing the object you want to modify, as follows:

1. Select the object by clicking the checkbox to the left of the object's icon and click Rename.

2. Enter a new id, making sure that the id you enter is unique for that particular folder; you cannot use the same id more than once in a folder.

2.4.2 Changing an Object Title

To change the title of an object on the Edit or Properties screen for the relevant object, do the following:

1. Click the object icon or title text in the right-hand frame of the management window, then enter the new title in the Title field.

2. Click Save Changes.

For example, to change the id and title of the image object we created earlier we would:

1. Select the object and click Rename.

2. Enter a new id and click OK (see Figure 2-21).

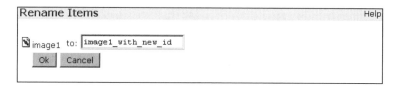

Figure 2-21: The new image id is image1_with_new_id

3. The image object now appears in the Contents view with its new id. Click it to open the Edit screen, shown in Figure 2-22.

Type	Name	Size	Last Modified
☐ ▨	image1_with_new_id (puzzled man)	2 Kb	2001-05-27 21:29

Figure 2-22: The id has been changed

4. In the Title field, enter a new title and click Save Changes, as shown in Figure 2-23.

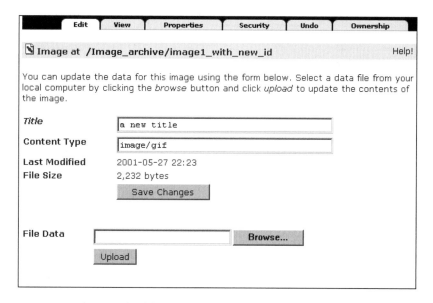

Figure 2-23: The new title of the image object should be "a new title"

Before you can try the following examples, you will need to create some more folders, methods, and documents as shown in Figure 2-24.

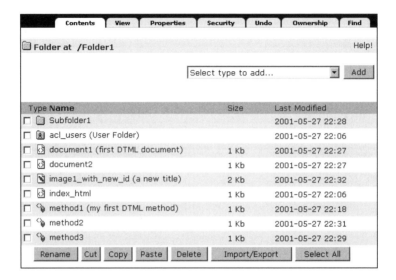

Figure 2-24: A sample folder with subfolders and other objects

2.4.3 Copying Objects

To copy objects or folders, click the checkboxes next to the objects you want to copy and click on the Copy button to copy the object to the clipboard. You can then paste the copied objects from the clipboard into target directories, either until another object is copied to the clipboard or until you exit the browser.

NOTE *For Zope's copy and paste functions to work, you must have cookies enabled in your web browser.*

Once the object has been copied, move to the target directory and paste the object or folder into it (the Paste button appears after you copy something to the clipboard). When you copy an entire folder, all its subobjects are copied along with it. If you copy an object to a folder containing an object with the same id, its id is changed to copy_of_<old Id>.

To copy objects from the example folder to Subfolder1.

1. Select the objects you want to copy (see Figure 2-25).

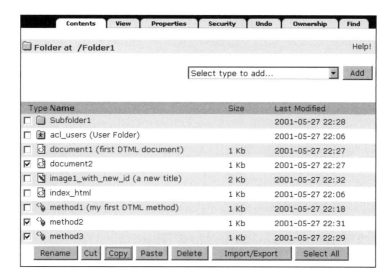

Figure 2-25: Three objects selected for copying

2. Click the Copy button and then switch to the folder Subfolder1. The Paste button appears.

3. Click Paste to insert the objects into the folder (Figure 2-26).

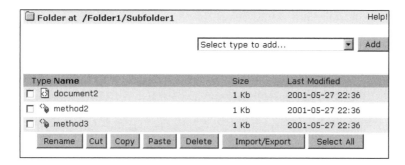

Figure 2-26: The same three objects copied to Subfolder1

2.4.4   Deleting Objects

To delete objects, click the check boxes next to the objects you wish to delete and press Delete. (You can only delete objects in the Contents view of the folder containing the object.)

NOTE   *Deleting a folder deletes all of its objects.*

2.4.5   Moving Objects

Unlike copying, when you move an object (or multiple objects) you remove it from its current directory and transfer it to another one. To move objects,

1.   Select the object or objects you want to move.

2.   Click the Cut button to remove the object from the current folder and save it to the clipboard.

3.   Change to the target folder and click Paste to insert the cut objects into the target directory.

NOTE   *Objects are not actually removed from the folder you cut them from until you actually paste them somewhere else.*

2.5   Acquisition and Standard Objects

To create an efficient information structure, Zope organizes the relationships between objects with the *acquisition* mechanism (the way objects acquire attributes from their superordinate folders). Acquisition is one of the most important and powerful mechanisms in Zope.

When you place objects in Zope's folders and subfolders, you create object hierarchies, which Zope considers complete information structures. Objects in a folder inherit the attributes (properties, methods, and other objects) of the folder that contains them. When combined with the attributes of the actual object itself, this collection of inherited attributes constitutes the context or *namespace* for every Zope server object. Objects have direct access to all attributes in their namespace.

An object's namespace includes both the attributes of its immediate parent folder and the attributes of all superordinate folders right up to the root directory. This allows attributes that are defined higher in the Zope folder hierarchy to be referenced by objects at or below these attributes without using an explicit path reference. Through acquisition, Zope is able to find attributes contained in an object's superordinate folders by name alone.

When an object attempts to call another object, it first searches its own folder for the object. If the object is not found there, it moves up the folder hierarchy, checking each folder above until it finds the correct object. (It will not search other branches of the hierarchy, however.) Thus, you can share code and data easily by placing the shared objects higher in your Zope hierarchy than the objects that call them.

NOTE   *Objects in the root folder can be accessed from all folders because they are located at the very top of the folder hierarchy.*

2.5.1 Standard Objects

As you may have noticed, the root directory contains a number of objects created upon installation of the Zope server. These *standard objects* ensure a consistent appearance for objects created using Zope, and, because they are in the root directory, they can be called by all other objects.

2.5.1.1 Standard HTML Header and Footer

For example, the standard objects standard_html_header and standard_html_footer define the header and footer in each text object and are inserted into every DTML method and document by default. The code in these files looks like that shown in Listings 2-1 and 2-2.

Listing 2-1: The standard header

```
<HTML><HEAD><TITLE><dtml-var title_or_id></TITLE></HEAD><BODY BGCOLOR="#FFFFFF">
```

Listing 2-2: The standard footer

```
<p>

<dtml-var ZopeAttributionButton>

</p>

</BODY></HTML>
```

These objects define an HTML header and footer. Both can be called at the start and end of DTML methods and documents to embed them in a basic HTML structure; they are missing only the body of the HTML document.

2.5.1.2 index_html

The method index_html defines the welcome screen from which you access the Zope management screen, among other screens. It looks like this:

```
<dtml-var standard_html_header>

<dtml-var zope_quick_start>

<dtml-var standard_html_footer>
```

NOTE *To create a new "home page" on your Zope server, you can modify this method.*

2.5.1.3 standard_error_message

The method standard_error_message is used to display Zope error messages in a uniform and consistent way. This can be modified to display error messages in any desired format.

2.5.1.4 Modifying Standard Objects

You can modify these standard objects to suit your own needs, but if you do, you must observe the acquisition mechanism. Remember that changing the contents of any methods in the root directory affects all objects that use that method.

To change only the appearance of specific objects, copy the applicable methods (see section 2.4.3), for example standard_html_header, to the folder at or above the objects you want to change, then change the copied methods. Thus, only the objects in the folder containing the changed methods (or in folders below) will be affected by the modifications; all other objects will still use the original methods.

Summary

You are now familiar with creating and manipulating objects in Zope. The next chapter will take you through Zope's tab bar and different management screens.

3

NAVIGATING ZOPE

This chapter will show you how to use the Zope tab bar to access important Zope functions, as well as the Help tabs and the Control Panel.

3.1 The Zope Tab Bar

The tab bar provides access to several interfaces you can use to configure Zope objects, specify basic settings, and so on. Its functions and tabs vary depending on the selected object and the permissions assigned to the current Zope user.

Let's have a look at the tab bar's basic functions.

3.1.1 The Contents Tab

When you click a folderish object on the management screen, the Contents view opens to display all objects in the folder together with their ids and titles, as shown in Figure 3-1.

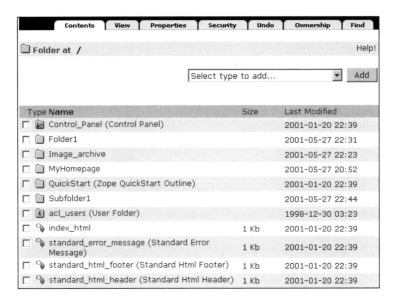

Figure 3-1: The Contents view showing all objects in the root folder

The Contents view lets you create, rename, copy, move, and delete objects using the buttons at the bottom of the screen, as follows:

Rename   Changes an object's id. See section 2.3.7, "Renaming Objects."

Cut   Moves objects. See section 2.3.10, "Moving Objects."

Copy   Copies objects. See section 2.3.8, "Copying Objects."

Paste   Pastes objects.

Delete   Deletes objects. See section 2.3.9, "Deleting Objects."

Import/Export Imports (in Zope versions later than 2.2.2) or exports an object. See section 3.1.9, "The Import/Export Tab."

Select All   Selects all objects in the folder (in Zope versions later than 2.2.2).

When you click a folderish object, its Contents view appears; when you click a nonfolderish object, the Edit screen appears. The Contents view's Add Objects menu lets you add new objects to the folder.

3.1.2   The Edit Tab and Edit Screen

You can edit nonfolderish Zope objects on the Edit screen, including the title and source text of DTML methods and documents. You cannot edit objects such as images or files, though you can change their titles and upload newer versions of the object in most cases. Other objects have different edit screens corresponding to their specific contents.

To open an object's Edit screen, click the object in the containing folder's Contents screen. Once you have the Edit screen open, you will see that the Edit tab is highlighted. If you switch from the Edit screen to another tab, you can return to the Edit screen by clicking the Edit tab. Figure 3-2 shows the Edit screen for the DTML method index_html.

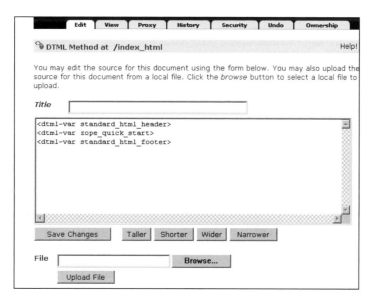

Figure 3-2: The Edit screen

You can edit the source text for the object in the text window, the size of which can be adjusted using the following four buttons:

Taller   Lengthens the text window.

Shorter   Shortens the text window.

Wider   Widens the text window.

Narrower   Narrows the text window.

The Save Changes button saves your changes. If you have changed the text or title, be sure to save your changes *before* using the buttons above to adjust the size of the text window or the changes will be lost.

Once you have your target object's Edit screen open, edit the source text in the text window (Figure 3-3) and click the Save Changes button when you are done. Provided there are no syntax errors in the code, your changes will be saved, and you will be returned to the Edit screen. If you clicked the View tab to check your changes, use the Back button in your web browser to return to the Edit screen.

```
<dtml-var standard_html_header>

<h1>Hello, <dtml-var AUTHENTICATED_USER></h1>
<p>
<h3>Hooray, the object is edited!</h3>

<dtml-var standard_html_footer>
```

Figure 3-3: Editing an object; to view your changes, click the View tab (see Figure 3-4)

Figure 3-4: View of the edited file index_html

3.1.3 The View Tab

The View tab, available on any object that can be viewed through a web browser, lets you preview any modifications you make to an object. When you click the View tab on a nonfolderish object such as a DTML method, the edited object is displayed just as it would be to a visitor to the web page.

When you click the View tab on the Contents screen of a folderish object, Zope attempts to display index_html. If index_html is not found in the current folder, Zope displays the next available index_html object, based on the acquisition rules. The acquisitions rules tell Zope to look in the parent folder if an object is not in the current one; if the object is not found there, to continue searching up the folder hierarchy. As a result, if the index_html object is contained only in the Zope root folder, the View tab will show it in every subfolder.

3.1.4 The Ownership Tab

All Zope objects, with the exception of the Control Panel and the root folder, can be assigned to an *owner* using the Ownership tab. When you create an object, you become its owner.

The Ownership screen tells users whether an object has an owner and offers an opportunity to make ownership permissions for a user either explicit (set directly on the object) or implicit (based on the owner of the parent folder). For more information, see section 6.1.2.

3.1.5 The History Tab

The History tab appears only on the Edit screen of DTML documents and methods and allows you to follow any changes made to these objects. When a user edits a DTML method or document and then saves the changed object by clicking Save

Changes, previous changes are not completely discarded. This creates a form of version management.

When you click the History tab, you see an overview of the various versions of the current object. From here you can view individual versions, compare two versions, or even restore old versions. Figure 3-5 shows the History screen for the DTML document index_html.

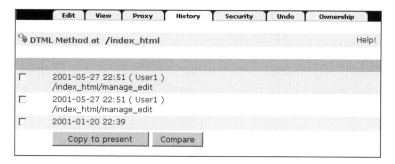

Figure 3-5: The History screen

Figure 3-5 shows two previous versions of index_html, both of which are displayed with the date, time, and username. To view a version, click the corresponding link in the overview.

The two buttons at the bottom of the History screen, Copy to present and Compare, offer these features:

Copy to present Restores old versions. Select the version to restore and click this button to update the current document to that version. You can restore only one version at a time; if you select multiple versions, only the first is restored. The current version is stored on the history list.

Compare Select two versions and click Compare to compare them. A screen appears comparing the versions. If you select only one version, it will be compared with the latest version of the object.

3.1.6 The Properties Tab

The Properties screen allows you to assign new properties to an object or delete or edit existing properties. Properties determine an object's characteristics and consist of a name, an associated value, and a property type. For example, you might assign a property named Price to a DTML document and then call Price in the document to use its assigned value. (The property type for Price should be an integer if you want to allow only whole numbers.) To change the value used for Price, you use the Property tab. If you change a value, all calls for the property in your document will be affected; they will be replaced with the new value.

The Properties screen (Figure 3-6) shows an overview of editable properties and includes a form for adding new ones. To add a new property, enter a name and value and then select the property type from the drop-down Type menu.

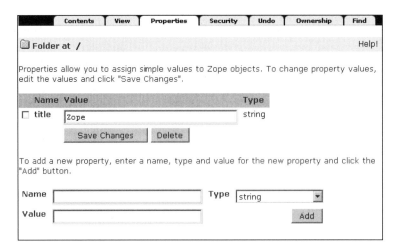

Figure 3-6: The Properties screen

The following property types are available on the Properties screen:

boolean	multiple selection
date	selection
float	string
int	text
lines	tokens
long	

The types boolean, float, int, long, and string roughly correspond to their namesake data types in other programming languages. (If you're not familiar with these concepts, see *Learning Python,* by Mark Lutz and David Ascher, O'Reilly & Associates, 1999.)

Let's take a brief look at the date, lines, multiple selection, text, selection, and tokens property types. (Chapter 7, "ZClasses," presents a comprehensive description of all property types.)

3.1.6.1 The Date Property Type
When assigning a date property, you must enter a date in the Value field because an empty field will be rejected.

3.1.6.2 The Lines Property Type
The lines type produces a list of multiple values. When using it, leave the Value field blank and enter a name for the property; the property name you entered will then appear in the list of properties. You can now enter item values in the property's text field, with each item value on a new line.

3.1.6.3 The Text Property Type
The text type is like the string data type (a sequence of elements, usually characters, considered as a whole), although it creates a multiline text field instead of a single line field as with the string type.

3.1.6.4 The Tokens Property Type

The tokens type is like the lines property type, except that token items are entered all on one line. For the tokens type, enter a string of several words separated by blank spaces, which will then be converted into a list.

3.1.6.5 The Selection and Multiple Selection Property Types

The selection type produces a pull-down menu with items derived from a selection variable specified by the selection property's value. The selection variable must be another property or method in the namespace of the object that returns or contains a list of string values—often a lines property set in a parent folder. You can select only one value at a time in a selection property.

The multiple selection is like the above except you can select several values at once.

3.1.7   The Undo Tab

Use the Undo tab to undo your actions. When you click the Undo tab, it displays all actions carried out on the selected object. If the selected object is folderish, it displays the actions carried out on all objects in the current folder and all subfolders. You can restore deleted objects, undo modifications, cancel copy actions, and so on.

Each action carried out on a Zope server is saved and listed in an overview, which can also be accessed via the Undo tab. To view all actions carried out on the Zope server, select the Undo tab in the root folder.

As shown in Figure 3-7, Undo shows the complete path to the object on which an action was performed, the method used, the user who performed the action, and the date and time of the action. This information lets you clearly identify an action and then undo it. To undo an action, select the appropriate check box and click the Undo button.

You can undo only actions that are attributed to your username, even if you see actions carried out by other users on the list. Also, you cannot undo an action if other actions were subsequently performed on that object, unless you undo those subsequent actions first. For example, if a DTML document was created and then subsequently edited, you can undo the create action only if you first undo the modifications made to the DTML document.

To facilitate the undo process, select the check boxes for all consecutive actions; then, when you click Undo, all actions will be undone simultaneously.

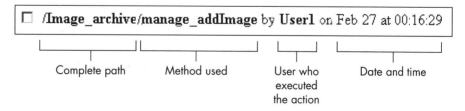

Figure 3-7: The Undo overview

3.1.8 The Find Tab

The Find tab offers a wide range of search functions that you can use to find objects on a Zope server. For example, you can search for specific objects if you know their ids or search for objects according to their meta type or other attributes (for example, you can search for all DTML documents modified since a certain date).

3.1.8.1 The Standard Search

Find offers the choice of a standard or advanced search. Figure 3-8 shows the standard search screen.

The four fields of the standard search—Find objects of type, with ids, containing, and modified—are described here.

Find objects of type Use this field to search for specific object meta types, all of which are listed on the field's menu (including all object types on the Available-Objects menu). You can search for individual objects, multiple objects, or all objects. To select multiple objects at the same time, click each one while holding down the CTRL (Windows) key.

with ids You can specify one or more ids to find. When listing several ids, separate them with a space.

containing Text entered here must be contained in the body of search objects, not in their ids.

modified Specify a time or date before or after which the objects you want to find were modified. To search for objects modified prior to a specific date, click the Before pull-down menu; otherwise, select After. Enter the date or time in the field next to the pull-down menu using the standard Zope date/time formats: YYYY/MM/DD hh:mm:ss; for example, 2000/01/01 00:30:00. In English, this corresponds to January 1, 2000, at 12.30 a.m.

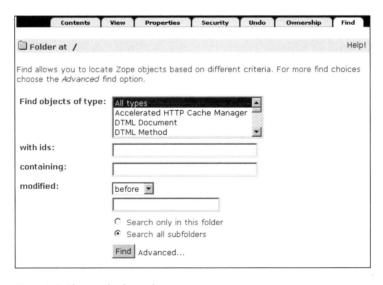

Figure 3-8: The standard search screen

Search only in this folder and Search all subfolders	Check one option to search for objects in a specific folder selected with the Find tab. Select Search only this folder to search through the current folder; select Search all subfolders to search the entire folder structure from the current folder down. To search the entire Zope server, open the root folder and perform your search from there, choosing the Search all subfolders option.
Find	Click here to start the search.

For example, here's how you might search for all DTML methods and documents that use the standard HTML header and that were edited after February 4, 2000:

1. Change to the root folder and click the Find tab.
2. Select DTML method and DTML document.
3. In the modified field, enter the date 2000/02/04.
4. In the containing field, enter `<dtml-var standard_html_header>`.
5. Leave Search all subfolders selected.
6. Click Find.

In response, the top of the screen should display links to all objects found that match the search criteria, as shown in Figure 3-9, which shows 12 found objects. Clicking one of these links opens the object so that you can edit it.

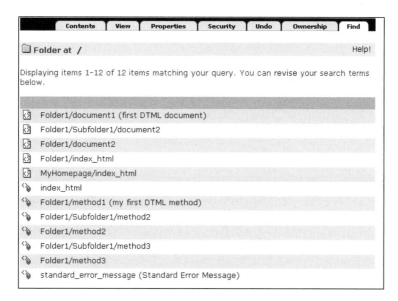

Figure 3-9: This example shows that twelve objects were found, each of which can be accessed using the links

3.1.8.2 The Advanced Search

To use the advanced search, click the Advanced link on the Find screen. Advanced search provides four categories in addition to those of the standard search:

expr	Use this category to specify a DTML expression that will be evaluated to determine whether it is true. (You must observe the DTML syntax rules, discussed in Chapter 4.) You can, for example, specify a property name to find only those objects that contain this property.
where the roles	Select one or more roles that must be assigned to an object for it to be found. See also Chapter 6, "Users, Roles, and Permissions."
have permissions	Select permissions that must be defined in the object for the selected role.
Sort results by	Sort the results of your search by type, id, or modification date (Last modified or Reverse).

For example, you might use an advanced search to find all objects for which a Price property has been defined and that can be accessed only by someone with the role of Manager. (The MailHost Services permission must be assigned to the Manager role.) To do so, follow these steps:

1. Change to the root folder, select the Find tab, and click Advanced.

2. Enter expr Price in the text field.

3. In the where the roles field, select Manager; then click mailhost services in the have permissions field.

4. Select Search all subfolders and then click Find.

   All found objects will be displayed as in a standard search.

3.1.9   The Import/Export Tab

Select the Import/Export tab (in version 2.2 or earlier) or the Import/Export button on the Contents screen (2.3 or later) to import and export objects (see Figure 3-10).

All objects created on a Zope server are stored in the Zope database, found in the Zope installation directory as the data.fs file. To use your objects on other Zope servers, you must export them to a file and then import that file to the target Zope server.

3.1.9.1   Exporting Objects

You can export only one object at a time, and that object must be in the folder for which you clicked the Import/Export button. When you export a folder or folder-ish object, all subobjects are also exported and, as with objects, you can export only one folder at a time. Here are the options for exporting:

Export object id	Enter the id of the object you want to export. You can also select the object in the folder before clicking on Import/Export to fill in the id value for you.
Download to local machine	Select this option to store the exported file on the client (the computer you are currently working on). The browser will ask you for a target directory.

Save to file on server	Select this option to store the exported file on the server (the computer on which the Zope server is running). The standard target directory here is the var folder for the Zope installation. (This variant is particularly useful if several Zope servers are running on a single server; it allows you to easily transfer objects from one Zope server to another.)
XML format?	Select this option to export an object in XML format. If you leave the box unchecked, the object is saved in binary format with the file extension .zexp.

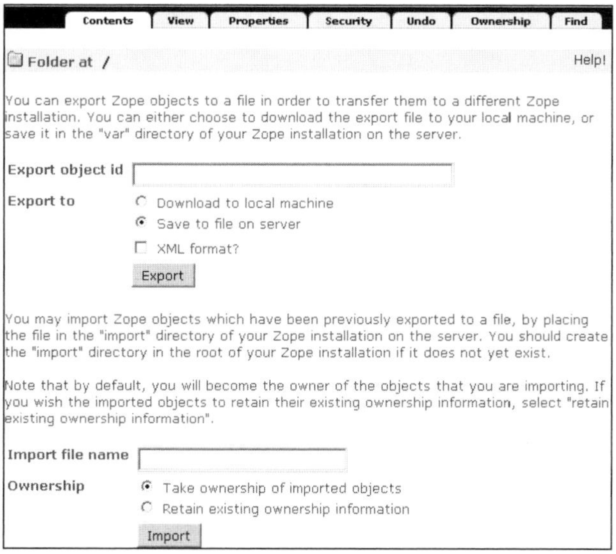

Figure 3-10: The Import/Export screen

You can also export an object by selecting it in the Contents overview and then clicking the Import/Export button. The Import/Export screen appears with the id of the selected object already in the id field. (If you select two objects on the Contents tab, only the first one will appear in the id field.)

3.1.9.2 An Export Example

The following steps show you how to export the DTML method index_html in XML format and save it on the machine that your Zope server is running on. You can find the exported file in the /var directory of your Zope installation.

1. Change to the root folder and click the check box next to index_html.
2. Click the Import/Export button.
3. Select both the Save to file on server and XML-Format? options.
4. Click Export.

You will be notified when the object is successfully exported, as shown in Figure 3-11.

index_html sucessfully exported to

C:\Programme\Zope_23/var/index_html.xml

Ok

Figure 3-11: The file index.xml is created and saved in the specified directory

If you have access to the server, you can view the XML file in your web browser or preferred editor.

3.1.9.3 Importing Objects

Before you can use an object exported from one Zope server to another, you must import it by placing it in the import directory of your Zope server. You should create the import directory in the root folder of your Zope installation, if it doesn't already exist.

When importing objects, you have these options:

Import file name	Enter the full name of the file containing the object to import.
Take ownership of imported objects	When activated, this option automatically makes you the owner of the imported objects.
Retain existing ownership information	Activate this option to retain the objects' current ownership settings.

3.1.9.4 An Import Example

Now that we've exported our file, we can import it. It makes little sense to import a file from the same server, so if you have several Zope servers running, change servers and proceed from there. Otherwise, just use your existing server.

1. Open the folder where you want to store the imported object.
2. Click the Import/Export tab or button.
3. Copy the exported file to the import directory of the Zope server where it is to be imported.
4. Enter the complete filename in the Import file name field: index_html.xml in this case.
5. Click Import.

3.2   The Help Button

Zope provides a really useful help system. The Help button at the top-right corner of each view on the management screen is your point of access. Click the Help hyperlink for information on the current view and related functions. When you click Help, a pop-up window opens containing relevant information, as shown in Figure 3-12.

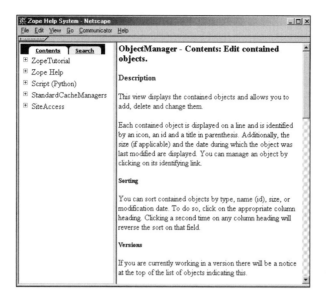

Figure 3-12: A Zope Help window

It's nice to know that if you get stuck while using Zope, you can always try its context-sensitive online help. In this section, we'll take a look at how to get the most out of Zope's built-in help.

The right frame of the Zope Help System lists the relevant help texts. The left frame contains a set of tabs, whose purposes are explained below.

3.2.1 Contents

The Contents tab provides an overview of all available help in a hierarchical tree; click the plus signs to expand a directory or click an item to read it. Zope Help and the ZopeTutorial appear by default in all installations. Figure 3-12 also shows another item, newProduct, which is additional user-created help designed to supplement Zope's documentation.

3.2.1.1 Zope Help

From Zope Help, you can call up help not only for the individual Zope tabs and functions but also DTML tags and the most important Zope objects, such as DTML documents or the ZCatalog.

3.2.1.2 ZopeTutorial

The ZopeTutorial contains a series of lessons on using Zope, each of which can be accessed individually.

3.2.2 Search

Click the Search tab to search through the help texts. The results link to the relevant text containing the search word.

3.3 The Control Panel

The Control Panel folder, located just below the root folder, is automatically created with each Zope installation. Its functions let you examine or change settings that affect the entire Zope server (see Figure 3-13). Like a system folder, the Control Panel folder cannot be deleted.

The first level of the Control Panel provides an overview of various system data relating to the currently running Zope server, including the following information:

Zope version The version of the current Zope server.

Python version The Python version used by the Zope server.

System platform The type of computer running the Zope server.

Process id The server program's process id number, which allows the Zope server to be identified in the operating system.

Running for The amount of time that the Zope server has been running.

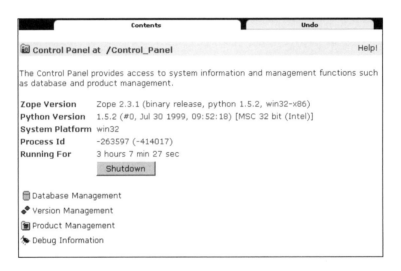

Figure 3-13: The Control Panel

3.3.1 Shutdown

When you click the Shutdown button you exit the Zope process, and you will be unable to access the Zope server until you restart it. Take extra care when using Shutdown; if several people are working on the same server at the same time, data may be lost because others will be unable to save their changes.

3.3.2 Restart

The Restart button appears only if the Zope server is running as a Win32 service or under daemon control in a Unix system. Clicking Restart stops and restarts the Zope server. Before using Restart, be sure to notify others using the same server to prevent lost data or similar problems—especially because when you restart, it may be quite a while before the Zope server can be used again.

3.3.3 The Database Management Screen

The Control Panel also provides access to functions that you can use to monitor the Zope database, manage the various Zope versions and products, locate errors, and perform debugging.

All objects on a Zope server are stored in the Zope Object Database (ZODB). The ZODB data is contained in the file Data.fs, located in the var directory of the Zope installation. The Zope Database Manager allows you to view the status of your database and to perform maintenance tasks, such as database packing and cache management. Its functions are accessed through the now-familiar system of tabs:

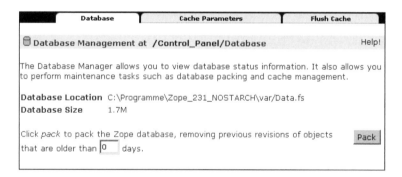

3.3.3.1 The Database Tab

Click the Database Management link to see information on the current status of the Zope database, like that shown in Figure 3-14. The Database Location field shows the complete path to the Zope database file (Data.fs); the Database Size field gives its size.

Figure 3-14: The Database tab

Click Pack to reduce the size of your database, but beware: Packing will remove Undo information from the database, preventing you from undoing certain actions. You can control this to some extent by specifying how old actions must be to be deleted from Undo. For example, entering 0 days tells Pack to delete all Undo information, whereas entering 7 will delete only information older than a week.

3.3.3.2 The Cache Parameters Tab

The Cache Parameters tab, shown in Figure 3-15, allows you to view and modify cache information, including the size and number of objects, as follows:

Total number of objects in the database
This field shows the total number of objects contained in the Zope database (in other words, stored in data.fs).

Total number of objects in all of the caches
This field shows the total number of objects currently in all caches.

Target size
This setting specifies the approximate maximum number of objects that can be contained in the cache at the same time. The smaller the number, the smaller the cache. The default setting of 400 is generally sufficient. Using a smaller number will make Zope use less RAM, but at the expense of performance; a larger number could be used for high-traffic sites, with lots of objects, if your server has enough RAM.

Target maximum time between accesses
This setting specifies how much time must elapse between accesses before an object will be automatically purged from the cache. The default setting of 60 means that objects that have not been accessed within the previous 60 minutes will be deleted from the cache.

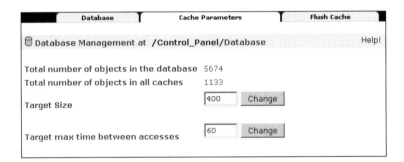

Figure 3-15: The Cache Parameters tab

3.3.3.3 The Flush Cache Tab

The Flush Cache tab, shown in Figure 3-16, lets you manually clear the contents of the cache, as follows:

Full Sweep
This option empties the cache. Specify the period of time during which an object must be accessed to prevent it from being deleted from the cache; the default setting of 60 seconds means that all objects not accessed within the past 60 seconds will be deleted.

Minimize
This option removes more objects from the cache than Full Sweep and requires slightly longer to carry out.

Figure 3-16: The Flush Cache tab

3.3.3.4 ZODB

Let's explore the basic principles of maintaining the internal Zope Object Database (ZODB). To begin, open the Zope management screen; you should see below Control_Panel a link labeled Database Management and an Undo tab that calls up the management screen for the Undo function, as shown in Figure 3-17.

The Database Size field on the Database Management screen tells you the size of the file Data.fs. The Database Location field tells you that the file is in the var directory of your Zope installation, which, for purposes of this chapter, is the Zope installation directory C:\Program Files\Zope\.

The file Data.fs logs all of your actions and contains all objects you created in Zope, including:

- DTML methods and documents
- Images or other Zope objects
- Instances of a ZClass
- Products defined inside Zope and their ZClasses
- Undo and version history data

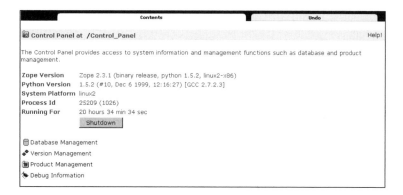

Figure 3-17: Management screen for Database Management

3.3.4 Managing Your Zope Database with Pack

Say you have been working with Zope for six months or so and, as a result, your undo list contains hundreds of entries. In such a case, the Data.fs file can become quite large, since it contains every revision of every object (including deleted ones) from the past six months.

Large Data.fs files cause two significant problems: they use excessive disk space and degrade performance due to the fragmentation of data in the file and on the disk. They can also greatly increase the time needed to restart Zope, which you'll need to do after installing new Products or modifying external Python code.

To eliminate this old revision data and reduce the size of the Data.fs file, you can pack the ZODB using the Pack button. You can decide how many days of undo information you want to keep after packing by entering that number in the relevant field; leaving this value at zero removes all undo information.

NOTE *When you click Pack, all entries for undoable actions are deleted from the Data.fs file. Zope then creates a backup of Data.fs and calls it Data.fs.old. The current version of Data.fs is then much smaller than Data.fs.old because it lacks all of the objects' previous revision information.*

Once you click Pack and the operation completes, click the Undo tab; you should no longer see a list of actions that can be undone, as shown in Figure 3-18.

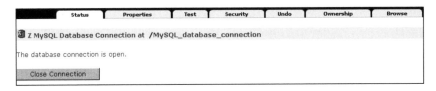

Figure 3-18: The Undo function management screen after you pack a database

3.3.5 Restoring Your Saved Data.fs File

If you inadvertently pack a database that contained changes you wanted to undo, replace the Data.fs file with the Data.fs.old file to turn back the clock. Do so as follows:

1. On the Control Panel, click Shutdown.

2. Delete the Data.fs file.

3. Change the name of the Data.fs.old file to Data.fs.

3.3.6 Copying Your Database to Another Zope Server

You can also copy databases from one Zope server to another, to create a backup Zope server, for example. For instance, to copy ZOPESERVER_A to Zope server ZOPESERVER_B, follow these steps:

1. Shut down both Zope servers.

2. Create a backup copy of the data.fs file on ZOPESERVER_B.

3. Copy the data.fs file from the var directory on ZOPESERVER_A to the var directory on ZOPESERVER_B and replace the data.fs file on ZOPESERVER_B with the data.fs file on ZOPESERVER_A.

Now the database from ZOPESERVER_A is available on ZOPESERVER_B.

NOTE *Make sure the same external products are installed on both servers, or any instances or code that relies on the missing products will not function on the backup server.*

NOTE *When you copy a database, all objects are copied, including passwords and login names!*

3.3.7 Version Management

Zope's versions feature allows you to make changes in Zope privately, without affecting others using the site while you are editing. When you have finished editing and are sure your changes are correct, you can apply your changes all at once to the original version of your site. (See Chapter 5, "Working with Zope Versions," for more information on versions and version management.) The Version Management screen (see Figure 3-19) makes it easy for you to work with versions. If you are not using versions, you will not need to use this tab.

Figure 3-19: The Version Management screen

3.3.8 Product Management

The Product Management link leads to the product overview of your Zope server, containing a list of all installed products, as shown in Figure 3-20. (See Chapter 7, "ZClasses," for more information on products, and section 12.3, "Products.")

The Product Management screen contains the same buttons as the Contents overview. You can use these buttons as usual on the listed products.

As with folders, click products to open them, access the contents of individual products, and view the objects in them using the Contents overview screen.

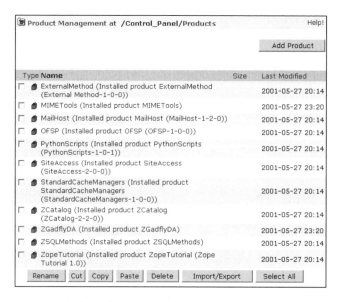

Figure 3-20: The Products view

3.3.9 Debugging Information

The Debug Information screen, shown in Figure 3-21, contains debugging information you can use to trace the source of an error. We'll discuss debugging in more detail in Chapter 13.

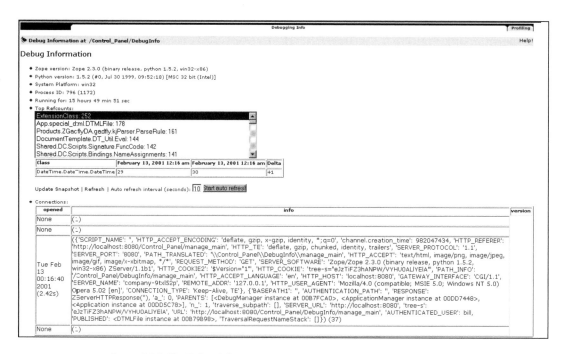

Figure 3-21: The Debug Information screen

Summary

You should now

- Be familiar with the fundamentals of using a Zope server, the Zope Management screen, and all Management screen components.

- Know how to navigate through the elements of the Zope server.

- Know how to work with Zope objects, including how to create, move, copy, delete, and rename them.

- Understand the principles underlying acquisition and the Zope object hierarchy.

- Be familiar with the Control Panel and how to manage the Zope database, Zope versions, and installed products (we'll cover these topics in more depth in Chapter 5).

We'll now turn our attention to the Zope's templating language, DTML, where we'll learn how to fill DTML documents with content to turn your ideas into reality.

4

DTML

4.1   Essentials

As a precursor to exploring how to create your own projects, this chapter will examine some concepts essential to understanding DTML, the most important of which are the first, second, and third tiers and the DTML namespace. It will also explain the concept of *variable data*, which differs little from the conventional definition of a variable.

4.1.1   First, Second, and Third Tiers

The *first tier*, Zope's programming level, is the base of all Zope applications. It includes the entire Zope source code as well as all modifications and expansions made using Python. Zope is usually expanded by creating a *product*, a third party software package that extends or enhances Zope's functionality.

The *second tier* refers to the management screen. You work in the second tier when you edit documents and methods, create objects, or use the Management screen's various functions (introduced in section 2.2). Figure 4-1 shows the second tier view of the newly created DTML document document_2.

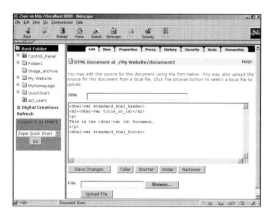

Figure 4-1: The second tier view of a DTML document

Users see the *third tier* when they view an object through the Internet as published by a Zope server. Although current third tier users generally see only content, as Internet applications and users become increasingly more sophisticated, they will increasingly be able to contribute content or control the look and feel of the website in some way. Because third tier users cannot see the Zope Management screen, the developer must create special custom interfaces in their applications to provide this functionality. Figure 4-2 shows document_2 as it appears in the third tier view.

Figure 4-2: The third tier view of a DTML document

The DTML code for an object is programmed in the second tier's edit screen. When a DTML object is viewed in the third tier, Zope evaluates the object's DTML code and returns the resulting text to the user's web browser by *rendering* it. Often, the text returned is HTML code (the code used to produce a standard web page), but it can also be plain text, XML, or any other textual document format. The important thing to understand is that DTML code is seen only by Zope and is never transmitted to the client user's web browser.

To view the generated HTML, display the document's source in your browser. The source text for our sample document is shown in Figure 4-3.

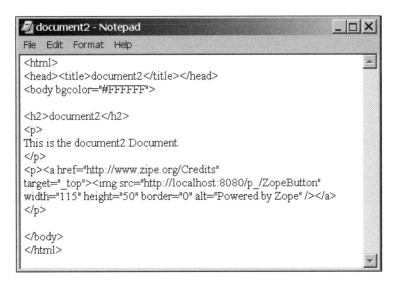

Figure 4-3: HTML source code of a DTML document

4.1.2 Variables

Zope regards nearly all things as objects, including methods, functions, documents, and so on. These objects can also act as variables.

A *variable* in the traditional sense consists of an indicator with a changeable value. For example, in the expression

```
x = a + b
```

The value of x depends on a and b. Zope variables act very much the same way. Like a and b in the expression above, the value of a Zope object depends on an indicator. For example, the value of the object ZopeTime depends on the time of day, which is automatically determined by the Zope system.

NOTE *In the following discussion, all references to variables refer either to Zope objects or attributes such as properties.*

4.1.3 The DTML Namespace

A *DTML namespace* is an object that contains names. Each DTML object has a namespace containing all names available to the object and their associated data. A *name,* therefore, is the indicator by which a variable is referred to and that may ultimately return a value. The DTML namespace is dynamic, meaning its content may vary; names can be defined at one time and then disappear later. When a variable is accessed, it is referred to by its name in the namespace. Names are case sensitive, so be sure they are correctly capitalized in your DTML code.

Names come to be in the namespace through Zope's automatic process of acquisition (see section 2.5) or by explicitly adding them with certain DTML constructs (see "The with Tag" and "The let Tag," sections 4.3.8 and 4.3.9). This creates an aggregate of the available object and attribute names called the *namespace stack* by moving upward through the object hierarchy and adding the objects and attributes found along the way. The object lowest in the hierarchy (usually the executing object or its parent) is topmost in the namespace stack. When a variable is accessed, the namespace stack is searched from the top down until its name is found or the entire stack is checked.

For example, suppose you had the Zope object hierarchy shown in Figure 4-4.

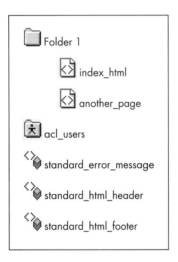

Figure 4-4: Example of a Zope hierarchy

When the DTML document index_html contained in the folder Folder1 is executed, its namespace stack would consist of the following sets of objects in order, shown in Figure 4-5.

4.2 DTML Syntax

The DTML programming language is intended to be easy to learn, and if you are familiar with HTML, you should soon become proficient in it. Zope supports several types of DTML syntax, the most common of which is similar to HTML.

Like HTML, DTML tags are enclosed within angle brackets. The opening bracket is followed by dtml-, as in <dtml- ... >, and the space between the brackets contains the name of the tag.

DTML tags can have one, several, or no attributes. The value of an attribute (the value can be optional) is enclosed within quotation marks after the equals (=) sign. If the value assigned to an attribute does not contain blank spaces, tabs, line break characters, or double quotation marks, it need not be enclosed in quotation marks.

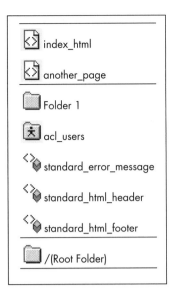

Figure 4-5: The namespace stack of the hierarchy in Figure 4-4

NOTE *It is generally considered good practice to surround all attribute values with quotation marks in DTML unless you have a specific reason not to, because unquoted values are sometimes treated differently by certain DTML tags, such as dtml-let.*

The resulting structure is

```
<dtml-Tagname Attribute1="Value1" Attribute2="Value2" ...>
```

For example, the following code displays in uppercase letters the name of the user accessing the document containing this line.

```
<dtml-var name="AUTHENTICATED_USER" capitalize>
```

In this example, the first attribute, called the *name attribute*, is assigned the variable AUTHENTICATED_USER as its value. The second attribute, capitalize (which is responsible for displaying the username with its first letter capitalized), requires no value and as a result appears with no value assigned to it.

4.2.1   Empty and Non-Empty Tags

The example above is known as an *empty tag* because it stands alone; it encloses no text between itself and an end tag. *Non-empty* DTML tags (also known as *container* or *block* tags) contain a tag body between start and end tags.

The *start tag* (Line 1 below) follows the attribute structure described above. The *end tag* (Line 3) is similar except that it contains no attributes and the opening angle bracket is followed by a forward slash:

```
1:      <dtml-Tagname Attribute1="Value1" Attribute2="Value2" ...>
2:          DTML Tag Body
3:      </dtml-Tagname>
```

The *tag body* (Line 2) contains text, HTML instructions, or additional DTML tags. The if tag, used to formulate a simple if-then-else construction, is an example of a non-empty tag, as follows:

```
1:      <dtml-if expr="1<2">
2:          2 > 1.<br>
3:          <h2>Two is always greater than 1</h2>
4:      </dtml-if>
```

Here, the expression in the start tag (Line 1), 1<2 (which is obviously true) is evaluated and the content of the tag body is output. The end tag (Line 4) delimits the tag body.

4.2.2   Old DTML Syntax

If you use DTML a lot, you will frequently encounter older versions of DTML tag syntax. These older syntaxes continue to work in current versions of Zope, but are generally avoided in favor of the <dtml-Tagname> syntax illustrated above. Let's take a look at two of them, just in case you come across some of them.

4.2.2.1 Syntax from Zope Version 1.x

The example given in section 4.2, which outputs the name of the user currently logged on, would look like this using Zope 1.x syntax (also known as "server-side include" syntax):

```
<!--#var name="AUTHENTICATED_USER" capitalize -->
```

This syntax follows the following form:

```
<!--#Tagname Attribute1="Value1" Attribute2="Value2" ... -->
<!--#/Tagname-->
```

4.2.2.2 Python String-Format Syntax from Zope 1.x

This format derives from the Python string formatting syntax used to dynamically create text strings in Python programs.

```
%(Tagname Attribute1="Value1" Attribute2="Value2")s
```

4.2.3 Abbreviating Attributes

Two special attributes, name and expr, can be assigned to virtually any DTML tag. There is a standard way to abbreviate each. For example, we could abbreviate the use of name in our earlier example—which was shown as

```
<dtml-var name="AUTHENTICATED_USER" capitalize>
```

to

```
<dtml-var AUTHENTICATED_USER capitalize>
```

To use the abbreviated form, omit the name attribute label, the equals sign, and the quotation marks. The first piece of information in the tag is automatically regarded as the name attribute's value.

The expr attribute (used to evaluate complex expressions) takes a similar approach, as shown below:

```
<dtml-var expr="1+1">
```

is abbreviated

```
<dtml-var "1+1">
```

NOTE *An expression must always be contained within quotation marks.*

Because the quotation marks are retained, the term between the quotation marks is regarded as an expression of the expr attribute.

NOTE *Although it is common to see these abbreviated notations for name and expr, they are discouraged in favor of the more explicit forms. Although choosing not to abbreviate requires slightly more typing, the resulting code is easier to read and debug.*

4.3 Using DTML Tags, Variables, and Attributes

The following sections will show you how to use the various DTML tags, variables, and attributes by giving explanations and concrete examples. Appendix A contains detailed tables of the different attributes used with each tag.

4.3.1 The var Tag

The var tag inserts the textual representation of variable data into your document's or method's output. As a result, text is generated even if you use var to call other non-textual attributes, such as image objects.

For example, imagine that you have an image stored in Zope called CompanyLogo. You want this image to appear somewhere in your document. To do so, you could use the following instruction:

```
<dtml-var name="CompanyLogo">
```

and Zope would insert source text like the following:

```
<img src="http://localhost:8080/CompanyLogo"
width="200" height="75" border="0" alt="My Company Title">
```

You should recognize this generated text as standard HTML. The user's browser would process this HTML and display the CompanyLogo image at the appropriate location when the document is viewed.

4.3.1.1 var Tag Attributes

Table 4-1 lists the most important var attributes along with examples and the corresponding screen output. See Appendix A for a complete list. Asterisked attributes require a value.

4.3.1.2 The name Attribute

The name attribute is used to obtain variable data from the DTML namespace. When this attribute is used, a variable is looked up by name and executed if it is a callable object (such as a DTML method); its value is passed to the relevant tag. In this way, for example, the system can search for a graphic object and then display it, as shown here again with the CompanyLogo name attribute:

```
<dtml-var name="CompanyLogo">
```

The following rules are imposed on names when they are used to access variable data using the name attribute:

1. They cannot begin with an underscore character (_).
2. They cannot contain characters that are significant to URLs, such as /, ?, &, :, and so on.

4.3.1.3 The expr Attribute

The expr attribute is used to evaluate complex expressions. The *attribute value*—that is, the expression to be evaluated—**must** be enclosed in double quotation marks. (See Chapter 9 for a brief introduction to the expression syntax.)

4.3.1.4 The fmt Attribute

The abbreviation fmt stands for *format;* text is formatted using the fmt attribute, meaning that the fmt attribute controls the appearance output of text generated by a tag. You can use standard, special, and C-style formats defined by the fmt attribute, as described in sections 4.3.1.5 and 4.3.1.6.

Table 4-1: Attributes for the var Tag

Attribute	Function	Example	Output
null	Defines a string that will be output instead of the value "null." If the value for null is omitted, no text is inserted.	null="The result returns an empty list."	The result returns an empty list.
missing	Defines a string to be inserted if the variable referred to by name is not in the namespace. If the value for missing is omitted, no text is inserted.	missing = "Not found"	Not found
lower	Changes all letters to lowercase.	title_or_id lower	testpage
upper	Converts all letters to uppercase.	title_or_id upper	TESTPAGE
capitalize	Capitalizes the first letter.	AUTHENTICATED_USER capitalize	Manager
html_quote	Characters significant in HTML are replaced with appropriate HTML entities.	teststring html_quote (teststring="<")	&lt;
url_quote	Characters not legal in URLs are properly escaped for insertion into href values.	teststring url_quote (teststring="<")	%3c
size	Displays only the specified number of characters from a string.	teststring size=6 (teststring="How're you?")	How're...
etc	Specifies a string that is inserted instead of the omitted characters (used with size).	teststring size=6 etc="--" (teststring="How're you?")	How're —
name*	See "The name Attribute" (section 4.3.1.2).		
expr*	See "The expr Attribute" (section 4.3.1.3).		
fmt*	See "The fmt Attribute" (section 4.3.1.4).		

4.3.1.5 Using the fmt Attribute

The fmt attribute is frequently used to format date and time information. For example, the object ZopeTime returns a value and displays it in the format specified by the fmt attribute. The syntax is as follows:

```
<dtml-var name="ZopeTime" fmt="format">
```

The format attribute can also be used to format numbers and strings.

Table 4-2 lists the most important fmt attribute formats; Table 4-3 contains special formats to use on other data types. A complete list appears in Appendix A.

4.3.1.6 C-Style Formats for the fmt Attribute

The C-style format lets you format various numeric types in scientific notation, as decimals, and so on. It can also be used for dates. It uses the printf syntax of the C programming language. (For a detailed description of C-style syntax, see your favorite C manual.)

C-style syntax consists of a percent sign, a conversion code, and an optional value placed before the converted value or a number that determines the number of places of the converted value. See Appendix A for a complete list of C-style formats.

Table 4-2: Standard fmt Attribute Formats

Name	Description
AMPM	Returns the time including seconds.
AMPMMinutes	Returns the time without seconds.
aCommon	The time is displayed in the format Mar 1, 2002 1:45 p.m.
ampm	Returns the suffix a.m. or p.m.
Day	Returns the full name of the day of the week.
day	Returns the day as a number.
fCommon	The time is displayed as March 1, 1997 1:45 p.m.
hour	Returns the time in 24-hour mode.
Month	Returns the full name of the month.
minute	Returns the minutes.
month	Returns the month as a number.
rfc822	Returns the date in RFC 822 format (the format used in HTTP headers).
second	Returns the seconds.
TimeMinutes	Returns the timestring for the object without seconds.
Time	Returns the timestring for the object with seconds.

Table 4-2: Standard fmt Attribute Formats (continued)

Name	Description
timezone	Returns the time zone in which the object is displayed.
year	Returns the object's calendar year.

Table 4-3: Special Formats that Can Be Used with the fmt Attribute

Special Format	Description
whole-dollars	Displays a numeric value with the dollar sign.
dollars-and-cents	Displays a numeric value with the dollar sign and two decimal places.
collection-length	Returns the length of a collection of objects.
structured-text	Renders the value as structured text, which generates HTML from Zope structured text data.

4.3.2 The Namespace Variable

Using the namespace variable, you can refer to variables within expressions that are not valid variable names in Python, including

- Names that do not begin with a letter
- Names that contain characters significant in expressions such as the dash (-), period (.), equals sign (=), space, and so on.

NOTE *The second rule shows why it is inconvenient to have periods in object names. This is the main reason Zope uses the name index_html instead of index.html: index.html is not usable as a variable name in expressions.*

The namespace variable is the underscore (_) character. To directly refer to something from the namespace, enclose the variable name in quotation marks and square brackets, as shown below. (Because this expression must be evaluated, make sure you use double quotation marks.)

```
<dtml-var expr="_['sequence-number'] / 5">
```

This example refers to a variable in our namespace named "sequence-number" (which is generally created by the dtml-in tag, discussed in Section 4.3.10). Because this variable contains a dash character (-), which means "subtract" in an expression, we must use the underscore variable to look it up here. If we did not, the expression would be incorrectly interpreted to mean "sequence minus number divided by 5"—that is, sequence - number / 5.

4.3.2.1 Using the Namespace Variable for Indirect Namespace Lookups

The underscore variable can also be used to look up names in the namespace that themselves are stored as variable data, a process called *indirection*. Indirection allows you write code that uses variable data without specifying its name directly inside the code. Instead, you specify the name outside the code through a property value, from the result of calling a function, or by passing the name when the code is executed. Thus you can modify the behavior of a piece of code without changing the code itself.

For example, say there is a property in the namespace called "message" with the value thank_you_message, and a DTML method with the id thank_you_message in the namespace as well. You could insert this DTML method using the following code:

```
<dtml-var expr="_[message]">
```

Notice there are no quotes around message, which tells Zope to use the value of the variable message and look it up in the namespace. In our example, that value is thank_you_message, so the DTML method with that name is found and rendered. If the value of the message variable is different the next time this DTML code is executed, it would insert different data from the object with the name corresponding to the new value. If the value of the message is not the name of any variable in the namespace, a Zope error will occur.

For a more complex example, say you wanted a page to present a different message depending on the day of the week. To do this, you could use the ZopeTime object's Day function and the underscore variable to insert the variable data corresponding to the current day of the week, as follows:

```
<dtml-var expr="_[ZopeTime().Day()]">
```

ZopeTime().Day() will return the string "Monday" or "Tuesday" or "Wednesday" and so on as appropriate. Placing this function inside the brackets following the underscore variable (without quotes) will look up the variable data associated with the name of the current day returned. For this to work properly, you must also create the seven day variables as properties or objects containing the message for each day.

NOTE *The namespace object always attempts to call or execute the object referenced if it can. This behavior is the same as the* name="…" *syntax. If however, you want access to an object and not just the result of calling it, use the* _.getitem() *function, described below.*

The namespace variable also accepts the useful attributes shown in Table 4-4 (see Appendix A for a complete list).

4.3.2.2 The Math Module
Perform mathematical calculations with the methods in the Math module. See Appendix A for a complete table of Math module attributes.

4.3.2.3 The String Module
The String module lets you perform extensive string manipulations. See Appendix A for a list of String constants and methods. Table 4-5 shows a few of the most important methods.

Table 4-4: Namespace Attribute Variables

Attribute	Function	Example	Output
float(number)	Converts a value to a floating point (decimal) number.	`"_.float(4)"`	4.0
getitem(name<, call>)	Looks up a name in the namespace like _[...], but also takes an optional second argument that determines if the returned object should be called. If this argument is omitted, the object is not called, which is the opposite of the behavior of _[...].	`"_.getitem('some_name')"`	Content of some_name
int(number)	Converts a value to an integer. Any decimal values are truncated, and no rounding occurs.	`"_.int(4.25)"` `"_.int('4.85')"`	4
len(seq)	Calculates the number of elements in a sequence.	`"_.len('Hello')"` `"_.len(['Me', 'You'])"`	5 2
range(count[, start][, step])	Returns a list of count integers (generally used for looping) starting at start (default 0) and incrementing by step (default 1).	`"_.range(4)"`	[0,1,2,3]
round(number, decimal places)	Rounds a number off to a specified number of decimal places.	`"_.round(2.1234, 2)"`	2.12
str(Object)	Converts a value into a character string.	`"_.str(AUTHENTICATED_USER)"`	manager
math	See Appendix A.		
whrandom	See "The Whrandom Module."		
string	See "The String Module."		
namespace (name1=Value1, name2=Value2, etc.)	Assigns variables including values to the namespace. See also "The with Tag" and "The let Tag" (sections 4.3.8 and 4.3.9).		

4.3.2.4 The whrandom Module

Generate random numbers using the methods in this module.

Attribute Name	Explanation	Example	Screen Output
choice(SEQ)	Selects a random element from a list.	"_.whrandom.choice(['1', '2', '3'])"	1 or 2 or 3
randint(a, b)	Selects a random integer from a to b.	"_.whrandom.randint(1, 5)"	1 or 2 or 3 or 4 or 5
random()	Selects a real number between 0 and 1.	"_.whrandom.random()"	for example, 0.5
uniform(a, b)	Selects a real number between the specified numbers.	"_.whrandom.uniform(1, 5)"	for example, 1.25

Table 4-5: String Module Methods

Attribute Name	Explanation	Example	Screen Output
capitalize(W)	Capitalizes the first letter of a string.	"_.string. capitalize ('hello')"	Hello
find(S, SUB[, START])	Returns the offset of the substring in the string S. If the substring is not found in the string, -1 is returned.	"_.string.find('Hello', 'e')" "_.string.find('Hello', 'a')"	1 -1
lower(S)	Converts all uppercase letters into lowercase.	"_.string.lower('Hello, How're you? ')"	hello, how're you?
split(S[, SEP[, MAX]])	Splits a string into a list; with the space character as the default separator.	"_.string.split('one two three')"	['one','two','three']
join(WORDS[, SEP])	Joins elements; the default value placed between elements is the space character.	"_.string.join(['one', 'two','three'])"	'one two three'
strip(S)	Removes spaces at the start and end of a string.	"_.string.strip(' Hello ')"	'Hello'
upper(S)	Converts all characters to uppercase.	"_.string.upper('Hello')"	HELLO

Table 4-6: RESPONSE Object Attributes

Name	Explanation
setHeader(name, value)	Sets an HTTP-Return-Header-Name with a value and deletes any previous value set for the header
expireCookie(name)	Removes an http cookie from the browser. The response contains an HTTP-Header that removes from the client the cookie called "name," if it exists, by sending a new cookie with an elapsed expiration date.
setCookie(name, value,…)	Causes the response to contain an HTTP-Header that sets up a cookie with the key name and the value "value" on browsers in which cookies are activated, thus overwriting all previously set values for the cookie in the response object. Additional cookie parameters can be inserted by specifying the keyword parameters expires, domain, path, max_age, comment, and secure.
getHeader(name)	Returns the value associated with an HTTP-Return-Header or None if no such header was set in the response.
redirect(location)	Redirects to another URL without resulting in an error.

4.3.3 Client-Server Communication over the Web

When you access a web page, a browser transmits an *http request* to the server. This request tells the server about the user, their browser, the computer it is running on, and the URL of the page being requested.

The server replies to the browser with an *http response*. This response consists of information about the server and, if a document corresponding to the requested URL is found and is authorized to be accessed, the data of the document requested. The response can also contain special headers that direct the browser to do things like redirect, store a cookie, or expire data in its cache.

Zope encapsulates the http request and response data into the REQUEST and RESPONSE objects, respectively. These objects are always available in the DTML namespace so that you can access their attribute values and methods. You use the REQUEST object to receive the data about the user, browser, URL, and data sent from a form or cookies from the client computer. You can also use REQUEST to store your own temporary variables.

4.3.3.1 The RESPONSE Object

The RESPONSE object is used to communicate back to the client. You can use it to set http headers like *Content-Type* (the MIME format of the page data), set or expire cookies, or redirect the browser to a different URL. Table 4-6 shows important attributes; see Appendix A for a complete list.

Appendix A also lists CGI-defined Web Query variables and http status codes.

4.3.3.2 The REQUEST Object

The REQUEST object has a very important attribute: the set method, with which you can insert variables into the namespace that remain defined for the duration of the web request (that is, until the document requested is rendered and returned to the client). The set method takes two arguments: the name of the variable as a string and the value to assign to the name, which can be any data type or object.

For example, to set a variable named "Price" to the value 1500, use the following DTML code (the call tag is discussed in Section 4.3.4):

```
<dtml-call expr="REQUEST.set('Price',1500)">
```

Notice how the first argument—'Price'—is quoted because it is a string value. The second argument is not quoted because it is a numeric value. You can also put an expression in the second argument to calculate the value of the variable you are setting. For instance, to calculate a tax of 8% on the value of Price and store the resulting value in a new variable Tax, you might use the following code:

```
<dtml-call expr="REQUEST.set('Tax', Price * 0.08)">
```

This may not work correctly in all cases, however. The REQUEST object is the last place names are acquired from because it is always at the bottom of the namespace stack; were there another variable in the namespace named Price, its value would be returned instead of the value you set in REQUEST above. To avoid this potential pitfall, you can explicitly tell Zope to look up a value in the REQUEST object only using the following syntax, which is the same construct we used earlier for looking up names in the underscore namespace variable:

```
<dtml-call expr="REQUEST.set('Tax', REQUEST['Price'] * 0.08)">
```

The construct REQUEST[name] is used to look up values directly in the REQUEST object rather than assuming they will be acquired from that object at the bottom of the namespace stack. This is especially useful if you need to access variables from REQUEST whose names are commonly used by other objects, like "title" or "id." You can also write this as REQUEST.name.

When data from an HTML form is submitted by the client browser or CGI query variables are passed on the URL to Zope, these variable names and values are stored in the form attribute of REQUEST. The REQUEST object also makes these variables available in the general namespace, but you can see exactly which variable data was passed by a form or CGI query by accessing the form attribute directly.

To display the contents of the REQUEST object, use this DTML code:

```
<dtml-var name="REQUEST">
```

The REQUEST data is returned in the format shown in Figure 4-6.

environ	
HTTP_ACCEPT_ENCODING	gzip
channel.creation_time	991008556
HTTP_REFERER	http://localhost:8080/Folder1/Subfolder1/method2/manage_edit
SERVER_PROTOCOL	1.0
SERVER_PORT	8080
PATH_INFO	/Folder1/Subfolder1/method2
HTTP_HOST	localhost:8080
REQUEST_METHOD	GET
PATH_TRANSLATED	\Folder1\Subfolder1\method2
SCRIPT_NAME	
SERVER_SOFTWARE	Zope/Zope 2.3.1 (binary release, python 1.5.2, win32-x86) ZServer/1.1b1
HTTP_ACCEPT_LANGUAGE	en
HTTP_ACCEPT_CHARSET	iso-8859-1,*,utf-8
HTTP_ACCEPT	image/gif, image/x-xbitmap, image/jpeg, image/pjpeg, image/png, */*
REMOTE_ADDR	127.0.0.1

Figure 4-6: Extract from a REQUEST

The ability to display the entire REQUEST object is particularly useful when you are developing and debugging a Zope application. It also allows you to view the values of the CGI-defined web query variables submitted by the client. Table 4-7 lists important REQUEST object attributes.

Table 4-7: REQUEST Object Attributes

Attribute Name	Explanation	Example	Screen Output
AUTHENTICATED_ USER	The user object of the user currently logged in. The user is "Anonymous User" if no user is logged in.	`AUTHENTICATED_USER`	For example, manager
AUTHENTICATION_ PATH	Path of the acl_users folder in which the current user is defined.	`AUTHENTICATION_PATH`	/Test/Folder1 (if the current user is defined in the acl_users folder in /Test/Folder)
PARENTS	Returns highest folder-like object in the object hierarchy starting from the current document backward. PARENTS[-1] always refers to the root folder.	`"PARENTS[0]['id']"` `"PARENTS[1]['title']"`	GWS_Training Zope
URL, URL0	Returns the full URL of the object requested by the client's web browser.	`URL`	http://localhost: 8080/Order1/ Test/index_html

(continued on next page)

Table 4-7: REQUEST Object Attributes (continued)

Attribute Name	Explanation	Example	Screen Output
URL1 - URLn	The URL path to the object up to the *n*th object above it in the path. Used to create links to objects higher in the Zope hierarchy.	URL1 URL2	http://localhost:8080/Order1/Test http://localhost:8080/Order1
BASE	Returns the base of the URL requested.	BASE BASE0	http://localhost:8080
BASE1 - BASEn	The URL path with *n* objects is added to the BASE.	BASE1	http://localhost:8080/Order1
cookies	The result is the values set as cookies in the form of a dictionary.	"REQUEST.cookies"	{'tree-s': 'eJzTiFZ3hANPW/VYHU0ALÏYEIA', 'dtpref_rows': '10', 'dtpref_cols': '65'}
form	The result is the values set by a form in dictionary format.	"REQUEST.form" "REQUEST.form['field1']"	{'field1': 'hello','myfield': 'you'} hello
has_key(name)	1, if the specified variable name is contained in the REQUEST; 0, if the specified variable name is not contained in the REQUEST.	"REQUEST.has_key('URL0')"> "REQUEST.has_key('URL9')"	1 (because URL0 is contained in the REQUEST) 0 (because URL9 is not contained in the REQUEST)
set(name, value)	Sets a variable in REQUEST with the specified name and value.	"REQUEST.set('myvar', 'Content of myvar')"	None (has no result which can be evaluated)
get(name[,default])	Retrieves a variable by name from REQUEST and optionally allows you to specify a default value if the variable is not set.	"REQUEST.get('myvar', ')"	The value stored in myvar or an empty string if myvar is not set

4.3.4 The call Tag

The call tag works like the var tag, allowing you to consult variables, carry out methods, and so on, except that it generates no text and does not carry out text substitution.

For example, the following call displays no result on the screen and is therefore not very useful.

```
<dtml-call name="AUTHENTICATED_USER">
```

The call tag is, however, very useful for methods whose results are not to be displayed. For example, many Python methods return the value None as a sign that they have run successfully. If you don't want this message displayed in your document, use the call tag.

The call tag is also frequently used to set variables. For example, should you want to create a list in a DTML method, you could do the following:

```
<dtml-var expr="REQUEST.set('list',['Schopenhauer','Freud'])">
```

The method called returns None and, because the var tag inserts this into the source text, "None" appears in the rendered output of the document. If you use the call tag instead, your list is generated without any text being added to the output, as follows:

```
<dtml-call expr="REQUEST.set('list',['Schopenhauer', 'Freud'])">
```

To prove that the lists were actually created, you can display the REQUEST object using the dtml-var tag.

The call tag is very useful if you want certain actions to be carried out without directly affecting the output of the document. For example, say you want to add a new element to a list (easily done with the list's append method), and you want the list to be displayed immediately. Were we to use the var tag on its own, we would not be able to achieve the desired results because "None" is returned by the append method. The best thing to do is execute the append method using the call tag and then render the list using the var tag:

```
<dtml-call expr="list.append('Nietzsche')">
<dtml-var  name="list">
```

The following text appears in the rendered output of this document:

```
['Schopenhauer', 'Freud', 'Nietzsche']
```

4.3.5   The if Tag

The if tag is used for the conditional evaluation of source text, meaning that Zope DTML source code is executed only if a specific condition has been fulfilled. This condition is specified in the name or expr attribute of the opening if tag. The value of the name or expression attribute is considered true if all the following criteria are met:

1. The result is not zero.
2. The result is not an empty string, list, dictionary, or other sequence.
3. The result is not None.

Conversely, the value is considered false if

1. The result is zero.
2. The result is an empty string, list, dictionary, or other sequence.
3. The result is None.

The if tag is a non-empty block tag that contains the DTML code to be conditionally executed between its start and end tags. The start tag contains the condition, which can be entered as either a name or expr attribute. For example:

```
1:    <dtml-if name="title">
2:          The title of this object is: <dtml-var name="title">
3:    </dtml-if>
```

In this example the condition is as follows: "Does the 'title' variable exist and return a true value?" Or more simply: "Does the object have a title?"

A check is carried out in the start tag (Line 1) to determine whether a title exists. If one exists, the text contained in the tag body (Line 2) is evaluated, and the object's title is retrieved and displayed. If the condition is not fulfilled, nothing happens.

NOTE *When specifying the condition using the name attribute, Zope returns a false value if the name is not in the namespace. In an expression, specifying a name not in the namespace will result in a Zope error.*

The above example illustrates only the most simple variant of the if tag. In fact, the if tag can be used in four ways, as shown in Table 4-8.

4.3.5.1 The else Tag Inside the if Tag
When inserted within the if tag, the else tag introduces the text to be processed by Zope if no condition above it is fulfilled, thus allowing alternative actions to be carried out. The else tag accepts no attribute. Thus, we can extend the above example as follows:

```
1:    <dtml-if name="title">
2:          The title of this object is:<dtml-var name="title">
3:    <dtml-else>
4:          This object has no title.<br>
5:          The Id of this object is:<dtml-var name="id">
6:    </dtml-if>
```

Table 4-8: Using the if Tag

if Tag Use	Example

The start and end tags enclose the tag body.	`<dtml-if Condition>`
	    `Tag Body`
	`</dtml-if>`

The start and end tags enclose the tag body and an else tag.	`<dtml-if Condition>`
	    `Tag Body`
	`<dtml-else>`
	    `Instruction`
	`</dtml-if>`

The start and end tags enclose the tag body as well as one or more elif tags.	`<dtml-if Condition>`
	    `Tag Body`
	`<dtml-elif Condition>`
	    `Instructions`
	`</dtml-if>`

The start and end tag enclose the tag body, one or more elif tags, and an else tag.	`<dtml-if Condition>`
	    `Tag Body`
	`<dtml-elif Condition>`
	    `Instructions`
	`<dtml-else>`
	    `Instructions`
	`</dtml-if>`

Here, a check occurs (Line 1) to determine whether there is a name title that can be consulted. If there is no title or a false value, the instructions defined by the else tag (Line 3) are carried out and the user is told that no title exists; the object's id is output instead.

4.3.6 The elif Tag

Just as the else tag can be used to carry out alternative actions, you can use one or more elif tags to formulate alternative conditions with corresponding instructions to be carried out. The elif tag is non-empty and accepts the var and expr attributes just like the if tag.

The following structure is used:

```
1:    <dtml-if Condition1>
2:        Code for condition1
3:    <dtml-elif Condition2>
4:        Code for condition2
5:    <dtml-elif Condition3>
6:        Code for condition3
7:    </dtml if>
```

Conditions are checked one after the other (Lines 1, 3, and 5) until one is fulfilled, at which point the instructions formulated within the tag are carried out. Once a condition is filled, all subsequent elif tags are ignored. If no conditions are satisfied, no actions are carried out. Therefore, you should pay particular attention to the sequence in which you code the conditions.

In the following example, we request the age of the current user (Line 1), then display a greeting appropriate to that person's age (Lines 2 through 4), then grant or restrict access to the site (Lines 5 and 6). To do so, the value "age" is taken from an HTML form and checked:

```
1:    <dtml-if expr="REQUEST.age >= 21">
2:          <h1>Welcome, </h1>
3:          You have unrestricted access to this site.
4:    <dtml-elif expr="REQUEST.age >= 18">
5:          <h1> Welcome, </h1>
6:          We're sorry . . . but your access to this site has been restricted.
7:    </dtml-if>
```

(Remember that form values are put into the REQUEST object.)

This example works by first checking to see whether the user is 21 years of age or older (Line 1); if not, a further check is carried out to determine whether the user is 18 years of age or older (Line 4). Depending on the result, the user is then provided with either unrestricted or restricted access to the website.

Let's look at why the sequence in which the conditions are formulated in the tag are so important. If the first check determined whether the user is 18 or older, users over 21 would also be given restricted access only. The second condition would then be ignored, and it would not be possible to carry out any further age differentiation.

The problem with this example is that users under 18 receive no message. To resolve this problem, we can add an else tag, as shown in this listing:

```
1:    <dtml-if expr="REQUEST.age >= 21">
2:          <h1>Welcome, </h1>
3:          You have unrestricted access to this site.
4:    <dtml-elif expr="REQUEST.age >= 18">
5:          <h1> Welcome, </h1>
6:          We're sorry . . . but your access to this site has been restricted.
7:    <dtml-else>
8:          We're sorry . . . but you are not allowed to access this site.
9:    </dtml-if>
```

Now users under 18 receive a message as well as those over 18.

Conditional operators that can be used in *dtml-if* expressions are shown in Table 4-9. The logical operators in Table 4-10 can be used to create complex conditional logic.

Table 4-9: Conditional Expression Operators

Operator	Description	Example
==	True if operands are equal	`"username == 'vincentp'"`
!=	True if not equal	`"size != 1"`
>=	True if greater than or equal to	`"size >= min_size"`
<=	True if less than or equal to	`"size <= max_size"`
>	True if greater than	`"x > y"`
<	True if less than	`"z < y"`

Table 4-10: Logical Operators

Operator	Description	Example
not	Negation: False values become true and true values become false.	`"not title"` (returns true if title is empty)
and	True only if both operands are true.	`"size!=1 and size<=max_size"`
or	True if any one operand is true.	`"x>y or z<y"`

4.3.7 The unless Tag

Like the if tag, the unless tag is used to insert text subject to certain conditions, but it carries out instructions only if a defined condition is not fulfilled (is a false value). The unless tag is a non-empty block tag and accepts the name and expr attributes, using the following structure:

```
<dtml-unless Condition>
    Instructions
</dtml-unless>
```

NOTE *Unlike the if tag, the unless tag cannot have else tags within it.*

4.3.8 The with Tag

The with tag is used to manipulate the DTML namespace. It is very useful in the following cases:

- To access different variables with the same names.
- To define new variables for a short period of time in the DTML namespace.
- To access objects or properties that are not in the namespace by default because they are not in the acquisition path.

Often you may need to access attributes of objects, such as title or id, that have the same names as those of the object containing the DTML code or method. Because the current or containing object (depending on whether you are in a DTML document or method) is first in the namespace stack, its attribute names will mask those of other objects we might want to access. To get around this, we can use the with tag to temporarily alter the namespace stack to search for the desired object first:

```
<dtml-with name="someObject">
    The title of someObject is: <dtml-var name="title"><br>
    The size of someObject is: <dtml-var name="get_size"> bytes
</dtml-with>
```

Inside the with tag, the object someObject is placed at the top of the namespace stack. This means that variable names will be sought in it first before the current or container object.

The with tag inserts an additional namespace at the top of the namespace stack. The object whose namespace is inserted is defined in the start tag of the dtml-with block. The tag body contains the instructions to be carried out and can also contain other with tags.

```
<dtml-with Object>
    Instructions
</dtml-with>
```

Here's how to access variables from subobjects not normally acquired by default:

```
<dtml-with name="Subfolder">
    The subfolder title is:<dtml-var name="title">
</dtml-with>
```

Also, with the aid of the underscore variable's namespace method, you can use dtml-with to temporarily set a new variable—including a value at the top of the namespace stack. This can be used to store the value of a calculation for use within the with block or to override the value of an existing variable in the namespace.

In the following fictional example, a function get_cost is called. This function looks up the cost of an item given its SKU number from an external database. The SKU number is passed from a CGI or HTML form variable. The get_cost function is complex and time consuming, so to increase the efficiency of our code, we store its value in a temporary variable named "cost." Further calculations and formatting will be performed on this value inside the with block.

```
<dtml-with expr="_.namespace(cost=get_cost(SKU))">
     Price breakdown for SKU <dtml-var name="SKU"><br>
     Cost: <dtml-var name="cost" fmt="dollars-and-cents"><br>
     Markup: <dtml-var expr="cost * .33" fmt="dollars-and-cents"><br>
     Retail Price: <dtml-var expr="cost * 1.33" fmt="dollars-and-cents"><br>
</dtml-with>
```

Inside the with block, the variable cost contains the result returned by the get_cost function. After the final with tag, the original namespace stack is restored and the variable cost is no longer defined.

4.3.8.1 The only Attribute

The only attribute can be used in the with tag to restrict the namespace to only the namespace stack of the object specified, thus allowing you to completely replace the namespace stack inside the with block. For example, in the following listing only the id variable's input using a form will be output:

```
<dtml-with name="REQUEST" only>
     <dtml-if name="id">
          The id specified is: <dtml-var name="id">
     <dtml-else>
          No id was specified.
     </dtml-if>
</dtml-with>
```

Because the REQUEST object is at the bottom of the namespace stack, it will be the only object that names are acquired from inside the with block.

NOTE *The only attribute does not turn off acquisition. Using only merely replaces the current namespace stack with that of another object, rather than just adding that object's namespace to the current one. Because of this, the only attribute has limited utility.*

4.3.9 The let Tag

The let tag is another construct for adding variables temporarily to the namespace. It is designed as a shortcut to using the with tag with the _.namespace() function as above. The let tag is a non-empty tag.

Let's say we wanted to place a new namespace at the top of the stack and then populate it with some variable data. Among other things, the let tag functions as if you were using the with tag and the namespace variable. The two examples below are functionally equivalent:

Example 1

```
<dtml-let cost="get_cost(SKU)">
     <dtml-var name="cost" fmt="dollars-and-cents">
</dtml-let>
```

Example 2

```
<dtml-with expr="_.namespace(cost=get_cost(SKU))">
    <dtml-var name="cost" fmt="dollars-and-cents">
</dtml-with>
```

The first line of each example creates a new namespace at the top of the namespace stack and adds a variable named "cost" to it. The value of cost is set to the result of the function get_cost, defined elsewhere. Because this new namespace is at the top of the stack, this value for the name cost supercedes any other variable data with that name that might exist farther down in the namespace stack. The second line then inserts the new cost variable data into our document, formatted as dollars and cents. The third and last line closes the block and removes, or pops, the namespace containing cost from the top of the namespace stack.

Multiple variables can be assigned to a namespace within a single let block. Each attribute of let defines a new variable name. The expressions and names are evaluated and referred to one after another. Thus, variables can be assigned values based on other previously defined variables in the same let tag as below:

```
<dtml-let x="5" y="10" z="y" result="x*y*z">
    <dtml-var name="result">
</dtml-let>
```

In this example, x, y, z, and result are evaluated in succession where z and result arise from the previous assignments. The value of the result variable, 500, is output.

NOTE *If the value following the variable name is double-quoted as above, the contents are evaluated as an expression just like in the expr attribute of other tags. However, if you omit the quotes around the value, it is called by name—similar to using the name attribute. This can be useful when the desired value is the result of a callable object, such as a DTML method or ZSQL database query.*

4.3.10 The in Tag

Using the in tag, sequences such as a list or the result set of a database query can be run in a loop, with the sequence to be run defined in the start tag. The tag body contains the instructions to be used for each individual list element. Before the tag body code is executed on each element, dtml-in creates a namespace containing any attributes of the element and some other helpful variables that can be used by the body code.

```
<dtml-in Sequence Attribute>
    Instructions
</dtml-in>
```

Table 4-11 lists the most important in attributes; Table 4-12 lists those defined inside the in body. All the values listed here require at least one value. See Appendix A for a complete list.

Table 4-11: Attributes for the in Tag

Name	Explanation
name	The name of the variable that returns the sequence to be iterated. See "The name Attribute" in section 4.3.1.2.
expr	An expression that returns the sequence to be iterated. See "The expr Attribute" in section 4.3.1.3.
sort	The sort attribute is used to sort a sequence of objects before the sequence is iterated. The value attribute is the name of the attribute (or the key if the mapping attribute is specified) according to which the items are to be sorted.
start	The name of a variable that specifies the starting sequence item of the current batch. If this is omitted, iteration starts at the first item.
size	The size of each batch of sequence items to iterate. If this is omitted, the entire sequence is iterated at once.
orphan	The number of items to expand the last batch to keep it from being too small. If this is omitted, this value defaults to 3.
overlap	The number of items that overlap between each batch. If this is omitted, there is no overlap.

Table 4-12: Variables Defined Inside the in Body

Name	Explanation
sequence-item	The current element being iterated.
sequence-key	The key associated with the sequence of an item; defined if an element is a two-item tuple. Its value is set to the first item and sequence item to the second item.
sequence-index	The index (where the first number is 0) of the current item being iterated.
sequence-number	The number of the current item being iterated, where the first item is number 1.
sequence-start	The variable is true if the current element is the first item of the current batch; if not, it is false. This is useful if text must be inserted at the start of an in tag, particularly if the text refers to a batch variable defined by the in tag.
sequence-end	The variable is true if the current element is the last one of the current batch; if not, it is false. This is useful if the text must be inserted at the end of an in tag, particularly if the text refers to a batch variable defined by the in tag.
sequence-even	Set to true if sequence-index is an even number. Can be used to alternately shade rows in a table.
sequence-odd	Set to true if sequence-index is an odd number.

Using the in tag you can, for example, iterate through the elements in a list in order to display them in a table. For example, consider the following code:

```
1:    <dtml-in expr="['Henderson', 'Jackson', 'Johnson', 'Jones', 'King', 'Smith']">
2:        <dtml-if name="sequence-start">
3:            <table border>
4:                <tr>
5:                    <th>sequence-start?</th>
6:                    <th>sequence-end? </th>
7:                    <th>sequence-index</th>
8:                    <th>sequence-item</th>
9:                </tr>
10:       </dtml-if>
11:       <dtml-if name="sequence-odd">
12:           <tr bgcolor="#eeeeee">
13:       <dtml-else>
14:           <tr>
15:       </dtml-if>
16:           <td><dtml-var name="sequence-start"></td>
17:           <td><dtml-var name="sequence-end"></td>
18:           <td><dtml-var name="sequence-index"></td>
19:           <td><dtml-var name="sequence-item"></td>
20:       </tr>
21:       <dtml-if name="sequence-end">
22:           </table>
23:       </dtml-if>
24:   <dtml-else>
25:       The sequence is empty.
26:   </dtml-in>
```

In this example, a list is passed as an expression to the starting in tag (Line 1). The in tag first determines whether the list is empty (contains no items); if so, a message to this effect is output using the else tag (Lines 24 and 25). Otherwise, the code in the body is executed for each item in the list in turn.

When we start the list, dtml-in sets the variable sequence-start to true. We test for this condition using dtml-if (Line 2), and a table header is defined when it is true (Lines 3 through 9). For each item in the list, a row is added to the table containing the values provided by some of the variables defined by the in tag. The dtml-in variable sequence-odd is tested to determine whether to shade the row (Line 11). If this value is true, the row is shaded (Line 12), otherwise it is not (Line 14). When the last item of the list is iterated, dtml-in sets the variable sequence-end to true. We test for this condition using dtml-if (Line 21), and the table is closed when it is true. The rendered output of this code would look like Figure 4-7 when viewed by a browser.

sequence-start?	sequence-end?	sequence-index	sequence-item
1	0	0	Henderson
0	0	1	Jackson
0	0	2	Johnson
0	0	3	Jones
0	0	4	King
0	1	5	Smith

Figure 4-7: The output of the code to iterate elements and display them in a table

The in tag defines several variables with which you can carry out statistical calculations on the sequence elements and that allow the batch processing of sequences. This can be very useful in the case of long sequences that are better displayed in several small batches instead of all at once.

See Appendix A for a list of summary and statistics variables, special element grouping variables, and batch processing variables.

4.3.10.1 Count Loops Using the in Tag

Another useful function of the in tag is its ability to repeatedly execute code. To do this, the in tag uses the range method, which can accept a maximum of three arguments:

```
range(Startvalue, Endvalue, Interval)
```

If only one argument is specified, the argument is the end value, the start value is zero, and the interval is 1. Using this method a list of the numbers is created, and the resulting list can be run through the in tag. For example, calling up range(5) creates a five-element list with the elements [0, 1, 2, 3, 4] so that you can use the in tag to define a loop to run the actions five times.

The following causes the line "Hello!" to be inserted ten times in the rendered output of a document:

```
<dtml-in "_.range(10)">
    Hello!<br>
</dtml-in>
```

4.3.11 The tree Tag

The tree tag is used to survey Zope objects in their hierarchy and present them as a tree structure with collapsible branches and leaves. Thus, you can create a tree structure view like the one used in the left-hand frame of the management interface. In the example in Figure 4-8, a folder named Folder1 contains several objects:

Type	Name	Size	Last Modified
☐ 📁	Subfolder1		2001-05-27 22:36
☐ 📁	Subfolder2		2001-05-28 02:17
☐ 🔲	acl_users (User Folder)		2001-05-27 22:06
☐ 📄	dtml_document2	1 Kb	2001-05-28 02:18
☐ 📄	dtml_method1	1 Kb	2001-05-28 02:19
☐ 📄	dtml_method2	1 Kb	2001-05-28 02:19
☐ 📄	index_html	1 Kb	2001-05-27 22:06

Figure 4-8: The objects in Folder1

To create a simple tree structure view, use the tree tag in a DTML method located in Folder1:

```
<dtml-tree>
<dtml-var name=" id">
</dtml-tree>
```

The tree view appears in the third tier view as shown in Figure 4-9.

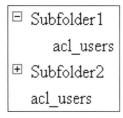

Figure 4-9: A simple tree structure view

The tree view in Figure 4-9 displays only folderish objects located in the current folder and is visually less attractive than the one used by the management interface. The tree tag itself is very complex and accepts a wide variety of attributes that can be used to format a tree view. For example, to start a tree from a location other than the one the DTML method is located in, you must specify the name of the object from which the tree should start, like so:

```
<dtml-tree name="Subfolder1">
```

The branches and branches_expr attributes are set as standard for the method tpValues. The method with which all objects and subobjects are found is called objectValues. These methods are defined for you in folderish objects.

To make sure that both objects and their appropriate icons are displayed in the tree view, use the following code:

```
<dtml-tree>
    <IMG SRC="<dtml-var name="icon">"> <dtml-var name="id">
</dtml-tree>
```

The most important tree tag attributes are listed in Table 4-13. See Appendix A for a complete list. Asterisked attributes require at least one argument.

Table 4-13: Attributes for the tree Tag

Name	Explanation
name*	See "The name Attribute" section 4.3.1.2.
expr*	See "The expr Attribute" in 4.3.1.3.
branches*	The name of the method used to find subobjects. The default is tpValues, a method that finds folderish objects. The method objectValues finds all objects and subobjects beneath another object. The value must be a method name.
leaves*	The name of a document that uses "leaves" to expand subjects that do not have subobjects.
header*	The name of a document to be displayed above any branch expansion. This allows you to mark a branch in a hierarchy.
footer*	The name of the document displayed beneath each expansion.
sort*	Sorts the branches before text is inserted. The attribute value is the name of the attribute by which the elements are to be sorted.

Additionally, the tree tag places in the namespace a number of variables that organize the display of the objects in a tree. Some of these variables are listed in Table 4-14.

Table 4-14: Variables in the tree Tag Body

Name	Explanation
tree-item-expand	True if the current element is expanded.
tree-item-url	The relative URL of the current element.
tree-root-url	The URL of the DTML document in which the tree tag appears.
tree-level	The depth of the current element.
tree-colspan	The number of tree nestings called.
tree-state	The tree status; output as a list of ids and sublists of sub-ids.

The following example displays a tree view containing all subordinate objects and additional image files inside Folder1.

```
1:    <dtml-var standard_html_header>
2:    <h1>Image Files</h1>
3:    <dtml-call expr="REQUEST.set('expand_all',1)">
4:    <dtml-tree name="Folder1" branches="objectValues">
5:        <dtml-if expr="meta_type == 'Image'">
6:            <IMG SRC="<dtml-var name="icon">">
7:            <a href="<dtml-var name="tree-item-url">"><dtml-var
              name="id"></a>
8:        <dtml-else>
9:            <IMG SRC="<dtml-var icon>"> <dtml-var id>
10:       </dtml-if>
11:   </dtml-tree>
12:   <dtml-var standard_html_footer>
```

On Line 3, the expand_all variable is set to true by calling REQUEST.set to instruct the tree tag to expand all of its branches down to the leaves by default. The tree tag is then opened (Line 4) and Folder1 is specified as the folder for the tree tag to recurse. The branches attribute of dtml-tree is set to objectValues (a method that returns all objects within a folder) in place of the default method tpValues (which returns only folderish objects).

Inside the tree body, we check to see if the current object is an image by using dtml-if (Line 5) to test the value of its meta_type, an attribute of all Zope objects. If the object is an image, we display its icon and construct a link to it using the variable tree-item-url supplied by the tree tag (Lines 6 and 7); otherwise only the icon and object id are inserted (Line 9). The body of the tree tag is then closed (Line 11). Figure 4-10 shows the rendered output of the document.

Figure 4-10: A complete tree structure view of Folder1

4.3.12 The sendmail Tag

The sendmail tag sends electronic mail using the Standard Mail Transport Protocol (SMTP). One feature of the sendmail tag is that no text substitution is carried out, meaning that email is sent without rendering text into your document. Since the text of the email will not appear to the user viewing the page containing the sendmail tag, a message confirming that the email was sent should be included elsewhere in the page.

The sendmail tag requires four parameters: an SMTP host address or a Zope mailhost object; a recipient's address; the sender's address; and a subject.

The last three items may either be specified as attributes inside the tag (as is customary) or they can be placed in a *header line form*. A header line form consists of the header followed by a colon, then a space, and then the relevant data. The header line of a sendmail tag should include the following fields:

To: [The email address of the recipient].

From: [The address of the sender comes next. This information is optional, although the header must not be omitted.]

Subject: [The subject of the email. This information is optional, although the header must not be omitted.]

The message's text follows these parameters. There must be at least one blank line between the subject line and the message text.

NOTE *The message is sent as soon as the sendmail tag is called. As a result, it is best to code the sending of email messages into a separate object that is called only for this purpose.*

4.3.12.1 "SampleMail" Example

For example, as a result of the code shown below, Ms. Smith will receive this email (although it would clearly make more sense to use a mail program to send this one-time email). If you enhance the sendmail tag with a number of DTML tags to achieve dynamic layout, you can use the sendmail tag to send email with variable content from a website.

```
<dtml-sendmail smtphost="mail.mycompany.com">
To: smith@company.com
From: Michael Haze <Michael@wproductions.cde>
Subject: Your last order
Dear Ms. Smith,
I regret to inform you that delivery of the goods you recently ordered will be
delayed by up to two days.
We apologize for any inconvenience and thank you for your patience.
Best regards,
Michael Haze
</dtml-sendmail>
```

The following examples illustrate two DTML methods. The DTML method form_dtml (Listing 4-1) generates a form in which only an address, a subject, and the actual message need to be entered. The data is then passed on to the DTML method sendmail (Listing 4-2), which contains the sendmail tag (see Table 4-15 for a list of sendmail tag attributes) used to send the message specified in the form.

Listing 4-1: The DTML Method form_dtml

```
<dtml-var standard_html_header>
<H2>Your Message:</H2>
<form action="sendmail" method="get">

Sender: <input type="text" name="name" size="40"><br>
Recipient: <input type="text" name="address" size=40><br>
Subject: <input type="text" name="subject" size=40><br>
<textarea name="message" rows="10" cols="50"></textarea><br>
<input type="submit" value="Send Message">
</form>
<dtml-var standard_html_footer>
```

Listing 4-2: The DTML Method sendmail

```
<dtml-var standard_html_header>
<dtml-sendmail smtphost="mail.mycompany.com">
to: <dtml-var name="address">
from: <dtml-var name="name">
Subject: <dtml-var name="subject">
<dtml-var name="message">
</dtml-sendmail>
<dtml-comment> The following message will be displayed when the message is
sent:</dtml-comment>
<h1>Your message has been sent </h1>
<a href="file_dtml">Compose another message</a>
<dtml-var standard_html_footer>
```

Recipient and sender addresses as well as the subjects and contents of emails are submitted from the form (Figure 4-11) to the sendmail method. The form data is then found in the namespace of the sendmail method. From here, the variables address, name, subject, and message are looked up and their values inserted into the body of the sendmail tag. Only then is the message sent. The user is then provided with a confirmation message that the email was sent.

Table 4-15: Attributes for the sendmail Tag

Name	Function	Example
mailhost	The Zope MailHost object that manages data required to send electronic mail. If this attribute is used, the smtphost is unnecessary.	`<dtml-sendmail mailhost="MailHost1">`
smtphost	The address of the SMTP server to be used. If this attribute is used, the MailHost attribute is unnecessary.	`<dtml-sendmail smtphost= "mail.mycompany.com">`
port	This attribute can be used only with the smtphost attribute, and the port number for a connection must be specified. If the smtphost attribute is used without the port attribute, the port number is set to 25 by default.	`<dtml-sendmail smtphost= "mail.mycompany.com" port="20">`
mailto	The recipient's address. Multiple addresses are separated by commas.	`<dtml-sendmail mailhost=MailHost1 mailto="abc@beehive.com" mailfrom="xyz@mycompany.com" subject="Meeting today">`
mailfrom	The sender's address.	
subject	The subject of the message.	

Figure 4-11: A simple email form

4.3.13 The MIME Tag and the boundary Tag

Often you will need to email not only text messages but also file attachments. To send attachments, you will need to use the MIME tag and one or more boundary tags, which are only permissible within the sendmail tag.

When you insert a MIME tag, the content of the message you are sending is automatically set to *multipart/mixed* so that files can be attached to the email using the boundary tags. The MIME tag is a non-empty tag and contains the required boundary tags.

The start MIME tag must be inserted on the last header line with no spaces between it and the subject header. You can use the MIME tag attributes to specify the message properties. If you want to send only files but no message text, you can omit the MIME tag attributes, as shown below:

```
<dtml-var standard_html_header>
<dtml-sendmail mailhost="MailHost1">
from: martina@beehive.com
to: martina@beehive.com
subject: Requested  files
<dtml-mime type="text/plain" encode="7bit">
Here are the files you requested:
```

A boundary tag for each file to be sent follows the message text, organizing their transport. The MIME and the boundary tag both use the same optional attributes, which are listed in Table 4-16. The file object(s) to be sent are inserted in a var tag immediately after the boundary tag (there must not be any blank spaces).

Table 4-16: Attributes for the MIME Tag and the boundary Tag

Attribute	Function	Example
type	Indicates the type and format of the data. The default value is application/octet stream.	Type="image/bmp"
disposition	Sets the content disposition of the following data. If the disposition is not specified in a MIME or boundary tag, the content disposition MIME header is not inserted into the message.	disposition="attachment"
name	Indicates the name of the file object to be attached. If the name attribute is used in the MIME tag, the message is sent as an attachment and not as standard text.	name="wordfile"
encode	Sets the encoding method for the files to be sent. The default value is base64, which is suitable for sending binary files to most mail clients. The following options are available: base64, uuencode, x-uuencode, quote-printable, uue, x-uue, and 7bit. If encode is set to 7bit, no encoding is applied. This is appropriate for textual document formats such as HTML.	encode=uuencode

Files sent using the sendmail tag must exist as file objects on the Zope server; you cannot send files directly from the file system. To send a file from the filesystem, first create a new Zope file object and insert the desired file. You can see your file object in the Management screen as shown in Figure 4-12.

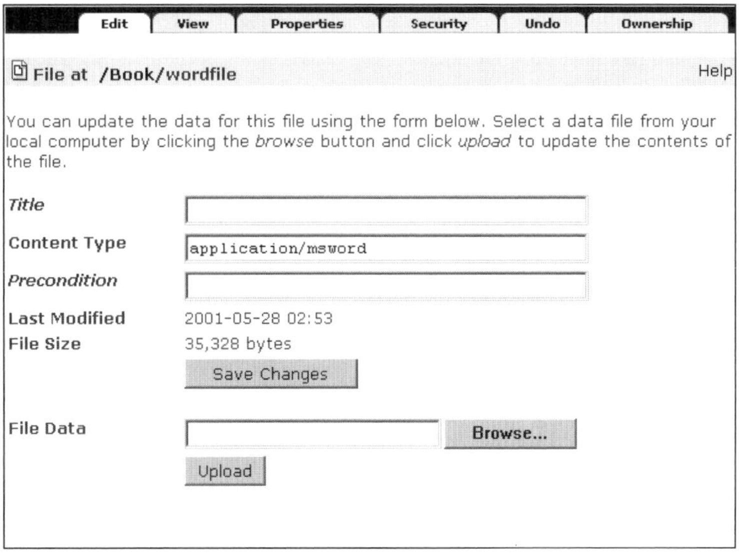

Figure 4-12: The properties of the file object, which contains the file to be sent

You can use this screen to determine which MIME content type to set in the corresponding boundary tag. When the content type is correctly set, the recipient will be able to click on a received file to open it in the associated program—depending, of course, on the mail program the recipient is using to view the mail.

You do not need to set the type attribute if you use as the name attribute a filename whose extension already identifies the file type sent. The file extension .doc, for example, indicates that a file was created using Microsoft Word. If the name attribute contain no extension, the mail client will be unable to find the appropriate application. In this case, the type attribute must be set, or the file will be regarded as an "unspecified type" and will not be associated with the appropriate application.

In the following example, we send two files: The first created in Microsoft Word has its full name given in the name attribute. (The type attribute is therefore not required.) The second is an image file for which no file extension is specified and for which the content type must be set.

```
<dtml-boundary name="Working with Zope Versions.doc" disposition="attachment"
encode="base64">
<dtml-var "wordfile">
<dtml-boundary type="image/bmp" name="spacecraft" disposition="attachment"
encode="7bit">
<dtml-var e_h.bmp>
```

```
</dtml-mime>
</dtml-sendmail>
Your message has been sent
<dtml-var standard_html_footer>
```

Netscape Messenger displays this message as in Figure 4-13.

Figure 4-13: The email message displayed in Netscape

NOTE *If a recipient lacks the correct application, the computer is improperly configured, or the mail program is incapable of doing so, the recipient may not be able to open attachments by clicking on them even though you set the correct content type.*

4.3.14 The comment Tag

The comment tag indicates text to be ignored by Zope. It is not an empty and contains the following text:

```
<dtml-comment>
     Comment text goes here.
</dtml-comment>
```

Zope ignores all text in the body of the tag, thus allowing you to insert comments explaining your source code, for example. The comment tag is also useful for fixing errors if, for example, you annotate parts of your DTML code to allow the focus to be placed on other parts.

Comment tags may be nested. And, because Zope ignores everything marked by the comment tag, you can annotate other comment tags so you can insert and check code sections piece by piece to fix problems.

```
<dtml-comment>
     This text is ignored by Zope.
<dtml-comment>
       This text is also ignored by Zope.
     </dtml-comment>
     And so is this text!
</dtml-comment>
```

Annotated text does not appear as a comment in the source text in the third tier view. Use the standard HTML comment if you want it to appear in the rendered source.

The comment tag accepts no attributes.

Unfortunately, the comment tag does not completely ignore DTML tags placed inside its body. Although no code inside a comment is ever executed, it must still be well formed and balanced for the DTML parser to accept the document. Because of this, it is not possible to comment out just the start tag of a dtml block (a dtml-if block, for example).

4.3.15 The try and the except Tags

You may sometimes wish to access a variable even though you do not know whether it has been defined or whether you can consult it. If you try to access a non-existent variable, Zope will generate an error message, just as when a faulty expression is called. You might also be making a call that relies on an external system that could fail, such as sending an email as above. These operations can be a problem in certain circumstances because the error message prevents you from displaying a document in the third tier.

Use the try and except tags to bypass error messages. The try tag is a non-empty tag and accepts no attributes. It contains the instructions to be carried out but which may generate a Zope error. It can also include one or more except tags, which may contain alternative instructions to be carried out. The except accepts an optional attribute that identifies the type of error it traps. If the attribute is omitted, the except block traps all errors not already trapped above it.

The following structure is used:

```
<dtml-try>
    Instructions that can fail or cause errors
<dtml-except Error>
    Instructions to handle the error or exception case Error
<dtml-except>
    Instructions to handle any other errors.
</dtml-try>
```

For example, say we have a variable that we want to use as a divisor in an expression and that we want to trap any errors caused if the expression tries to divide by zero. To trap the error and bypass a Zope error message, use the try tag as follows:

```
<dtml-try>
    The result is: <dtml-var expr="100/x">
<dtml-except DivideByZeroError>
    The result could not be displayed.
</dtml-try>
```

The code above bypasses the error message so that the remainder of the document can be displayed. The person viewing the document is informed that the result could not be displayed.

4.3.16 The finally Tag

The finally tag can only be used within the try tag. To define a block of instructions that will always be carried out regardless of whether an error message needs to be bypassed, use the finally tag instead of the except tag, as follows:

```
<dtml-try>
    Instructions
<dtml-finally>
    Instructions to be carried out in all cases
</dtml-try>
```

4.3.17 The raise Tag

Use the raise tag to cause and generate your own Zope error message. You can define your own names for your error messages and define the error text to be displayed.

The raise tag is non-empty. The error message belongs in the start tag and the error text is placed in the tag body. The error message must consist of individual words. You can specify entire texts for the error text.

```
<dtml-raise Errormessage>Error text</dtml-raise>
```

The following code produces a simple error message:

```
<dtml-raise MyError> This is the problem.</dtml-raise>
```

The error output is shown in Figure 4-14.

Zope Error

Zope has encountered an error while publishing this resource.

Error Type: MyError
Error Value: This is the problem.

Figure 4-14: The self-defined error message

You can also use dtml-raise to generate internal Zope errors. One such error, Unauthorized, can be raised to log the current user out of Zope:

```
<dtml-raise Unauthorized>You are logged out.</dtml-raise>
```

4.3.18 The return Tag

The return tag can be used to interrupt the execution of DTML at any time and return a value without raising an error. Normally DTML objects return only text, but with dtml-return they can return any type desired—including other objects.

The following example returns only the number 25; all of the other text that would normally be returned is ignored.

```
The document id is: <dtml-var name="id">
<dtml-return expr="25">
```

Summary

You should now be familiar with the DTML syntax and know the most important general DTML tags, which will allow you to create websites with dynamic content. Among other things, you can

- Insert and format content from variables, objects, or expressions using dtml-var.
- Use the namespace variable (_) to look up names and call utility functions.
- Communicate between client and server using the REQUEST and RESPONSE objects.
- Call objects without insertion using dtml-call.
- Conditionally execute code using dtml-if.
- Manipulate the namespace stack using dtml-with and dtml-let.
- Iterate lists and sequences using dtml-in.
- Traverse and iterate a hierarchy of objects using dtml-tree.
- Send mail messages and file attachments using dtml-sendmail.
- Catch and raise errors using dtml-try and dtml-raise.
- Return arbitrary values using dtml-return.

5

WORKING WITH ZOPE VERSIONS

The more complex your website, the more complex its structure will be, and the more you will need to maintain it—yet remain unseen by your everyday user. The challenge, of course, is to make your changes without affecting your site's functionality.

This chapter will present the solution to this problem: Zope's versions feature. Zope versions let you modify objects without immediately affecting your application and without displaying changes in process to your users until you're ready.

Briefly, when using Zope's versions, you do your testing and modifications (editing, creating, and deleting objects) within one or more temporary version workspaces. Then, once you are sure that everything is working properly, you save your version's changes, in turn updating all of the modified objects simultaneously. Your updated web pages, with their new content and functionality, then appear to your users.

This chapter will show you how to create versions; access, edit, exit, and delete them; and how to save or discard the changes you make. We'll follow our discussion with a simple example.

5.1 Creating a Version

You can create a new version in any folder you want, but it is a good idea to create it in the folder where the website objects to be changed are located. If you are working on several separate subprojects at once, you can create additional versions in other folders and later associate the various changes with the correct subproject.

NOTE *Placing a version in a particular folder does not mean that the version affects only that folder. Versions are global and work the same regardless of where they are created in your Zope hierarchy. Placing versions in the folder you are working in is merely a convenience.*

To begin working with versions, open the Available-Objects menu in the desired folder and select Version. Once you enter an id and a title, you will have created a version, which will be shown in the contents view with a red diamond icon.

5.2 Joining and Leaving a Version

You must join a version before you can work in it. To join a version, click the version you want to join and, on the Join/Leave screen that appears, click Start Working in Version id, as shown in Figure 5-1. Then begin your work.

Figure 5-1: Joining a version with the id update

Once you join a version, a button labeled "Quit Working in Version id," shown in Figure 5-2, will appear in that version's Join/Leave screen. Click this button to leave the version. (You can work in only one version at a time.) When you leave a version, you return to the default Zope workspace, where changes immediately affect your users.

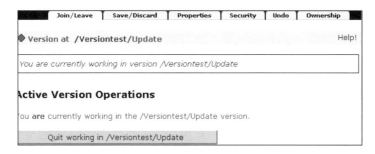

Figure 5-2: Leaving the version

When you are working in a version, a line on each Zope screen tells you which version you are working in. To be sure that you are working in the correct version, check the version name on the Join/Leave screen so you don't get lost when you have created multiple versions. It is helpful to use a somewhat descriptive id for each version (such as a subproject's name) so that you can tell at a glance what changes should be made in it.

5.3 Working in a Version

When working in a version, you can make and test changes as usual. Edited objects are marked by a small red diamond. When you create an object, both the new object and the folder above it are marked with a diamond.

NOTE *Multiple users can join and work in the same version simultaneously.*

If you leave a version without applying your changes, the edited objects are locked and can be edited only when you rejoin that version or once the version's changes have been saved or discarded. Locked objects are indicated by a small blue lock and details of the locked version; for example:

If you create or delete an object or change its properties or security settings when working in a folder without saving your version's changes, that entire folder will be locked, and you will be unable to add or delete objects in that folder or modify its properties outside of the version. By locking objects changed in a version, Zope prevents conflicts that would occur if an object could be changed in two versions at the same time.

NOTE *Be very careful when working in a version in your root folder, especially if several people are working with the server at once. If you fail to save your changes properly, you could unintentionally lock the root folder for all other users.*

When you finish working in a version, you can choose to save or discard all of the changes you made in it at once.

5.3.1 Updating Objects

To make your changes to a version visible to the outside world, you must save it. Do so on the Save/Discard screen, accessed by selecting a version and then clicking Save to make the update.

NOTE *It is a good idea to enter a brief comment in the text field above the Save (or Discard) button. This comment then appears on each modified object's history screen and helps you identify the action if you need to undo it later.*

Discard changes by clicking Discard on the Save/Discard screen and entering a comment if you like. If your version's changes have been saved, you can no longer discard them in that version, but must use Undo instead. (If you added comments when you saved, it should be easy to find the desired one to undo.)

5.3.2 Saving and Discarding Changes Using the Control Panel

The Control Panel can also be used to save or discard changes to one or several versions. To do so, open the Control Panel and click Version Management, where you should see a list of all versions that can be changed. To save or discard changes for a version, select the check boxes next to each and click Save or Discard, as shown in Figure 5-3.

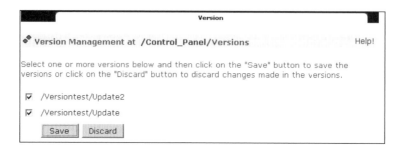

Figure 5-3: The changes in both versions are saved in one step

5.4 Deleting a Version

Before you can delete a version, you must make sure that all changes made to it have been saved or discarded. To check, view the version's Save/Discard screen and see whether any changes need to be saved or discarded. Or, open the Control Panel and use Version Management to see whether the desired version appears in the list there. If it does not, you can be sure that all changes have been saved or discarded, and the version can be deleted. If you try to delete a version that contains unapplied changes, an error message appears.

To delete a version, select the check box beside the version you want to delete and click Delete.

5.5 Working with Multiple Versions

When working with multiple versions, remember these tips:

- Always leave one version before moving to another. If you don't, you will need to undo the changes belonging to the version you accidentally joined, and you will have to make them again in the correct version. Always pay attention to the following information at the top of the management screen:

```
You are currently working in version [path for the current version]
```

- Limit the number of versions you work with to reduce the risk of confusing them, particularly if versions are in the same folder and one version locks another.

- Although you can create a new version while working in another, you will not be able to join the new version until you leave the old one. Consequently, the new version can be joined only after you save the changes to the original version you created it in.

5.6 An Example

Let's make versions a bit more concrete with this example.

1. In the root folder of a Zope server, create a folder called Versiontest that includes a user folder and public interface, as shown in Figure 5-4.

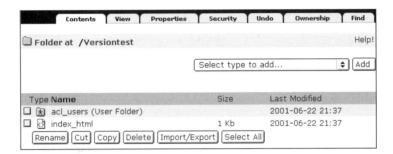

Figure 5-4: The Versiontest folder

2. Create two version objects called Update and Update2, then join the version called Update as shown in Figure 5-5.

3. Create a user named Meyer and assign the role of Manager to him.

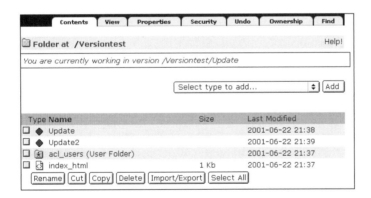

Figure 5-5: Joining Update

4. Enter the Properties screen for the folder, change the value of the title property, and save the changes.

5. Leave this version (Update) and join Update2.

As you can see in Figure 5-6, the folder Versiontest is locked by Update because the change you made to the title property affects the entire folder. Consequently, you can edit only the index_html object, but you cannot delete or create any objects in the folder.

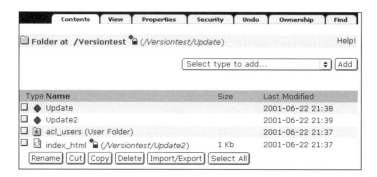

Figure 5-6: Leaving Update and joining Update2

6. Change the code in the file index_html working in version Update2 as follows:

```
<dtml-var standard_html_header>

<h2>Hello <dtml-var name="AUTHENTICATED_USER"></h2>

<p>

This is the <dtml-var id> Document.

</p>

<dtml-var standard_html_footer>
```

7. Leave the version (see Figure 5-7).

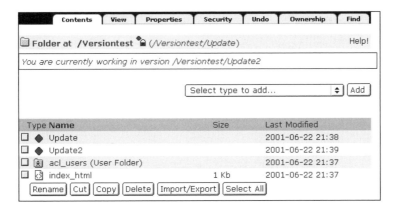

Figure 5-7: index_html is locked by Update2

If you now view the index_html object (Figure 5-8), you see no changes. Your modifications will be visible only to general users when that version's changes have been saved.

Figure 5-8: Accessing index_html before saving the version

8. On the Control Panel, use Version Management to apply the changes to both versions simultaneously.

Notice on the Contents screen that the locks on the edited objects have been removed, and all users can see the changes you made while in the versions (Figure 5-9).

Figure 5-9: Accessing index_html after saving the version

9. Finally, delete both versions. Once you save your changes within a version, you may discard it unless you plan to work in it again.

Summary

This chapter has shown you how to work with versions in Zope, including how to create or modify a version and how to apply your changes. You should now be able to delete individual versions and manage multiple versions simultaneously using the Control Panel. Armed with this information, you should be able to edit your projects to meet your requirements and make modified objects available to your users in a controlled and testable manner.

6

USERS, ROLES, AND SECURITY

This chapter will look at the Zope security structure. We will create and edit new users using both the Management screen and DTML. We will also create new roles and take a closer look at the various permissions that Zope provides for users. Finally we will explore Zope's procedure to authenticate users.

6.1 Zope's Security Structure

One of the most important and powerful security functions provided by Zope is its ability to define roles, which can then be used to assign and remove user permissions.

NOTE *This book uses the terms "rights" and "permissions" synonymously.*

The following two examples demonstrate the uses of roles and permissions:

1. A group of developers is working together on different parts of a Zope project. You want to ensure that individual team members cannot change parts of the project that are outside their area of responsibility.

2. Large companies consist of several departments in which various people have overall responsibility. If this type of company wants to establish an Internet presence, care must be taken to ensure that no one individual user in a group (in this case, a department) can make changes in another department's areas, and that if problems do arise, it is easy to determine who is responsible.

These are only two of the many ways that Zope's roles and permissions allow you to achieve the desired distribution of responsibility and control.

6.1.1 User Roles

Each Zope user has a specific role (or roles) within Zope, regardless of whether that user works directly managing Zope or merely with pages published by Zope on the Internet or intranet. Through those roles, each user is assigned specific permissions and access rights. Roles may have been previously created, or they can be created as needed by authorized users.

6.1.2 Zope Roles: Anonymous, Manager, Owner

The roles already present in Zope are Anonymous, Manager, and Owner. New roles can be created and assigned only by users who have the rights or permissions needed to do so.

The permissions assigned to each role (and hence to each user assigned to that role) determine what actions the user can carry out with regard to the objects and management functions in Zope. Permissions determine whether and where users can view, create, or modify Zope objects or perform management tasks.

6.1.2.1 Anonymous

By default, Zope automatically assigns the Anonymous role to all users who have not explicitly logged in. Users assigned the Anonymous role can only view pages for which the View permission has been assigned to the Anonymous role, which by default is all Zope objects except the Control_Panel folder.

Of course, the permissions for the Anonymous role can be expanded to include actions other than View, as we'll describe in Section 6.1.4. In addition, when you create a new user in Zope (see Section 6.2.1), you specify the role(s) assigned to that user and define new roles and their permissions.

By default, the role Anonymous has the Access contents information and View permissions for all objects. (In section 8.3.4, "Assigning Permissions for login_html," we'll remove this permission from the Anonymous role for a specific object to restrict Anonymous users' access to that object.

6.1.2.2 Manager

By default, the Manager role is assigned all existing permissions, for all objects. Whereas you can change the permissions assigned to the Manager role for specific objects, we recommend against doing so because it is very easy to deactivate the wrong permissions, thus removing access to the object instead.

NOTE *Zope allows you to define a special emergency user, which can be used to fix such a situation. To define this user you use the zpasswd.py program (see section 1.5.3.3).*

6.1.2.3 Owner

The Owner role has no permissions by default. It is used primarily to determine the permissions of the owner (or creator) of an object. When a user creates an object in Zope, that object is automatically given the local role Owner (see section 7.1 for more information on local roles).

6.1.3 Assigning and Creating Roles

If you wish to assign a new role, such as Manager, to a user, you must first create a user object in Zope and assign the username, password, and roles to it. Do so in the User Folder (*acl_users*) for the object the user is to access, or in a higher folder (see section 6.2.1).

When you create a new role, it initially has no permissions, so you must assign the necessary permissions to your role on the desired objects after you create it.

As described above, roles and permissions control an individual's ability to perform actions in Zope. Each role can be assigned any desired permissions. For example, Anonymous users can view various published pages but cannot open the Zope management screen to change these pages unless they have been assigned the View management screens permission. Even if they have this permission, they may lack other specific permissions for actions taken in the management screen such as adding, modifying, or deleting objects.

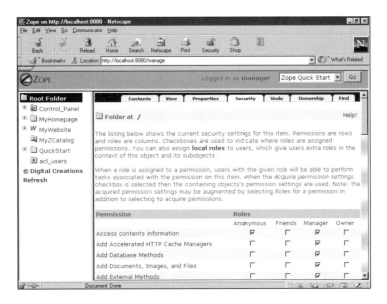

Figure 6-1: Security screen in the root folder

You can edit roles and permissions for an object from the Security tab in the management screen (see Figure 6-1); if you have the Manage permissions permission for that object, you make the necessary changes to the Security settings. If you do not have this permission on an object, you will not see its Security tab.

When you work with folderish objects, the specified roles and permissions apply to the folderish object for which they were defined as well all objects within that folder, unless you specify not to acquire certain permissions for these objects. (See section 6.1.4 for an explanation of permission acquisition).

6.1.3.1 View Management

To view, create, or modify Zope objects or to perform management tasks, the user must be authorized to view the management screen in Zope (see section 2.2). The permission that allows users access to the management screen is called "View management screens."

/manage

You can manage every Zope object by typing the suffix /manage after the object's URL, provided your role authorizes you to do so. (We will discuss how to create roles and assign permissions in Sections 6.2.3 and 6.1.4.) If, for example, you want to manage the DTML document my_document in the folder my_folder, simply enter the following URL:

```
http://localhost:8080/my_folder/my_document/manage
```

To see the third tier's rendered view of the DTML document, omit the suffix /manage from the end of the URL. To view an object, your role must have the View permissions for that object.

Whenever a user tries to perform an action, Zope checks to see if the proper permissions are assigned to the user's roles. If a user tries to perform an action for which that user is not currently authorized, Zope will first ask the user to *authenticate* or log in. In response, the user must enter a username and password that Zope recognizes as belonging to a role with permission to perform the action. If the username and password are invalid or do not correspond to a user with the proper permissions, Zope generates an *Unauthorized* error message.

6.1.4 Assigning Permissions Using Acquisition

As explained in section 2.5, acquisition plays a pivotal role in Zope. Like other attributes of objects, such as properties, permissions settings can be acquired by an object from its parent objects, all the way up to the root folder.

It works like this: Imagine a folder as an object with a long list of permissions—such as Access contents information, Add Database Methods, and so on—shown in the Security screen. Each permission has a checkbox to the left of it, in the Acquire permission settings? column, as shown in Figure 6-2.

NOTE *Folderish objects contain all permissions available for all object types it can contain. Installing new Zope products often allows you to create new types of objects that have their own additional permission settings. This is why the permissions list is so much longer for folderish Zope objects than it is for non-folderish objects.*

Permission	Roles			
Acquire permission settings?		Anonymous	Friends	Manager	Owner
☑ Access contents information	☐	☐	☑	☐
☑ Add Accelerated HTTP Cache Managers	☐	☐	☑	☐
☑ Add Database Methods	☐	☐	☑	☐
☑ Add Documents, Images, and Files	☐	☐	☑	☐
☑ Add External Methods	☐	☐	☑	☐
☑ Add Folders	☐	☐	☑	☐
☑ Add MailHost objects	☐	☐	☑	☐
☑ Add Python Scripts	☐	☐	☑	☐
☑ Add RAM Cache Managers	☐	☐	☑	☐

Figure 6-2: Activated "Acquire permission settings?" checkboxes

6.1.4.1 Acquire permission settings?

The right-hand columns in the permissions list define the roles for the current folder. When the Acquire permission settings? checkbox is checked (the default, shown in Figure 6.2), acquisition is active for the relevant permission, and the current folder acquires its permission and role settings from the next highest folder.

If Acquire permission settings? is active in that next highest folder, that folder acquires the settings from the one above it and so on, up the hierarchy to the root folder. Thus, the permissions set for the roles in a folder (or folderish object) can spread quite far, depending on how extensively the setting Acquire permission settings? is activated in the object hierarchy.

Acquisition is more complicated than this, however. If you look at the roles in the Security screen (Figure 6-3), you see checkboxes beneath them as well. These checkboxes allow Zope managers to allocate permissions among roles differently from their superordinate folders.

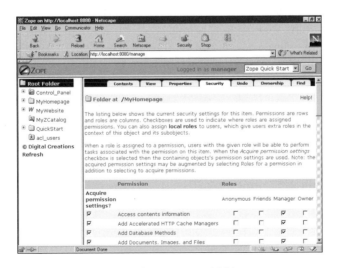

Figure 6-3: Security screen for an Activated folder

For example, imagine that we have a folder hierarchy consisting of a State folder, containing a County folder, which in turn contains a City folder (Figure 6-4) We see the permission Access contents information in the Security tab of all three folders. If Acquire permission settings? is activated for this permssion in both County and City (as it is by default), then all roles in City will acquire their settings for Access contents information from the County and State folder and all folders above State up to the Root folder via acquisition. Changes to the permission made in State will also affect County and City. Changes made to County will affect City (but not State), and changes made to City will only affect itself.

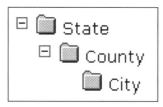

Figure 6-4: Example folder hierarchy

Acquiring permissions works well, assuming you want the subordinate folders to have the permissions granted in their parents; but what if you want the Access contents information permission granted to a particular role in State, but not to County contained in it?

In County, first deactivate Acquire permission settings? for the Access contents information permission and make sure that the checkbox opposite Access contents information under the role you are restricting is also deactivated. Deactivating Acquire permission settings? means that *none* of the roles in County will inherit this permission setting from State—so you may need to manually activate the checkboxes for other roles to which you still want to grant this permission.

If, however, you want to reactivate the permission for the role in the City folder contained by County, you will no longer be able to use acquisition because the permission is not set for the role in the County folder. Instead, you would need to set the permission explicitly in City using the checkbox under the role to the right of the Access contents information permission.

We see here that deactivating the Acquire permission settings? for Folder X in a hierarchy breaks the acquisition chain for this permission. If you then activate Acquire permission settings? for this permission in a subfolder of Folder X, a new acquisition chain begins from that subfolder and continues down through successive layers of folders thereafter.

NOTE   *The example given above also applies to non-folderish objects—which are always at the end of the acquisition chain because they cannot contain additional subobjects.*

By combining acquisition (using Acquire permission settings?) with directly activating or deactivating roles, you can modify permissions to meet your security requirements. (This will be illustrated in section 8.3, "Example: Authentication," with a simple but important example of authentication.)

Because acquisition can make it difficult to see exactly which permissions are granted to each role on a given object, it can sometimes be beneficial to deactivate Acquire permission settings? for all permissions and set them all explicitly. This is especially true of objects that must be tightly secured because they have the potential to be destructive or to expose sensitive data.

Acquisition makes it easier and more efficient for Zope programmers and administrators to create and manage websites. For example, using acquisition the Zope programmer can create all necessary roles in the root folder and set the permissions according to their defaults. Once these changes are saved, the settings apply to all existing folders and subfolders in Zope as well as all folders that you later create. To set different permissions for one or more objects, we simply deactivate the appropriate Acquire permission settings? checkbox for the relevant object and change the permissions as required. (Remember that in so doing you are breaking the security acquisition chain.) All subobjects default to the same permissions as the object where the acquisition chain was broken (if the Acquire permission settings? checkbox is still activated for the subobjects).

Because administrators cannot always know when roles are added or changed through the hierarchy, you should devote adequate time to designing the security structure in large projects. Carefully consider which permissions are required and how many different user roles there should be.

6.1.5   Ownership

The user who creates a new object in Zope automatically becomes that object's owner, granting them the permissions assigned to the owner role on that object. The Ownership tab on an object is used to inspect and modify the current ownership of an object.

When you click on the Ownership tab (shown in Figure 6-5), you open the Ownership screen for the object (Figure 6-6). The Ownership screen shows who owns the object—that is, the object's creator. Objects created during the Zope installation are unowned.

Figure 6-5: The Ownership tab

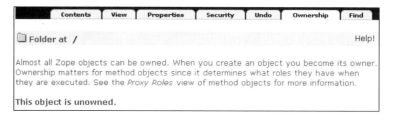

Figure 6-6: Ownership screen of the root folder (unowned)

6.1.5.1 Ownership When Importing

When you import objects (Figure 6-7), you can retain their current ownership settings or become their new owner (for more information on importing, see section 3.1.9.3, "Importing Objects").

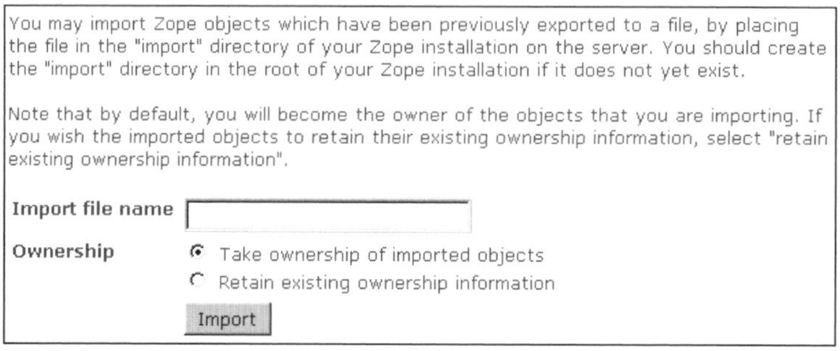

You may import Zope objects which have been previously exported to a file, by placing the file in the "import" directory of your Zope installation on the server. You should create the "import" directory in the root of your Zope installation if it does not yet exist.

Note that by default, you will become the owner of the objects that you are importing. If you wish the imported objects to retain their existing ownership information, select "retain existing ownership information".

Import file name [   ]

Ownership   ⦿ Take ownership of imported objects
                 ○ Retain existing ownership information
                 [Import]

Figure 6-7: Importing an object

The Ownership screen shows the user who owns the object. Users who do not own the objects see only the text indicating who does own the objects (although users with permission to Take Ownership see the Take Ownership button (shown in Figure 6-8). If you click the Take Ownership button, you become the owner of the object.

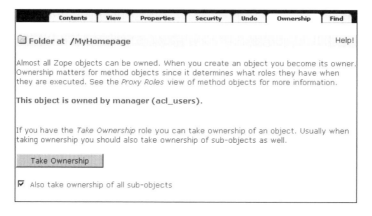

Figure 6-8: Ownership screen with Take Ownership button

The ownership of an object is especially important for executable objects such as DTML Methods or documents. When an executable object is rendered (executing its code), the permissions granted to its owner's roles are used to determine the permissions available to the executing code. If the owner does not have sufficient permissions (via their roles) to execute the code in the object, the code cannot be run by any user, even if the user viewing the object has the permissions (via their roles) needed to execute the code. This prevents so-called "Trojan Horse" attacks, where a user with lesser security privileges writes harmful code that they cannot themselves execute, and then deceives a user with greater privileges into executing it for them.

6.2 Managing Users

The following sections show how to create and manage users using the management screen and discuss how to create new roles.

Users are managed in Zope with User Folders (acl_users). However, you can create only one User Folder per folder, and you cannot copy a User Folder or cut and paste users in it into another folder (This is a security feature: if users could switch their access permissions to different areas in Zope, security would be undermined.) Users in a User Folder can log in anywhere at or below the folder where the User Folder lies in the hierarchy. This could be used, for example, to create a user who can log in with the Manager role to only one section of your website.

6.2.1 Creating Users

To create a new user in Folder A, first open the folder acl_users in Folder A. (If Folder A does not contain an acl_users folder, create one by clicking the Add Objects menu for the Folder A and selecting User Folder.) When you click on acl_users, the Contents screen opens, wherein you can edit or create users. To create a new user you will need the following, as shown in Figure 6-9. (The Name, Password, Confirm, and Roles fields must be completed; Domains is optional.)

Name   The user's name (if you want that user to be able to log on). Usernames can consist of one or more words separated by spaces and can contain special characters. (Multiple spaces are reduced to just one space.) You cannot change a user's name once it has been created.

Password   Enter the user's password for logging on.

Confirm   Re-enter the password. If the password and confirmation do not match, click "OK" in the dialog box. You will be returned to the Management screen for the User Folder, where you must recreate the user.

Roles   Users must be assigned at least one role. To select multiple roles, hold down the CTRL button and click on the desired ones. The permissions available to the user are determined by adding all of the permissions granted to all of the roles assigned to that user. If a user has the Manager role, no other roles are generally needed because the Manager role is already granted every available permission.

Domains   This optional field lists the Internet domains that this user can log in from. This can contain one or more IP addresses, subnets, or Internet domain names separated by a space. Restricting where the user can log in from helps prevent a malicious user from logging in as a Manager over the Internet, for instance. If you leave this field blank, the user will be able to log in from anywhere.

Figure 6-9 shows the management screen of a User Folder in a folder named "My_Homepage."

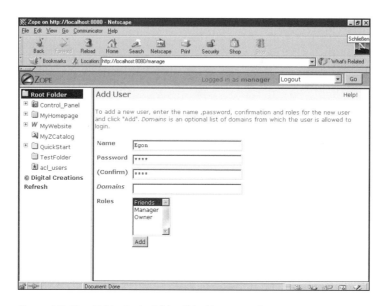

Figure 6-9: User Folder in the folder "My_Homepage"

NOTE   *Once you create a user, the only way to change the username is to delete and recreate the user.*

6.2.2   Modifying a User

To delete a user, go to the User Folder and activate the checkbox in front of the name of each user to delete, then click on the Delete button. To change the properties for an existing user, click on the relevant user to open a form like the one for creating a user. Use this form to change the user's password, domains, or role(s).

NOTE   *You will notice that the number of characters in the password field may not match that user's actual password. This happens because, as a security feature, the actual password is not populated in the form.*

6.2.3   Creating New Roles

If you want to assign roles other than the standard ones in Zope, you can create new roles in the Security screen of any folderish object. These new roles apply in the hierarchy from the point at which they were created; they will not be available to objects higher in the hierarchy. To define a role that applies throughout Zope, create it in the root folder.

To create a new role:

1. Enter the name of the new role in the Security screen's User defined roles input field (Figure 6-10).

New roles are not assigned any permissions. After creating a role, you will need to assign its permissions on the appropriate objects.

Figure 6-10: Input fields for new roles

2. Now click the Add Role button. The new roles appear in the list in the Security screen beside the existing roles.

6.3 Managing Users in DTML

If you want new visitors to your website to be able to create Zope users for themselves, you must code this functionality in your application. Allowing anonymous visitors access to the Zope management screen is not an option for a secure application. To implement this function securely, create an HTML form for visitors to enter their information into. Then you will create a DTML method with the relevant DTML commands to create a user based on the data from the form.

6.3.1 Creating Users in DTML

Now that we know the details Zope requires to save a user in its database, we can perform the same actions with DTML. To do so, we need the names of the methods Zope uses to save users.

6.3.1.1 Python Module User.py

Zope users are managed with the Python module User.py, found in the Zope folder AccessControl (/lib/python/AccessControl). This module contains all methods needed to create and manage users.

6.3.1.2 manage_users() Method

Like most objects in Zope, the User Folder is created with Python. Several Python methods define the object's class, which, in the case of the User Folder, allows us to create, edit, or delete users.

The Python method for creating, changing, or deleting a user is manage_users. It requires three arguments: submit a string with the value Add, Change, or Delete (with which the method determines the action), REQUEST, and RESPONSE (see Appendix A and B).

manage_users is called for the User Folder acl_users as follows (expressed in Python by the period between acl_users and manage_users):

```
<dtml-call expr="acl_users.manage_users('Add', REQUEST, RESPONSE)">
```

6.3.1.3 REQUEST.set for Creating Variables

To create a new user using this call, put the user's information into REQUEST first, using the REQUEST.set command, which creates a variable in REQUEST and saves the desired data into it. You call this command from DTML as follows:

```
<dtml-call expr="REQUEST.set('name', 'Egon')">
```

When you call REQUEST.set, the variable name is entered first as a quoted string value, followed by a comma and the variable's value (which in this case is also a quoted string).

With the name now set, all that REQUEST needs are the password, the password confirmation, any applicable domains, and the role(s) for the new user.

The command looks slightly different for domains and roles because both values are lists. A list is written as a comma-separated sequence of values between square brackets ['item 1', 'item 2', . . . ,'item n']. The roles variable needs to be set to a list of role names (as string values) for the user. Setting roles would be coded as follows:

```
<dtml-call expr="REQUEST.set('roles', ['Manager', 'Owner'])">
```

The complete code required to create a new user using DTML would look something like this:

```
<dtml-call expr="REQUEST.set('name', 'Egon')">
<dtml-call expr="REQUEST.set('password', 'hello')">
<dtml-call expr="REQUEST.set('confirm', 'hello')">
<dtml-call expr="REQUEST.set('domains', [])">
<dtml-call expr="REQUEST.set('roles', ['Manager', 'Owner'])">
<dtml-call expr="acl_users.manage_users('Add', REQUEST, RESPONSE)">
```

Listing 6-1: DTML Code for Creating a User

NOTE *In Listing 6-1, we passed an empty list for domains so that there is no domain restriction for the user. The literal value [] is used to denote an empty list.*

Say we have a DTML document called user_create_form that contains a form into which you can enter all information needed to create a new user. The form might look something like this:

Listing 6-2: DTML Document Form "user_create_form"

```
<dtml-var standard_html_header>
<h2>Create a new user</h2>
<p>
Please complete the following table to create a new user:
</p>
<FORM ACTION="create_user " METHOD=POST>
<table>
<tr>
    <th>Id (Name of User):</th>
    <td><input type=text size=20 name=name></td>
</tr>
<tr>
    <th>Password:</th>
    <td><input type=password size=10 name=password></td>
</tr>
<tr>
    <th>Confirm Password:</th>
    <td><input type=password size=10 name=confirm></td>
</tr>
<tr>
    <th>Domains:</th>
    <td><input type=text size=20 name="domains:tokens"></td>
</tr>
<tr>
    <td><input type=submit value="Create user"></td>
    <td><input type=reset></td>
</tr>
</table>
</FORM>
<dtml-var standard_html_footer>
```

The form in this DTML document refers to another object, user_create (using the ACTION attribute of the Form tag), which is a DTML method that creates the user. It has the following code:

Listing 6-3: DTML Method "user_create"

```
<dtml-var standard_html_header>
<h2><dtml-var title_or_id></h2>
<dtml-call expr="REQUEST.set('roles', ['Friends'])">
<dtml-call expr="acl_users.manage_users('Add', REQUEST, RESPONSE)">
The user <dtml-var name="name"> has been added.
<dtml-var standard_html_footer>
```

When add_user_form is submitted, Zope puts the values supplied on the form into the REQUEST variables: name, password, confirm, and domains. We do not want the user to be able to select a role other than Friends, so we put that value into REQUEST manually using REQUEST.set in create_user.

6.3.2   Problems When Creating Users in DTML

Table 6-1 shows several reasons that an attempt to create a new user might not work.

Table 6-1: Possible Problems with Creating Users

Problem	Result
A user with this name already exists.	The new user is not created; the existing user is not changed.
Password and Confirm do not match.	The new user is not created.
There is no User Folder in the current folder.	The new user is created in the next highest User Folder with the id acl_users.

In each of these three cases, the manage_users call either does not work or does not work as desired. The problem is that no message is returned and, as a result, you do not notice that the new user was not created. To solve this problem, create users with Zope's Add User form (addUser.dtml in the directory /lib/python/AccessControl/dtml) so that error messages will be displayed if any of the problems above occur.

You can change the layout of addUser.dtml to suit your own requirements, because as designed it works only in the Zope management screen. The ACTION in the Form tag of the HTML form in acl_users/manage_users must be changed because you will be creating a new custom DTML method to create users not contained in the acl_users User Folder (User Folders can only contain User objects). The DTML method you create will call the User Folder's built-in Python method manage_users.

One problem with using the addUser.dtml form is that, once the user has been added, the Contents view of the User Folder (acl_users) appears because manage_users() redirects the browser to this page. Visitors to the website as well as users with the role Friend are not authorized to access the Zope Management screen. If a visitor attempts to access the Contents view of the User Folder, Zope recognizes the current visitor as unauthorized and displays the login window.

6.3.3   Changing Users in DTML

You can use the command acl_users.manage_users() to change a user in much the same way as you would create a user. Following is an example of how to use DTML to see whether a user already exists in the current acl_users folder and, if so, how to change that user:

Listing 6-4: Changing a User after Checking

```
1:     <dtml-var standard_html_header>
2:     <dtml-call expr="REQUEST.set('name', 'Billy')">
3:     <dtml-call expr="REQUEST.set('password', 'hello')">
4:     <dtml-call expr="REQUEST.set('confirm', 'hello')">
5:     <dtml-call expr="REQUEST.set('domains', [])">
6:     <dtml-call expr="REQUEST.set('roles', ['Manager', 'Owner'])">
7:     <dtml-if expr="acl_users.getUser(REQUEST.name)">
8:         <dtml-call expr="acl_users.manage_users('Change', REQUEST, RESPONSE)">
9:         <p>User <dtml-var name="name"> updated.</p>
10:    <dtml-else>
11:         <p>User <dtml-var name="name"> does not exist.</p>
12:    </dtml-if>
13:    <dtml-var standard_html_footer>
```

Listing 6-4 first uses REQUEST.set (Lines 2 through 6) to create variables containing the user's updated information. This data could also be passed from a form (as in Listing 6.3), in which case you could omit these calls.

Next, dtml-if (Line 6) determines if the specified username exists by calling the getUser method of the acl_users User Folder and passing it the name of the user in REQUEST.name. If that user exists, it is returned by the method, and the expression is evaluated as true. If the user does not exist, getUser returns None, which is evaluated as false.

If our user exists (the dtml-if expression is true), we call the acl_users.manage_users method (Line 7), passing it the value 'Change' as its submit argument. This tells the method we want to change an existing user (as opposed to adding one as in the previous example). After this call, a message is returned indicating that the user was updated (Line 8).

If our user does not exist (the dtml-if expression is false), it cannot be updated, so we simply return a message in the else clause (Lines 10–11) stating this fact.

6.3.4   Deleting Users in DTML

To delete users, set the submit argument for manage_users to Delete. You can delete one or more users simultaneously, but either way the user name(s) must be transferred as a list. In addition, the variable name for this list is names, and not name (as with Add and Change).

Listing 6-5: Deleting One or More Users

```
<dtml-call "REQUEST.set('names', ['Egon'])">
<dtml-call "acl_users.manage_users('Delete', REQUEST, RESPONSE)">
```

As you saw in the example for changing a user, User Folder objects have additional methods that are useful in certain circumstances. The example "Changing Users in DTML" above used the method getUser() to determine whether a user with a certain name exists. You could also call this method on other user folders for which you have adequate permissions. To do so, formulate an expression that walks down the folder hierarchy to the desired acl_users folder. Because objects contained in folderish objects are considered attributes of their parent container object, you can use the dot notation to traverse down through the hierarchy in an expression.

If you are in the folder My_ Homepage (Figure 6-11), the following examples are possible (the folder you are currently in must not be explicitly named when calling up the method):

1. `acl_users.getUser()`

2. `Test_folder.acl_users.getUser()`

3. `Test_folder.subfolder.acl_users.getUser()`

4. `second_folder.acl_users.getUser()`

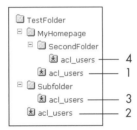

Figure 6-11: Access instructions for the various user folders

6.3.5   User Folder Methods

Table 6-2 lists available user folder methods.

Table 6-2: User Folder Methods

Method	Description	Example
getUser(name)	Returns the user object with the name specified or None if no user with that name exists.	`"getUser('Casey')"`
getUserById(id[, default])	Similar to getUser, except it returns an optional default value (or raises an error) if the user does not exist.	`"getUserById('Duncan')"`
getUsers()	Returns a list of all user objects in the user folder.	`"getUsers()"`
getUserNames() user_names()	Returns a list of all the names of the users in the user folder.	`"getUserNames()"` `"user_names()"`

Listing 6-6 shows a simple query that checks to see whether the user currently logged in exists in the User Folder.

Listing 6-6: Checking Whether a User Exists in the Current User Folder

```
<dtml-if "acl_users.getUser(AUTHENTICATED_USER.getUserName())">
    Currently logged in user exists in User Folder.
<dtml-else>
    Currently logged in user does not exist in User Folder.
</dtml-if>
```

`AUTHENTICATED_USER.getUserName()` returns the name of the user currently logged on.

To check a user in a folder other than the current User Folder, you must access the relevant User Folder through the also folder(s) and/or subfolder(s).

```
<dtml-var "Folder.acl_users.getUser(AUTHENTICATED_USER.getUserName())">
<dtml-var "Folder.subfolder.acl_users.getUser(AUTHENTICATED_USER.getUserName())">
```

Section 8.2.1 documents additional methods available in AUTHENTICATED_USER.

Summary

This chapter covered the basics of Zope's security system and management using roles and permissions. You have learned about the various objects and attributes Zope uses for security and how to affect them through the management screen and through DTML. Chapter 7 will look at roles and permissions in more depth.

7

LOCAL ROLES AND PERMISSIONS

Sometimes, you may want to give users in one role the same permissions as another; for example you might wish to give a Friend the same permissions as a Manager for one particular object (for example, a DTML document or a specific folder), in which case there is little point in assigning the user (let us call him "Egon") the role of Manager, because he will then be able to see and use the management screen for the whole of Zope. Egon should only be able to modify the folder My_Homepage. Similarly, if you give the role Friends the same permissions as Manager, all users in the Friends role will have Manager permissions for the folder My_Homepage.

7.1 Local Roles

It is at this point that local roles come into play. Local roles allow us to assign a different role to a user created in the acl_users folder for a specific object, be it a folder or individual document.

7.1.1 *Example*

To give Egon the same permission as a Manager for the folder My_Homepage, we must first open the Security screen for the folder My_Homepage, shown in Figure 7-1. Notice the link local roles in the introduction text.

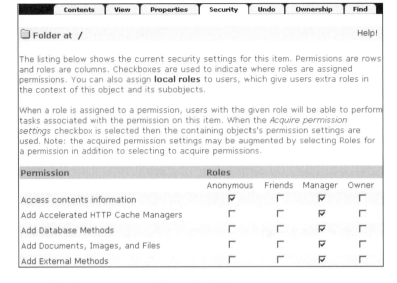

Figure 7-1: Security screen with local roles link

Clicking the local roles link opens another page (Figure 7-2) that contains a list of all local roles already set up for this object. As you can see in Figure 7-2, only the local role Owner has been set for the user who created the folder My_Homepage in our example.

Figure 7-2 also shows two multiple-select lists: To the left is a list of all users for whom local roles can be set, and to the right is a list of all local roles that can be used for this object.

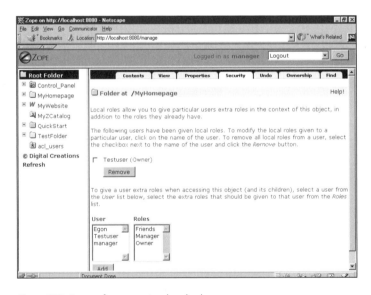

Figure 7-2: Screen for managing local roles

We now select Egon from the list of users and Manager from the list of roles. When we click on the Add button under the two lists, Egon appears in the list of set local roles (with the local role set for him contained in brackets after the name). Egon can now carry out all activities in the folder My_Homepage that could normally be carried out only by a Manager.

NOTE *Say you have created a form for sending email (for example, sendEMailForm), a DTML method (for example, sendEMail) with the sendmail command, and a MailHost. If you want to allow only certain users (for example, Egon) to send email this way, you may think that it a good idea to assign the local role of Manager to Egon for the DTML method sendEMail, because this DTML method contains the sendmail command. This will not, however, produce the desired results. To allow Egon to send email, he must be assigned the Manager local role in the MailHost object. Of course, this also means that he will be able to change the MailHost object—a possible drawback you should consider.*

7.2 Proxy Roles

Proxy roles serve a purpose similar to local roles, but proxy roles are object-related whereas local roles are user-related. Proxy roles allow all users who access the object to have the same permissions, regardless of the role assigned to them.

Let's take a look at an example:

Suppose you have created a new DTML document index_html with the standard source code (see "Access contents information" below). To assign the proxy role Anonymous:

1. Go to the Edit view of the DTML document and click the Proxy tab to call up the Proxy view, where you'll find a list of all roles that can be assigned as a proxy role for this object.

2. Select Anonymous from this list and click the Save Changes button.

3. Now go to the containing folder's Security view and deactivate acquisition for the permission Access contents information.

4. Save the changes to the folder's permissions.

This interrupts the acquisition chain and removes the Access contents information permission from the Anonymous role. However, this permission is needed to view a DTML document that contains the DTML command

```
<dtml-var id>
```

—which the standard code for a DTML document contains. If you (or any other user) now try to view your just-created DTML document, you will be unable to do so regardless of the roles assigned to your authenticated user (even the Manager role). This is because the proxy role of Anonymous assigned to index_html overrides all other roles assigned either directly to the user or via local roles.

7.3   Permissions

Let's take a closer look at some of the permissions available in the Security tab of the management screen. Different objects can perform different actions and have different management screens, so the permissions available vary from object to object. Folderish objects, which can contain other objects, also show all the permissions of the objects they can contain. This is so that you can affect the permissions of all objects that could be contained in the folderish object from one central location. Because of this, permissions settings in the root folder are the most general, because they affect the largest number of objects.

Figure 7-3 shows a typical security screen for a non-folderish object.

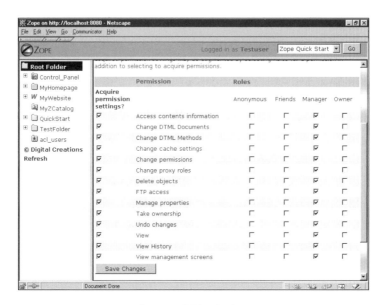

Figure 7-3: Security screen for a non-folderish object

We cannot possibly cover all permissions that Zope users may encounter, because each new product may bring with it its own set of permissions, each of which is added to the list of Zope's existing permissions once the product is installed. Thus, the following sections concentrate on the permissions provided by Zope.

7.3.1   Permissions for Non-Folderish Objects

As mentioned in Section 7.3, you can set many more permissions for folderish objects than for non-folderish ones, because folderish objects allow you to assign all permissions available for all object types that can be contained within them. This list will grow if you add Products or ZClasses that allow you to create additional object types.

In all of these permissions, if the permission is set for a specific object and a specific role (either by acquisition or directly under the role), a user with that role can carry out actions on that object defined in this permission. If a user lacks this permission, a permission is neither set in the object itself nor via acquisition for any role assigned to the user.

For example, a user with the role Friends can open a DTML document in the third tier view if the permission View has been assigned to the Friends role for that document. The user cannot view the management screen, however, if the permission View management screens is not assigned to the Friends role for that document.

Access contents information

This permission allows a user to view information, such as the Title or id, relating to the object for which the permission is set. Take, for example, the standard content of a DTML document, as shown in Listing 7-1. Zope automatically inserts this content into the document by default when you create a new DTML document. (This code also appears in the DTML document index_html, created automatically by Zope if you activated Create public interface when creating a new folder).

Listing 7-1: Standard Content of a DTML Document

```
<dtml-var standard_html_header>
<h2><dtml-var title_or_id></h2>
<p>
This is the <dtml-var id> Document.
</p>
<dtml-var standard_html_footer>
```

<dtml-var title_or_id> returns the Title or, if there is no Title, the id of the object; <dtml-var id> returns only the id of the object.

If a user lacks this permission on a DTML document with this code, they will be unable to render the document, and thus unable to view it even if they have the View permission. Zope requires that the user log in as a user who belongs to a role permitted to view this object information. Consequently, you will often need to set this permission in conjunction with View to allow users to view a DTML document.

NOTE *This permission is granted by default to the Anonymous role.*

Change DTML Documents/Change DTML Methods

These permissions must be set so that changes to existing DTML documents and methods can be saved. If a user lacking the appropriate permission attempts to save changes by clicking the Change button, the user is asked to enter a password. Without this password—that is, without the appropriate permission—the user can only view the source code of the DTML document or method in the Edit screen.

Change permissions

This permission allows changes to be made to the permission settings in the Security tab of the object. For example, if you are logged in as a user without this permission, the Security tab is not displayed in the management screen for the object, meaning that you cannot access the Security screen to create roles and assign permissions.

NOTE *Normally only the Manager role should have this permission. If you grant this permission to another role, users in that role can then assign themselves any additional permissions they like, defeating any restrictions you might have imposed on them.*

Change proxy roles

If this permission is set for a role, the Proxies tab appears in the management screen of a DTML document or method. If a user has this permission, that user can assign a proxy role to a DTML document or method, so that the DTML document or method can then access Zope resources to which the user does not actually have permission. Change proxy roles lets you assign the access permissions of any roles present in the folder to the DTML document/method.

NOTE *Only a Manager can assign all existing roles as proxy roles to a DTML document or method. Other roles can only be assigned to their own or Anonymous roles as proxy roles.*

Delete objects

Without this permission, users cannot delete, move, or rename objects; Zope will not display the Delete button in the management screen for them.

FTP access

If you have this permission, you can use FTP (file transfer protocol) to copy Zope objects to or from your hard drive or to include them in external files or folders in Zope. For example, you can use an FTP client to integrate folders or files stored on your hard drive into Zope without having to create each file manually using the web interface. FTP makes it easier to move files back and forth between Zope and your hard drive.

NOTE *Zope's FTP port is 8021 as opposed to the usual 21. This can be changed by modifying the Zope start script (see section 1.5.3.6).*

Manage properties

If this permission has not been set, the Properties tab is not displayed in the management screen, and you will not be able to add new properties or change existing ones. Properties are created in the Properties screen of an object when you click on the Properties tab. The title of an object is also a property in Zope, but you can change it in the Edit and Properties screen of many objects.

For example, say you have a DTML document that frequently uses the word "Boston." To replace "Boston" with the words "New York," you could create a property called "City" with the value Boston. As a result, the variable <dtml-var City> would appear in place of the word Boston. To change "Boston" to "New York," all you would need to do is change the value of variable to "New York." Then, throughout the document, New York would replace Boston.

Take ownership

From Zope 2.2.0 onward, this permission adds a button labeled "Take ownership" to the Ownership screen, provided the current user does not already own the object. Although the role Manager is normally given all permissions by default, this right is not. This permission is assigned by default only to the Owner role.

Undo changes

This very important permission makes the Undo tab appear in the management screen. To use the Undo changes permission, you may need to set additional permissions depending on what you want to undo. In general, though, if you can perform an action, you can also undo it.

NOTE *As of Zope 2.2.0, the Undo screen displays only actions carried out in the current folder or its subfolders, not all actions in the Zope installation as was previously the case.*

View

When this permission is set for an object for a given role, users assigned the role can view the object in the third tier view. This permission is often set in conjunction with Access contents information (see above). It does not allow users to access the management screen using the /manage URL extension.

NOTE *This permission is granted by default to the Anonymous role.*

View history

Users with this permission see a History tab in DTML documents and methods. This tab leads to the History view, which lists all actions carried out on the current object, from which you can compare the current version of a DTML document with a previous version.

View management screens

Users with this permission can access the management screen using the URL for an object together with the /manage URL extension. For example, the URL to access the management screen for a DTML document named index_html in a folder named My_Folder would be http://localhost:8080/My_Folder/index_html/manage.

This permission does not allow a user to do any more than view these screens. Additional permissions must be granted for a user to be able to add, edit, or delete objects, for instance.

7.3.2 Permissions for Folderish Objects

As mentioned in Section 7.3, folderish objects have many more available permissions than non-folderish ones. These include the permissions for non-folderish objects, permissions created as a result of new product installations, and permissions provided by Zope for folders. We will now take a look at this last group of permissions: permissions provided by Zope for folders.

Following are the permissions that appear in the Security screen for a folder:

Add Database Methods	Change Versions
Add Documents, Images, and Files	Change cache managers
Add External Methods	Change cache settings
Add Folders	Change configuration
Add MailHost Objects	Change proxy roles*
Add Python Scripts	FTP access
Add RAM Cache Managers	Import/Export objects
Add Site Roots	Join/leave Versions
Add User Folders	Manage ZCatalog Entries
Add Versions	Manage Vocabulary
Add Virtual Host Monsters	Manage users
Add Vocabularies	Open/Close Database Connections
Add Z Gadfly Database Connections	Query Vocabulary
Add ZCatalogs	Save/discard Version changes
Add Zope Tutorials	Search ZCatalog
Change Database Methods	Undo changes*
Change External Methods	Use Database Methods
Change Images and Files	Use mailhost services
Change Python Scripts	

NOTE *The following descriptions use the phrase "add menu" to refer to the Select type to Add... or Available Objects menu (depending on your Zope version) found in the Contents screen of folderish objects. This menu contains the object types a user can create inside the folder.*

NOTE *The contents of the add menu in a folderish object varies according to the objects that can be contained in the folder and the permissions assigned to the current user. In fact, if you can add only one type of object, the drop-down menu is replaced with an Add button. If you do not have permissions to add any object types, the menu disappears completely.*

Add Database Methods
If this permission is set, Z SQL Method appears in the add menu.

Add Documents, Images, and Files
As the name suggests, this permission allows you to create DTML documents (and methods), images, and files in a folder. This permission is also needed, along with Delete objects, for users to rename existing objects of these types. This permission also allows users to create a Z Search Interface, which will assist you in creating a query interface for Z SQL Methods and ZCatalogs.

Add External Methods
When this permission is set, users can create external methods, which create a connection between your own Python modules and Zope. To add an external

These items were discussed under section 7.3.1.

method object, you must first place the module file containing the method's function definition in the Extensions directory of your Zope installation. The following is an example of an external method file, showing its code and the corresponding External Method object values.

```
Python File:  pythonmeth.py
Content:
     def my_PyMethod(arg1, arg2):
          """Description"""
          Instruction Block


Details for the External Method object in Zope:
     Id:      my_ExtMeth (SampleName)
     Title:
     Function name:      my_PyMethod
     Python module file: pythonmeth (without .py extension!)
```

Zope automatically adds the .py extension to the module filename.

In the above example, a Python module file "pythonmeth.py" is written containing a function named my_PyMethod. The module file is saved into the Extensions directory in the Zope installation. To make the function accessible from within Zope, an external method object is added that tells Zope the name of the module and function. The function is now callable from your DTML code by calling the external method object.

Add Folders
When this permission is set for a role in an object, users with this role can create additional folders in that object.

Add MailHost Objects
This permission allows users to create a MailHost, which is used to send email with Zope. The permission Use mailhost services must also be set before the MailHost can be used.

Add Python Scripts
This permission (available in Zope 2.3 and later) allows you to create a Zope Python Script, which allows you to write Python code inside Zope instead of using external methods. (See Chapter 14.)

Add RAM Cache Managers
This permission (available in Zope 2.3 and later) allows you to create RAM Cache Managers, which give you the ability to enhance the performance of frequently accessed pages and objects by holding them in RAM on the Zope server.

Add Site Roots

This permission (available in Zope 2.3 and later) allows you to create virtual site roots inside Zope. These site roots are used to do virtual hosting in Zope. Virtual hosting allows multiple websites with different Internet domain names to be hosted by a single Zope server.

Add User Folders

With this permission, users can create User Folders, but only one for each folder. (Zope cancels attempts to create a second User Folder in the same folder.) Users are created in the user folders.

Add Versions

Remember that versions allow users to make changes in an object without making the changes visible to all users and without permanently changing the object. (Only users working with the same version will see these changes.)

The permission Add Versions is required to create a version. (Note that the permission Join/leave Versions is also needed in order to work in a version. Furthermore, the permission Save/discard version Changes is needed in order to discard or save the changes so that they are visible to all users.)

Add Virtual Host Monsters

This permission allows you to add Virtual Host Monster objects that affect the URLs generated by Zope objects, thus allowing you to use Zope seamlessly with a front-end webserver or accelerator (such as Apache or Squid), which rewrites certain incoming URLs to correspond to your Zope server. Normally, inserting URLs in Zope (in a DTML document, for instance) with the URL attribute of the REQUEST object or the absolute_url() method will create a URL based on the name of the Zope server and the absolute path of the object. Virtual Host Monsters allow you to affect the output of these built-in attributes to correspond with your URL rewriting rules.

Add Vocabularies

As of Zope Version 2.2.0, the ZCatalog includes a vocabulary (see Chapter 11). The permission Add Vocabularies allows users to create a general vocabulary that can be shared by several ZCatalogs.

Add Z Gadfly Database Connections

This permission allows you to create a Z Gadfly database connection in a folder. Gadfly is a simple SQL database system included with Zope. However, Z Gadfly Database Connections appears in the drop-down menu only when another permission that allows you to add objects is set (for example Add Documents, Images, and Files or Add Folders). The database connection is automatically opened when you create it; to close it, you must have the permission Open/Close Database Connections.

Add ZCatalogs

When the permission Add ZCatalogs is set, you can create a ZCatalog in a folder. ZCatalogs are folderish objects that allow you to index and query other Zope objects. To find and index objects in the ZCatalog, you must have the permission Manage ZCatalog Entries.

The permission Search ZCatalog lets a user search the ZCatalog for objects, but no other operations, such as management, can be performed.

Add Zope Tutorials

Zope versions since 2.2.0 include an introductory Zope tutorial. To view it, you must first create a Zope Tutorial object, which you'll only be able to do if you have this permission.

Change Database Methods

This permission must be assigned for you to be able to change SQL methods. You must also set this permission in order to display the Test tab in the management screen and to test an SQL method.

Change External Methods

This permission allows you to modify External Method objects and to reload the external file corresponding with the External Method, if it has been modified.

Change Images and Files

This permission lets users change images and files included in Zope, meaning that they can edit their properties or upload new data from a file. They cannot, however, rename the image or file objects.

NOTE *When you upload a new version of an image or file, the old version may still be displayed if it is still in your computer's cache. To remedy this, empty your browser cache.*

Change Python Scripts

This permission allows you to save changes made to Python Scripts (available in Zope 2.3 and later).

Change Versions

With this permission, you can open an existing version in the Properties screen and change its title. To view the other screens for an object, you will need the permissions Join/leave Versions and Save/discard Version changes.

NOTE *You may be asked to enter your password when you confirm the title change, because the OK button in the message "Your changes have been saved" refers to the version's Join/leave screen in the background, for which you may not have permissions. Although Zope responds as if you need the permission Join/leave Versions, your changes to the title will still be saved.*

Change cache managers

This permission is needed to change the objects cached by a RAM Cache Manager object.

Change cache settings

This permission allows users to adjust the parameters used by a RAM Cache Manager object.

Change configuration

This permission is needed in order to make changes to a MailHost object.

Import/Export objects

With this permission, you can move objects from one Zope installation to another, for example from one computer to another. Zope's ability to import and export objects regardless of whether they are non-folderish objects (like a file) or an entire folder (including its subfolders and other objects) will prove extremely useful.

If this permission is set for the role of the current user, the Import/Export button appear in the management screen.

NOTE *When you import, you add objects to a folder. To import a file into a folder, you must have the permissions necessary for creating the objects you are importing in that folder (the permissions Add Documents, Images, and Files or Add Folders must be set for this folder and its roles). If not, Zope asks for your password.*

Join/leave Versions

This permission lets you start or stop working in an existing version.

Manage ZCatalog Entries

This permission must be set if you want to manage a ZCatalog.

Manage Vocabulary

With this permission, you can access the screens for a vocabulary (see Chapter 11), including the Vocabulary and Query screens. The Vocabulary screen displays all words contained in the Vocabulary in groups of 20. The Query screen is used to query the Vocabulary.

Manage users

You must set this permission if you want to manage existing users, including changing their passwords, domains, and roles, or creating new users. To rename a user, you must create a new user with the desired name; you cannot change the name of an existing user.

Open/Close Database Connections

This permission allows you to open and close external SQL database connections. (See "Add Z Gadfly Database Connections" above.)

Save/Discard version changes

This permission allows you to save or discard changes you make to a version.

Search ZCatalog

This permission must be set so that you can search a ZCatalog using this search page, which includes a page with a form in which you specify the search criteria as well as another page to display the results. Both pages can be created using Z Search Interface from the add menu.

Use Database Methods

This permission is needed if you want to call Z SQL methods.

Use mailhost services

Using the permission Use mailhost services, you can restrict users who can send email. To send email with Zope, you must create a MailHost object, typically in the root folder. (The actual composition and sending of emails is carried out using the DTML command sendmail.)

The following example code in Listing 7-2 uses a mailhost object to send an email programmatically. A user would need the Use mailhost services permission to execute this code.

Listing 7-2: Example of sendFeedback

```
<dtml-sendmail mailhost=MailHost>
To: admin@test.com
From: <dtml-var sender>
Subject: Feedback
<dtml-var text_to_email>
</dtml-sendmail>
```

Summary

You now have the knowledge you need to manage the roles and permissions of your Zope objects and keep your applications secure. Chapter 8 will be explore the many additional functions and methods available to you in Zope's security modules.

8

HODS FOR THE
USER.PY MODULES

‹ at the functions of other interesting and sometimes extremely useful methods for the Role.py and User.py modules, which can be called in DTML documents or methods.

These methods can be used to inspect and modify the security settings and permissions of objects programmatically. For example, methods defined in the Role.py module can be used to determine and modify the permissions assigned to roles on an object. The methods defined in User.py allow you to determine the permissions a user has on an object or the roles assigned to a user; it also includes methods to create and modify user objects as in our example in section 6.3.1, "Creating Users in DTML."

8.1 Calling Methods

Use the following command format to call the methods in a DTML document or method:

```
<dtml-var expr="object.method()">
```

If you do not want to display the result of the method on the current page, use the call tag instead of the var tag:

```
<dtml-call expr="object.method()">
```

`object` above represents the Zope object (DTML document, User Folder, and so on) with which you want to do something. If you omit `object`, Zope assumes you wish to execute the method on the object at the top of the name-space stack.

The modules Role.py and User.py are in the system under /lib/python/AccessControl. Let's begin with the Role.py module.

8.2 Methods for the Module Role.py

The following methods, in file Role.py in the Zope directory lib/python/Access-Control, are available on any Zope object with a Security tab, which is nearly all Zope objects.

acquiredRolesAreUsedBy*(permission)*
The result of this method is 'CHECKED' (for use in an HTML checkbox), if the acquisition Acquired permission settings? is active for the object's permission named *permission*. If not, an empty string is returned.

NOTE *Permission names are case sensitive and vary in their capitalization. See the Security tab for the object you are calling to find its exact name.*

has_local_roles()
This method returns the number of local roles set for the object.

get_local_roles()
This method produces a list of tuples (a special immutable list), each of which contains the username as the first element and a list of local roles set for these roles as the second element.

For example:

```
[('TestUser1', ['Manager']),
 ('TestUser2', ['Manager','Owner']),
 ('manager', ['Owner'])]
```

get_valid_userids()
This method gives a combined list of all user names from all User Folders in the object's acquisition chain.

get_local_roles_for_userid*(userid)*
This method results in a list of all set local roles for the specified user name in *userid*.

manage_addLocalRoles(*userid*, ['*role1*', '*role2*',...])

This method expects a *userid* as an argument as well as a list of roles. If the method is called using inappropriate arguments, the userid (if it exists) is created with the relevant role as a local role. You can do the same thing using the method manage_setLocalRoles(userid, ['role1', 'role2', ...]).

manage_defined_roles(*submit*, REQUEST)

With this method you can add or delete roles using 'Add role' or 'Delete role' for *submit*. To use this method, first specify a role, such as Role2, in the REQUEST under the variable role.

```
<dtml-call expr="REQUEST.set('role', 'Role2'')">
```

Once you have specified a role you can call the method manage_defined_roles in both forms:

```
<dtml-call expr="manage_defined_roles('Add role', REQUEST)">
```

or

```
<dtml-call expr="manage_defined_roles('Delete role', REQUEST)">
```

manage_delLocalRoles(*userids*, REQUEST)

This method allows you to delete local roles you have set. It requires a list of users (*userids*) and *REQUEST* as arguments.

permission_settings()

This method returns all permissions for an object in the form of a list of dictionaries. Each element has the following form:

```
{
        'acquire':  'CHECKED',
        'roles':  [ {'name': 'p0r0', 'checked': ''},
                {'name': 'p0r1', 'checked': ''},
                {'name': 'p0r2', 'checked': 'CHECKED'},
                {'name': 'p0r3', 'checked': ''} ],
        'name': 'Access contents information'
}
```

acquire   'CHECKED' if Acquire permission settings? is activated for the relevant permission, otherwise an empty string is returned.

roles   Contains a list of dictionaries as a value. The value for 'name' is a combination of letters and numbers (p*a*r*b*). 'p0r0', for example, indicates the zero permission (p=permission) of the zero role (r=role). (Zero is used because Python starts counting from zero.) If the value of 'checked' is 'CHECKED', the role has this permission.

The values *a* and *b* indicate the number of the permission/role as it stands in the order of the Security screen for the object; permissions from top to bottom and roles from left to right.

name   The name of the permission. From here you can read the name of the permission corresponding to the value *a* in *parb*: thus, Access contents information would be the zero permission.

permissionOfRole(*role*):

This method requires a role as a transfer argument and returns all activated permissions for this role in the form of a list of dictionaries.

```
[{'selected': 'SELECTED', 'name': 'Access contents information'}, ...]
```

Each dictionary has the keywords 'selected' and 'name'. The keyword 'name' contains the name of the permission as a value. If the value of the 'select' keyword is 'SELECTED', the permission is activated for the role.

possible_permissions():

This method returns a list of all permissions present in Zope even if you use them on a non-folderish object.

rolesOfPermission(*permission*):

This method returns a list of dictionaries you can use to determine the *permission*'s roles.

```
[ {'selected': '', 'name': 'Anonymous'},
 {'selected': '', 'name': 'Friend'},
 {'selected': 'SELECTED', 'name': 'Manager'},
 {'selected': '', 'name': 'Owner'} ]
```

If the 'selected' keyword has the value 'SELECTED', the role that appears after 'name' has the permission specified by the name.

valid_roles():

Using valid_roles() you receive a list of the roles permitted as local roles. In other words, roles that can be assigned to users as local roles.

validate_roles(*roles*):

validate_roles(roles) requires a list of roles as a transfer argument and returns a true value if all roles in the list are valid. The method returns a false value if at least one of the roles in the list is invalid.

userdefined_roles():

The method returns a list of roles defined in Zope by any user for the current object. Roles defined in other objects (for example, the superordinate folder) do not appear in the list.

8.2.1 Methods for the User.py Module

In the section "Creating, Changing and Deleting Users in DTML" we used some of the methods contained in the module User.py, for example getUser() and getUserNames(). The same methods are described below as well as some other methods from this module which may be of interest to you.

This module contains more Python methods in the folder AccessControl (Zope/lib/python/ AccessControl) than are described below. They cannot, however, be called up using DTML.

The following User.py methods must always be used on a user object and cannot be called up for themselves alone. Here are some examples:

```
<dtml-var expr="AUTHENTICATED_USER.getRoles()">
<dtml-var expr="acl_users.getUsers()[0].getUserName()">
```

In these examples, the user objects AUTHENTICATED_USER and acl_users.getUsers()[0].(getUsersName() return the first user contained in acl_users).

The syntax of the following examples are incorrect because no user object has been specified:

```
<dtml-var expr="getRoles()">
<dtml-var expr=" getUserName()">
```

authenticate(*password*, REQUEST):

If you use this method on a user, a true value is returned if the user has the password *password*; a false value is returned if the password does not belong to this user. You can use this process to verify the input of a password.

If, for example, you obtain the name and password of a user using a form, you can then check the password using the following command:

```
<dtml-if expr="acl_users.getUser(REQUEST.user).authenticate(REQUEST.password,
REQUEST)">
  Password correct.
<dtml-else>
  Password incorrect.
</dtml-if>
```

getUserName():

When used, for example on AUTHENTICATED_USER, this method returns the name of the user currently logged on as a string.

```
<dtml-var expr="AUTHENTICATED_USER.getUserName()">
```

getRoles(*userid*):

getRoles() returns a list of roles for the relevant user. (See getUser().)

getRolesInContext(*object*):

This method returns a list of the relevant user's roles in relation to an *object*, including their general roles and any local roles in effect for that user on the object specified.

getDomains():

This method returns a list of the Internet domains from which the user can log on in Zope.

has_role(*role*[, *object*]):

If the user you are using this method on has the role *role*, this method returns a true value; if not it returns a false value. *role* can also be a list of roles, although all roles must match to produce a true value. *object* is an optional argument; when specified, local roles in effect on the object are also compared. The method refers to the current object if no value is specified for the *object*.

Example:

```
<dtml-if "AUTHENTICATED_USER.has_role('Manager')">
  User is a Manager.
<dtml-else>
  User is not a Manager.
</dtml-if>
```

has_permission(permission, object):

The method returns a true value if the user has the permission *permission* for the object *object*. If not, it returns a false value. Unlike has_role() above, both arguments must always be specified.

NOTE *When testing user rights on a given object, it is generally better to test individual permissions for the user rather than roles. This makes your code easier to maintain and more reusable because the available roles are application-specific, whereas the available permissions are generally the same across applications.*

The following methods in the User.py module are used on the User Folder (acl_users) and not on individual users:

getUser(*userid*):

Returns the object for the relevant user; not just a string but also an object that can be used for other methods. If, for example, you have a user called Test1 in the current acl_users folder, you can find out the user's role using the command:

```
<dtml-var expr="acl_users.getUser('Test1').getRoles()">
```

getUserNames() , user_names():

Returns a list of users contained in the User Folder. The usernames are presented as strings. getUserNames() and user_names() are two different methods with the same function.

getUsers():

This method returns the list of user objects in a user folder.

manage_users(*submit*, REQUEST):

This method is described in detail in section 6.3.1, "Creating Users in DTML."

8.3 Example: Authentication

Let's say we want to create a simple homepage consisting only of a static welcome page. We want our page to be accesible to all users in the third tier, and to have a link that allows our friends to log in. Once a user logs in, a personalized greeting appears on our homepage; the result is a dynamically created homepage.

Figure 8-1 shows a schematic of this process, using the example of two visitors to the page. In this example, Egon has a user created in Zope while Bill does not and is regarded as "Anonymous."

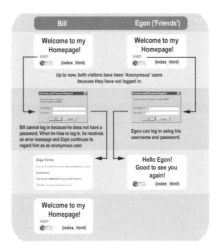

Figure 8-1: Schematic process for the Login example

To create our homepage, we first create a folder (see Figure 8-2) called My_Homepage. When creating this folder, select both the Create public interface and Create user folder options to automatically add an index_html DTML document and an acl_users folder.

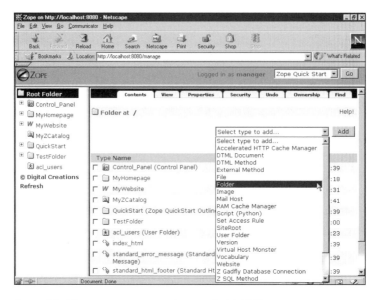

Figure 8-2: Management screen with expanded Add Objects menu

We want to give our friend Egon special permissions to access functions unavailable to Anonymous users. To do so, we create a new user called Egon (with the role Friend and a user-defined password) in the User Folder (acl_users) for the My_Homepage folder, as shown in Figure 8-3. (To create the Friend role, use the folder's Security tab.)

	Folder at /MyHomepage		Help!
	Select type to add... ▼		Add
Type	**Name**	Size	Last Modified
☐ [x]	acl_users (User Folder)		2001-05-20 22:41
☐ 🗋	index_html	1 Kb	2001-05-27 13:20
☐ 🗋	login_html	1 Kb	2001-05-27 13:24

Rename | Cut | Copy | Delete | Import/Export | Select All

Figure 8-3: Object list for the My_Homepage folder

In addition to the welcome document (index_html), which generates both the normal and special welcome pages, we have also created a DTML method called login_html in the folder My_Homepage. This page contains a redirect to the welcome page index_html, meaning that the page login_html will not be displayed and the browser will be redirected back to the DTML document index_html. (The function of the DTML method will soon become apparent, but first we must specify the code for both pages.)

8.3.1 DTML Method login_html

The DTML method login_html simply consists of the following line:

```
<dtml-call expr="RESPONSE.redirect('index_html')">
```

The method redirect of the RESPONSE object is used to send a browser to a different URL than was originally requested.

login_html calls up a password query to authenticate the user (see Figure 8-6), as explained below when we deal with setting permissions for login_html. If Zope recognizes the user at the password query, the page index_html displays a custom message according to the user's role.

8.3.2 DTML Document index_html

The DTML document which login_html refers to (index_html), is shown in Listing 8-1:

Listing 8-1: Code for index_html

```
<dtml-var standard_html_header>
<dtml-if expr="AUTHENTICATED_USER.has_role('Friend')">
        <h2>Hello <dtml-var name="AUTHENTICATED_USER">!</h2>
        <p>Good to see you again!</p>
<dtml-else>
        <h2>Welcome to my Homepage!</h2>
        <a href="login_html">Login</a>
</dtml-if>
<dtml-var standard_html_footer>
```

8.3.3 The two views of index_html

This DTML document can create two different views. The first view is only visible to users with the role Friends who have logged in. The other view (after <dtml-else>) is initially seen by all visitors to the homepage. While unauthorized users cannot proceed beyond this screen, authorized users proceed to the special greeting once they have logged in.

We must retain the default permissions for index_html so that all users can see the page. As you know, users can see this page because Zope has assigned the View permission to the Anonymous role. Each user initially sees the page index_html as shown in Figure 8-4.

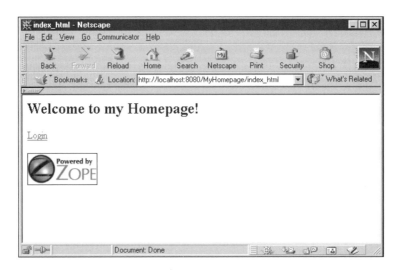

Figure 8-4: View of index_html before login

8.3.4   Assigning Permissions for login_html

Several permissions may be needed in order to successfully render a page. At the very least, the visitor must have the View permission for the object. However, since we also have only formulated the method login_html as a redirect, the user does not actually see a new page if they click on the link (Login), which leads to login_html. Access to this serves only as a gateway to the special welcome page view of index_html.

Initially, all users have the permission that allows them to access login_html as a result of Zope's automatic assignment of permissions to roles by acquisition. The purpose of the login_html method, however, is to test the permissions of the current users and make them authenticate if they do not have the role Friend.

To accomplish this, the default permission assignment for login_html must be deactivated since, by default, login_html acquires the View permission for the Anonymous role from the root folder. Once this is turned off neither Anonymous users or Friends are permitted to access login_html. If a user clicks on the Login link, Zope attempts to display login_html and recognizes that the user does not have permission to access login_html via View and requests authentication.

To give Egon access, we must set the View permission for the role Friend separately. Once enabled, when Egon enters his correct user name and password, he is transferred by the redirect to index_html. There he is classified as an authenticated user with the Friend role during the 'if' query and is shown the special welcome page. Since no other Anonymous users can authenticate, they are not redirected and do not see the special welcome page. This differentiation is achieved as follows:

1. Click on the object login_html in the list of objects in the My_Homepage folder.

2. Click on the Security tab on the tab bar to access the Security screen for login_html, as shown in Figure 8-5.

3. Deactivate the Acquire permission settings? checkbox in front of the View permission (the default setting is activated) so that the permissions set for the superordinate folders are not acquired. This breaks the acquisition chain and allows you to apply the permissions you want.

4. Activate the View permission for the Friends role.

5. Click on the button at the bottom of the list to save these changes.

You have now saved all of the settings needed to allow users to authenticate through login_html.

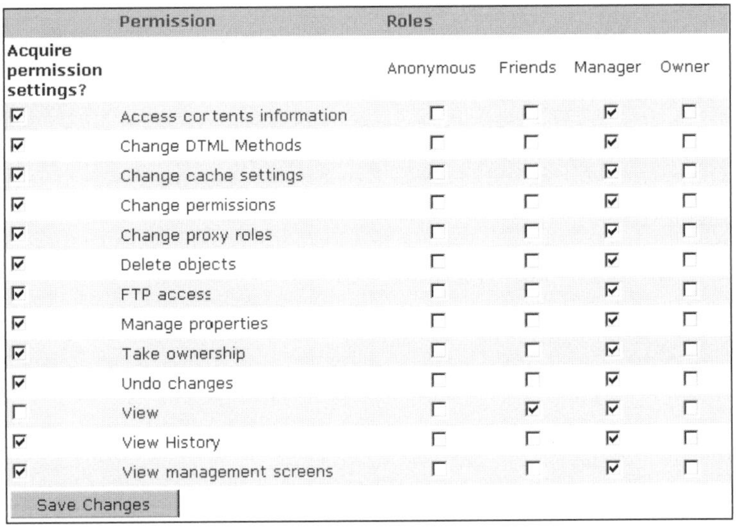

Permission		Roles			
Acquire permission settings?		Anonymous	Friends	Manager	Owner
☑	Access contents information	☐	☐	☑	☐
☑	Change DTML Methods	☐	☐	☑	☐
☑	Change cache settings	☐	☐	☑	☐
☑	Change permissions	☐	☐	☑	☐
☑	Change proxy roles	☐	☐	☑	☐
☑	Delete objects	☐	☐	☑	☐
☑	FTP access	☐	☐	☑	☐
☑	Manage properties	☐	☐	☑	☐
☑	Take ownership	☐	☐	☑	☐
☑	Undo changes	☐	☐	☑	☐
☐	View	☐	☑	☑	☐
☑	View History	☐	☐	☑	☐
☑	View management screens	☐	☐	☑	☐
Save Changes					

Figure 8-5: Assigning permissions for 'login_html'

When a visitor to the site clicks on the Login link, the password window appears, as shown in Figure 8-6.

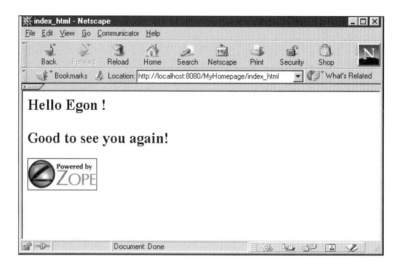

Figure 8-6: Password query

Since Egon exists as a user in Zope, when he enters his username and password (which we created and passed on to him when we created the user in the User Folder for My Homepage) he is returned to the index_html page because the login_html page only consists of a redirect. He is then regarded as a user with the role Friend during the 'if' query and can view the custom text, as shown in Figure 8-7.

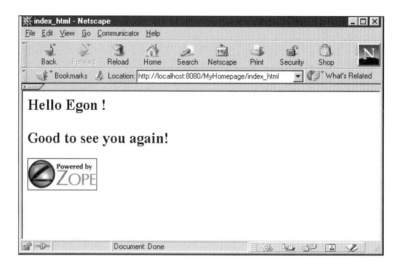

Figure 8-7: View of index_html after Egon logs in

Visitors to the site who have not been created as a Zope user do not have a username or password and cannot log in during the password query. If such a visitor attempts to log in, even if the user is not registered, an error message is displayed after the third unsuccessful attempt, as shown in Figure 8-8.

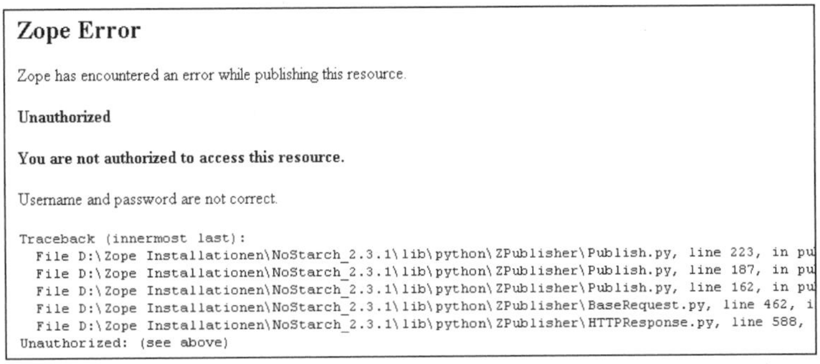

```
Zope Error

Zope has encountered an error while publishing this resource.

Unauthorized

You are not authorized to access this resource.

Username and password are not correct.

Traceback (innermost last):
  File D:\Zope Installationen\NoStarch_2.3.1\lib\python\ZPublisher\Publish.py, line 223, in pu
  File D:\Zope Installationen\NoStarch_2.3.1\lib\python\ZPublisher\Publish.py, line 187, in pu
  File D:\Zope Installationen\NoStarch_2.3.1\lib\python\ZPublisher\Publish.py, line 162, in pu
  File D:\Zope Installationen\NoStarch_2.3.1\lib\python\ZPublisher\BaseRequest.py, line 462, i
  File D:\Zope Installationen\NoStarch_2.3.1\lib\python\ZPublisher\HTTPResponse.py, line 588,
Unauthorized: (see above)
```

Figure 8-8: Error message for unsuccessful login

NOTE *Once a user logs in, they remain authenticated until they exit their browser or attempt to perform an action for which they do not have sufficient permissions. In the latter case, the password window will appear again for the user to specify a new username and password.*

Summary

In this chapter, we explored the many functions and methods available to you in the Zope security system. We also created a working example of how to authenticate users and create dynamic content based on their roles.

In Chapter 10 we will look at how to create and change users, roles, and permissions using external methods. But before we get there, let's have a look at ZClasses.

9

ZCLASSES

You now know how to create objects such as folders, DTML methods, and files in Zope as building blocks for applications. By combining these objects in various ways, you can create myriad applications in Zope. However, limitations and drawbacks to using these general objects still exist and, often, a better approach to designing your application is to create your own specialized objects that are custom tailored to the problems at hand. To create your own object types in Zope, you create a ZClass that describes their interface and functionality.

Using ZClasses, you can create these custom Zope objects, either based on existing Zope objects (to extend these objects' functionality) or from scratch. ZClasses can encapsulate the data, interface, and behavior of specific parts of an application, entirely through the Zope management screen with little programming. As such, programmers and non-programmers can use ZClasses to quickly create complex web application functionality.

In this chapter we explore the process of designing, creating, and incorporating ZClasses into Zope applications, as we use Zclasses to create a web application for a small online bookstore. Once you've completed this chapter, you should find it easy to create ZClasses for use in your own web applications.

9.1 Why Use ZClasses?

In a nutshell, *ZClasses* are special classes in Zope that can be used to describe your own objects—such as cars, jobs, and CDs—and to develop unique solutions to your own tasks, such as selling cars on the Internet or creating an online job bank.

ZClasses are special because you don't need to know how to program in Python to create your own custom object class; you simply create a new product using the Product Management screen in the Control_Panel and then create the necessary ZClasses in this product. You can also export your ZClasses to other Zope installations for other users to use. ZClasses also allow you to easily reuse components from one application in another or distribute your components online.

You might use ZClasses in a company application to create objects that describe the work of individual employees, workgroups, or entire departments. For example, a class called Sales Staff could be used to create objects that describe the employees responsible for sales. Or you could create a ZClass called Software to describe software objects such as graphics applications, computer games, photo CDs, and so on, or a ZClass called Jobs to describe job advertisements.

9.1.1 Example ZClass Application: Bookstore

This application will allow you to manage pages and create objects to sell books. You can add and delete objects as well as change the individual specifications of an object or an entire object class using a web browser. You can also specify how the objects (the individual books, CDs, and so on) are listed: for example, by price, name, or publication date. Figures 9-1 through 9-4 show where we'll end up with our online bookstore.

Title	Book Id	Author	Publisher	Year of Publication	Genre	Price	Delivery Time	Photo
The Sickness Unto Death	B09362	Soren Kierkegaard	Pengiun USA	1989	Philosophy	13.95	3 days	No Photo Available
A Man in Full	B16630	Tom Wolfe	Jonathan Cape	1998	Mystery	19.99	5 days	No Photo Available

Go To Order Form

Figure 9-1: Website from which users can order merchandise

9.2 Classes and Objects

Before you start creating your own ZClasses, you need to familiarize yourself with several basic principles. As mentioned in Section 9.1, you first create a product and then add your ZClasses to it. A ZClass (like all classes) determines certain properties for objects. For example:

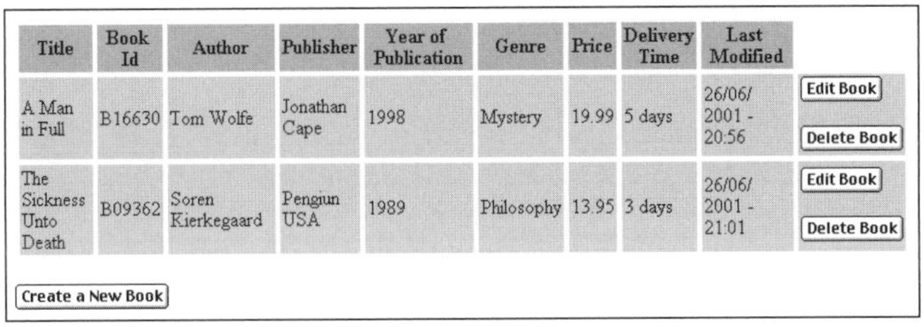

Title	Book Id	Author	Publisher	Year of Publication	Genre	Price	Delivery Time	Last Modified	
A Man in Full	B16630	Tom Wolfe	Jonathan Cape	1998	Mystery	19.99	5 days	26/06/ 2001 - 20:56	Edit Book / Delete Book
The Sickness Unto Death	B09362	Soren Kierkegaard	Penguin USA	1989	Philosophy	13.95	3 days	26/06/ 2001 - 21:01	Edit Book / Delete Book

Create a New Book

Figure 9-2: Managing the goods available on your website

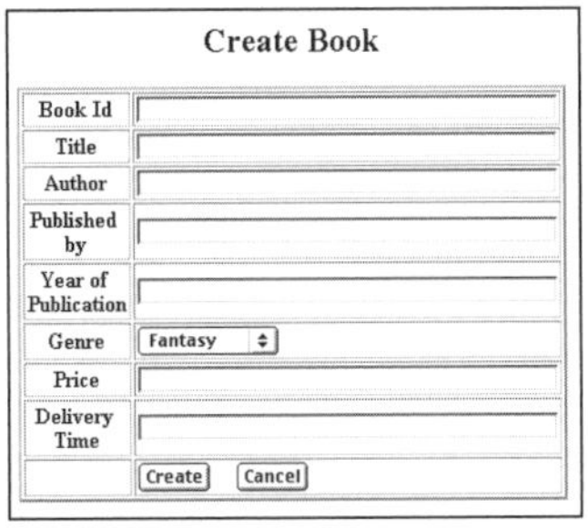

Create Book

Book Id	
Title	
Author	
Published by	
Year of Publication	
Genre	Fantasy
Price	
Delivery Time	

Create   Cancel

Figure 9-3: Input form to add new books

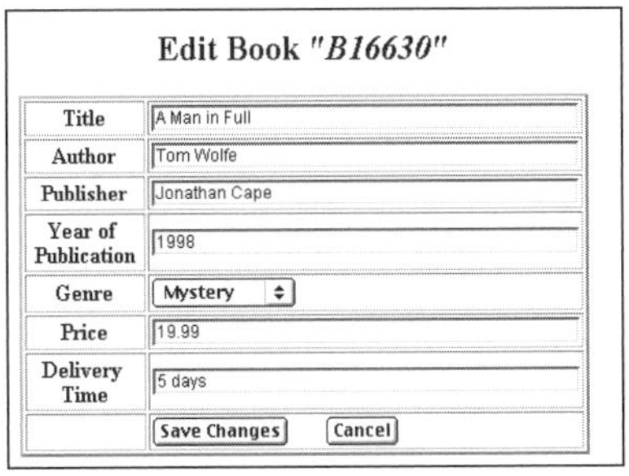

Edit Book "B16630"

Title	A Man in Full
Author	Tom Wolfe
Publisher	Jonathan Cape
Year of Publication	1998
Genre	Mystery
Price	19.99
Delivery Time	5 days

Save Changes   Cancel

Figure 9-4: Input form to change data for existing books

- The ZClass CarClass can set the properties for a particular car (for example, manufacturer, engine, color, and so on).

- The ZClass ApartmentClass can set the properties for an apartment (such as the number of rooms, year of construction, heating, and so on).

An object derived from a class is called an *instance*. Instances created from a class take all of the class's properties and methods, as you will see. Each instance represents an individual member of a class. For example, an instance of CarClass would be an individual car, an instance of ApartmentClass a specific apartment, and so on. (For more information on classes, instances, and objects, see section 2.3.1).

9.2.1 Creating a ZClass

There are four steps to creating a ZClass:

1. Create the product with Zope's Control Panel (see section 9.3.1) to house your ZClass and its associated objects. (A single product can hold multiple ZClasses.)

2. Create the ZClass and specify certain information about it such as the id and title (see section 9.3.2).

3. Define any property sheets and instance methods for the ZClass (see section 9.3.7).

4. Establish views for the ZClass.

9.2.2 Example: CarClass

Suppose you create a ZClass called CarClass that defines the object type Car, after which you create a number of different Car instances. The Cars you create all have the properties defined in the ZClass CarClass (for example, manufacturer, model, year). Individual instances of Cars can then be described by their properties—such as manufacturer, model, year of manufacture, and so on. For example, the properties of a Car object might be Audi (manufacturer), Quattro (model), and 1993 (year of manufacture).

NOTE   *Changes you make to an existing class are applied to all of the class's instances; this powerful feature allows you to make sweeping changes across an application from one central point.*

9.2.2.1 Class Property Example
If you add the property ISBN_Number to the ZClass Books, an ISBN_Number field is added to each object created (in other words, each book) using this class.

9.2.3 Identification Numbers

Each object and each ZClass is automatically assigned a unique *identification number*, or OID, that Zope uses to store the item in the internal Zope Object Database (ZODB). (Do not confuse this with the user-defined id described later.) Normally you do not need to be aware of this internal id.

9.2.4 Property Sheets

A *property sheet* is a list of properties that acts like a container; you create object properties (like the properties for a book) on a property sheet. Properties specify the characteristics used to describe an object of your ZClass. Each property has a name, a property value, and a *data type*.

Data types define the type of property in question, such as text, numeric, and so on, and control the type of data that can be stored in the property, much like the data type of a field in a database table. For example, for a property called Title, you would select the string data type. An overview of all of the data types is contained in section 3.1.6.

You use *views* to manage an object's properties. A view is a management screen defined in your ZClass to manage its instances in Zope. Each view creates a tab in the management screen that executes an instance method of the object when you click on it. (Sections 9.3.5 to 9.3.8 provide more information on property sheets and properties as well as views.)

The property sheets you define in your ZClass describe the schema of the data stored in the instances of the class. Property sheets also provide a convenient user-interface that you can use to examine and modify the data contained in the ZClass instances.

9.3 Creating a ZClass

Now that you have a sense of the stages involved in creating a ZClass, let's look at how to create a product and then how to create a ZClass in this product. In this scenario, you are the owner of an online bookstore, and you need to track your business and inventory in several ways.

9.3.1 Creating a Product

First we'll create a small Zope product called "Sales" that will contain a ZClass you create. To create Sales, follow these steps:

1. Click Control_Panel and then click Product Management. A list of currently available products appears.

2. Click Add Product to add a new product, as shown in Figure 9-5.

Figure 9-5: Management screen for creating a product

3. In the id field, enter `Sales`. Make sure that the name you enter is not already in the list of currently available products.

4. In the Title field, enter `Sale of Books`. For practical reasons, always enter a short, precise description of the ZClass in the Title field, even though this field is not compulsory.

5. Click Generate to create your product. The product Sales should now appear in the list of currently available products, as shown in Figure 9-6.

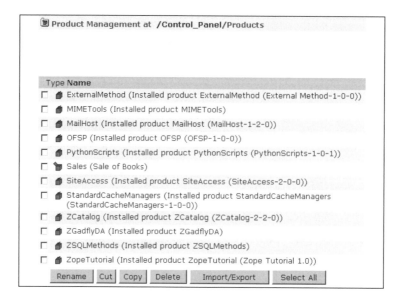

Figure 9-6: Management screen after creating the product Sales

9.3.2 Adding a ZClass to the Product

Now that we have created the product Sales, let's create a ZClass called BookClass within it. Start by creating the ZClass BookClass and defining certain information in it.

1. Click Sales (Sale of Books). Once you have created the product Sales, Zope automatically adds an object called Help (Sales) to the product (Figure 9-7), to which you can add files, images, and help topics. (See section 9.3.9, "Creating Help Topics" for more information.)

Figure 9-7: Help object, automatically created by Zope

2. Select ZClass from the list of available objects. The screen shown in Figure 9-8 appears.

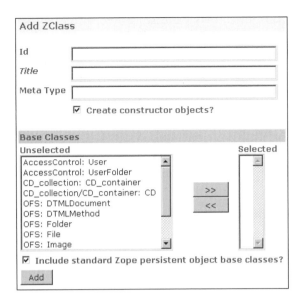

Figure 9-8: Management screen for creating a ZClass

3. In the id field, enter BookClass. Always enter a name in this field so that Zope can identify the object. Be sure that the name contains no accented characters, spaces, or other special characters.

4. In the Title field, enter ZClass for Books. This field is optional and exists solely to hold a short description.

5. In the Meta Type field, enter Book. Book then appears in the list of available objects, allowing you to add new books to any folderish object in Zope. The term *meta type* indicates the type of objects you are creating using your ZClass. You can enter any name you like for meta type, but it makes sense to use a term that relates to the objects created in the ZClass. Meta types can be multiple words with spaces, but keep them short enough so that they fit on the Add Objects menu.

NOTE *Each meta type must be unique within Zope. For example, a ZClass named Graphic_CD and the meta type CD could not co-exist with a ZClass WIN98_Games that contained the meta type CD, because the meta type CD is duplicated. If the meta type is duplicated, you'll receive an error message, just as if you tried to create two objects in the same folder with the same id.*

6. Select the checkbox Create constructor objects? (it will contain a check mark by default). Section 9.3.3 explains why this is important.

7. From the list of *base classes* (other object classes you can base your ZClass on—see section 9.3.6), select ZCatalog:CatalogAware and click the right-pointing arrow button to move ZCatalog:CatalogAware to the Selected list. Then add a second base class, ZClasses:ObjectManager to the Selected list following the same steps.

8.   Make sure that the checkbox Include standard Zope persistent object base classes? is checked so that your ZClass has the standard Zope object base classes that allow its instances to be stored in the ZODB (Zope Object DataBase). Your Zope management screen should now look like Figure 9-9.

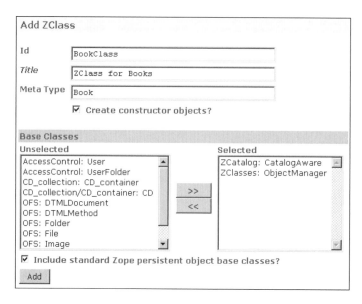

Figure 9-9: Creating the ZClass BookClass

9.   Click Add to create the new ZClass.

You have now created the ZClass BookClass. The following sections will explain the components we've created, and will show you how to modify them to suit the needs of the bookstore application.

9.3.3   The Create Constructor Objects Checkbox

When you selected the checkbox Create constructor objects? in Step 6 of Section 9.3.2 and clicked Add, Zope created four constructor objects for you in addition to your ZClass. These constructors tell Zope how to create the instances of your ZClass. Had you deactivated the checkbox, Zope would have created only the ZClass BookClass, and you would have had to create the following four objects yourself:

•   A DTML method called BookClass_add, which provides the framework for the code used to create an instance of the ZClass BookClass.

•   A DTML method called BookClass_addForm. This serves as the basis for the input form used to enter the new instance's properties, such as its title and id. This form calls the BookClass_add method above when it is submitted.

- A Zope permission called BookClass_add_permission. This creates a new security permission (available in the Security tab of folderish objects) for adding instances of your ZClass.

- A factory object called BookClass_factory. This object adds an item to the add menu of folderish objects for the book ZClass and instructs Zope to display BookClass_addForm when the menu item is selected. It also associates the BookClass_add_permission with this action.

NOTE *The two DTML methods Zope creates for you are intended only to assist you in getting started. You will learn how to modify these and add more functions in section 10.1, "Modifying the Constructor Methods."*

9.3.4 Changing the ZClass Information

Once you have specified the general information for the ZClass, click BookClass and then use the tab bar to define its properties. The tab bar that appears when you click BookClass and enter the directory tree ZClass at /Control_Panel/ Products/Sales/BookClass offers the options described below.

9.3.4.1 Methods Tab

Click Methods (see Figure 9-10) to create your own instance methods for use on your ZClass instances.

For example, in our BookClass we could create methods that allow us to view and upload an image of the book's cover. One of these methods could also be used as a view, allowing it to be easily accessed from the Zope management screen.

Figure 9-10: Methods: Creating methods in a ZClass

9.3.4.2 Basic Tab

Click Basic (see Figure 9-11) to change the title, class ID, and meta type for your ZClass at a later stage. *Class ID* is the identification number automatically assigned to a class by Zope and the identifier Zope uses to associate object instances with their ZClass.

This screen also allows you to create a custom icon for your Zclass, just like those of the built-in Zope objects, which can be viewed in the management screen. To create a custom icon for your ZClass instances, upload an image that is 16 x 16 pixel, in either GIF or JPEG format.

Under normal circumstances you should not change this identifier, unless you wanted to replace an existing ZClass with a new one that, for instance, had different base classes. (Base classes of an existing ZClass cannot be changed.)

Thus, you could associate existing instances with the new ZClass by copying the Class ID value of the original ZClass into the new one and deleting the original ZClass. (You must be very careful doing this however, because this can easily break all of the original ZClass's instances.) You can also specify an image on your local computer and then use it as an icon for the ZClass instances so that they have icons in the management screen like other objects.

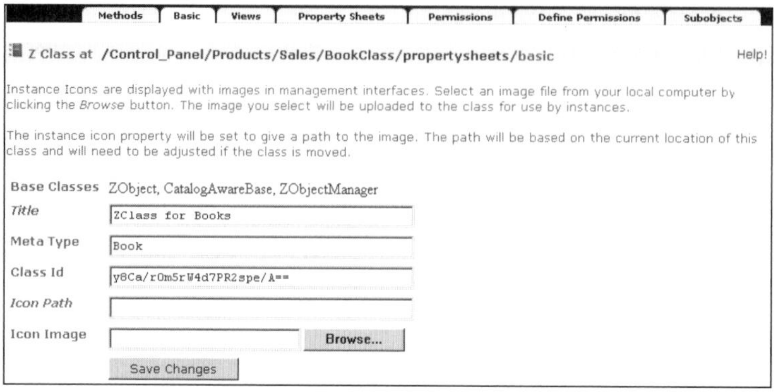

Figure 9-11: Basic: Changing ZClass information after it has been created

9.3.4.3 Views Tab

Click Views to create views for your ZClass instances. A view consists of a tab in the management screen's tab bar and a method called when the tab is clicked. To understand this better, see the bottom of Figure 9-12, which contains a view called Contents, automatically created by Zope. The management screen in Figure 9-11 shows an example of the Basic view, in which you can change certain information relating to the ZClass.

Views allow you to perform various functions on objects, including:

- Displaying and editing an object's contents
- Editing an object's properties
- Previewing an object
- Changing an object's security permission

The Contents view in Figure 9-12 shows a tab called Contents, which appears in the tab bar if you click a class instance. If you open the folder Books and click the object Book01, the Contents tab appears in the tab bar. If you then click Contents, the Python method manage_main is called; this method (inherited from the ObjectManager base class) displays the contents of a folderish object.

We can create views for our BookClass that will allow us to inspect and modify the properties of an object and view it as it appears to users in the third tier.

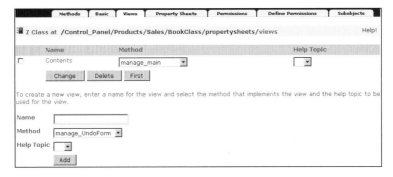

Figure 9-12: Determining the views for the ZClass

9.3.4.4 Property Sheets Tab

Click Property Sheets to create property sheets that describe class instances. Most ZClasses will have only a single property sheet, but if you have many properties, it sometimes make sense to create separate sheets to organize them. For example, as a bookstore owner you might create one property sheet for a book's properties, and another for a distributor's properties. Figure 9-13 shows the property sheet Book_description. (You'll see how to create this section 9.3.7.)

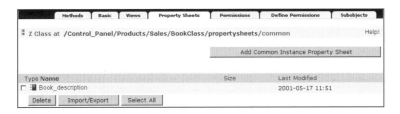

Figure 9-13: Property Sheets: Establishing property sheets and properties

9.3.4.5 Permissions Tab

Click Permissions to set permissions. (See Chapter 6 for more information.)

9.3.4.6 Subobjects Tab

Use the Subobjects screen (shown in Figure 9-14) to specify the types of objects (images, DTML methods, files, and so on) that an instance of BookClass can contain. (You must have selected the base class ObjectManager in Step 7 when you created the ZClass for the ZClass to contain subobjects.)

For example, if you want the object Book01 to contain an image (of the book cover, perhaps) and perhaps text, go to ZClass at /Control_Panel/Products/Sales/BookClass and click Subobjects. Press and hold the CTRL key and then click File and Image in the list.

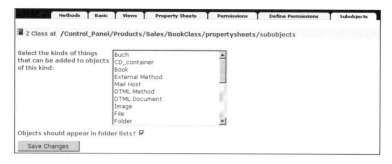

Figure 9-14: Management screen for creating subobjects

Make sure that the checkbox Objects should appear in folder lists? is selected so that you can later select File and Image from a pull-down menu when specifying the contents for a book. Then click Change.

NOTE *To control the objects contained in a folderish ZClass instance programmatically, deselect the Objects should appear in folder lists? so that users cannot add subobjects manually. With this option disabled, the object types selected can only be added from DTML or Python code.*

9.3.5   Base Classes and Their Views

A base class name is formatted as Product Name: Class Name. For example, OFS: File. Here are the two base classes we selected in Step 7 of the example in section 9.3.2:

ZCatalog:CatalogAware   This base class catalogs objects in your application using a ZCatalog. It must be the first base class selected for it to function properly. (See Chapter 11 for more information on ZCatalog.)

ZClasses:ObjectManager   This base class allows an instance of a ZClass to contain other Zope objects (for example, a Book object could contain an image). In other words, it makes the instances folderish. If you click Subobjects in the tab bar of the ZClass, you can select the object meta types that a class instance can contain. (For more information on this subject, see section 9.3.4.6, "Subobjects Tab.")

Zope automatically creates default views, which are displayed in the tab bar under Views when you selected base classes when creating your ZClass. (See section 9.3.2, Step 7.) Table 9-1 shows the views created with each base class.

9.3.6   Creating a Property Sheet and Properties

Once you have created your first ZClass, you will need to create a property sheet for it. In a property sheet, you define various characteristics (properties) that apply to the individual class instances.

Before creating a property sheet, take a few moments to consider exactly which properties the objects should have. Although you can always change your property definitions, plan ahead or you may also need to modify the code you write to access the properties. Changing a property's data type can be problematic too because, once instances of your ZClass have been created, they will continue

Table 9-1: Base Classes and Their Associated Views

View: Function	No Base class selected	User	User Folder	DTML Document	DTML Method	Folder	File	Image	Generic User Folder	CatalogAware	ZCatalog	Object Manager
Security: manage_main	x	x										
Contents: manage_main			x			x			x		x	x
Security: manage_access			x	x		x	x	x	x	x		
Undo: manage_UndoForm			x			x			x			
Edit: manage_main				x	x		x	x				
Upload: manage_UploadForm				x	x		x	x				
Properties: manage_propertiesForm				x	x	x	x	x	x			
View:				x	x		x					
Proxy: manage_proxyForm				x								
Define Permissions: manage_access					x							
View: index_html						x						
Find: manage_findFrame						x						
View: view_image_or_file								x				
User List: manage_listUsers									x			
Cache: manage_cache									x			
User Info: manage_userInfo									x			
Cataloged Objects: manage_catalogView											x	
Find Items to ZCatalog: manage_catalogFind											x	
MetaData Table: manage_catalogSchema											x	
Indexes: manage_catalogIndexes											x	
Status: manage_catalogStatus											x	

to contain property values in the old property type even after you've changed the type in the ZClass. Too, removing a property from a ZClass with instances does not remove the actual property value attribute from the instances, although the property will no longer show up in the property sheets.

To create a property sheet for the ZClass BookClass, do the following:

1. Go to Product at /Control_Panel/Products/Sales/. Then click BookClass.
2. Click Property Sheets on the tab bar of the management screen (see Figure 9-15).
3. As you can see, your current ZClass has no property sheets. Click Add Common Instance Property Sheet to create one. A screen appears containing two fields: Id and Title.
4. In the Id field, enter Book_description; you can leave the Title field blank.
5. Click Add to create the property sheet Book_description.

You can now click your property sheet Book_description and specify individual properties for it.

Figure 9-15: Management screen for creating property sheets

9.3.6.1 Defining Properties in a Property Sheet

A property (attribute of an object) consists of an id and a default value, as well as a property type. The following property types are available (see section 3.1.6 for more information):

Property Type	Description
boolean	A property with two discrete values: true or false. Represented on the property sheet by a checkbox.
date	A date and time value that cannot be left empty in the property sheet. This property shares all of the functionality of the DateTime and ZopeTime objects. (See Appendix A for more information on working with dates.)
float	A floating point decimal number, often used to represent fractional or monetary values. Floats must always have a value assigned.
int	An integer, either positive or negative in value with no fractional part. The range of values may vary on different operating systems, but will always have a precision of at least 32 bits. Int properties will not allow an empty value.
lines	A list of text strings with each list item on a separate line. Useful for multiple word keywords or an arbitrary number of values.
long	An integer value without an upper or lower value range. Use this property for extremely large numbers that may exceed several billion in value.
string	A single line string of text of unlimited size. This is probably the most commonly used property type.
text	A multiline string of text of unlimited size. Uses a multiline text area on the property sheet, and is often used for long string values such as descriptions, or long passages of text data.

tokens	Another list of strings like the lines type except that this property consists of a single line with each list item separated by a space. This property is useful for storing keywords.
selection	A string type with a discrete set of allowed values, only one of which can be selected at a time. The value field points to a property or method that returns a list of the allowed values (a lines property defined in a parent folder or the root is often used for this list). Selection properties are represented by a drop-down list on the property sheet.
multiple selection	Like a selection, except that multiple values can be selected at one time. These selected values are kept as a list of strings in the property.

Now establish the properties for Book_description. The book should have the following properties:

- **title** with the string type
- **author** with the string type
- **publisher** with the string type
- **date_of_publication** with the string type
- **genre** with the selection type
- **price** with the string type
- **delivery_time** with the string type

Let's create the title property as an example (see Figure 9-16):

1. In the Id field, enter title.
2. Leave the Value field blank. This specifies a blank string as the default title.
3. For the type, select string from the pull-down menu.
4. Click Add to create the first property.

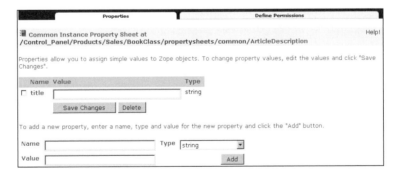

Figure 9-16: Management screen for creating properties

If you enter a value in the Value field, every object you create using this ZClass is initially assigned this value for the title property. The Value field creates a default value that can be modified later for each object you create.

You must specify a property value for any boolean, int, long, float, or date properties. These property types will not accept a blank default value.

Now create all remaining properties except the genre property. (The genre property requires extra explanation, provided in section 9.3.7.2.)

9.3.7 Creating a Selection or Multiple Selection Property

To use selection and multiple selection type variables, you must first create a lines property in the root folder, which allows you to use the values from the lines property in your ZClass. This property type represents a selection list for a selection or multiple selection type property.

You can also use a DTML method or Python script as the source for the items in a selection list. To use a method, it must return a list of strings. In DTML, you can use the dtml-return tag to accomplish this.

9.3.7.1 The Selection Type

The selection type specifies a pull-down menu and contains the values from a lines property contained in a superordinate folder. Only one value can be selected at a time. One example of an object that uses the selection property is a selection list called Delivery with the values Available for Delivery and Not Available for Delivery.

9.3.7.2 The Multiple Selection Type

The multiple selection type also specifies a selection list that contains the values from a lines property located in a superordinate folder, but you can select multiple values. One example of an object with the multiple selection property is a selection list called "Interests" with the values Sport, Internet, Finance, and Music.

Therefore, to create the Genre property, you first create the necessary lines property as follows:

1. Open the root folder.
2. Click the Properties tab.
3. In the Id field, enter book_genre and select the lines type from the pull-down menu. Leave the Value field blank.
4. Click Add.
5. Enter the following values in the text field for book_genre; each book genre must be on a separate line:

   ```
   Romantic Novel
   Science Fiction
   Thriller
   Philosophy
   Short Stories
   ```

6. You should now see the screen shown in Figure 9-17.
7. Click Save Changes.

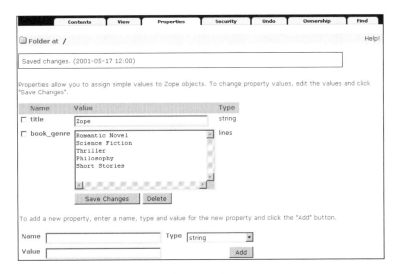

Figure 9-17: Management screen for the book_genre property

This selection list should now be available throughout the hierarchy beneath the root folder, but it must still be assigned to the genre selection list property.

To create the genre property using the selection type, do the following.

1. Go back to the property sheet Book_description in which you have already created the properties title, author, publisher, year of publication, price, and delivery time. (You'll find the values you just entered for book_genre here.)

2. In the Id field, enter genre and choose selection from the Type menu. In the Value field, enter book_genre.

3. Click Add.

Zope will now create the genre property, which can use the values in the book_genre property as its own. Once you have created all of the properties, your management screen should look like Figure 9-18.

NOTE *The float type is not used for the Price property because you may announce a product whose price is unknown, and you need to be able to enter Not Known in the Value field. Similarly, string is selected for Year of Publication so that you can enter a value such as: December 2000.*

9.3.8 Establishing Views

Once you have specified your properties, you will need to establish views for your ZClass so that you can manage the properties of the book instances you create, so that content managers will be able to view and edit the properties using the Zope management screen. Follow these steps to create the view:

1. Click Control Panel and then choose Product Management. Click Sales and then BookClass. The directory tree should look like the following:

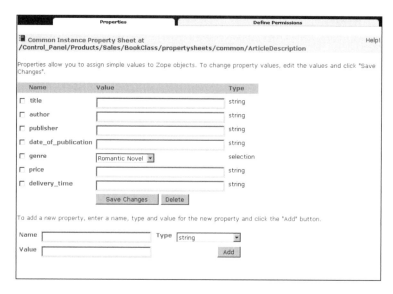

Figure 9-18: Management screen after you create all properties for a BookClass object

---

`Control_Panel/Products/Sales/BookClass/propertysheets/methods`

---

2. Click the Views button in the tab bar. Your management screen should look like Figure 9-19. You will now create a new view called "Properties" so that you can view and edit the property values of Book instances.

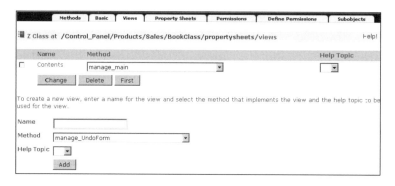

Figure 9-19: Management screen for adding views

3. In the Name field, enter `Properties` and select propertysheets/ Book_description/manage from the Method pull-down menu. The following items are available:

View method	Description
manage_UndoForm	Shows the standard Undo information and allows users to undo actions carried out on the object (or subobjects).
manage_access	The method used for the Security tab. Allows Zope managers to change permissions and roles.
manage_main	The main object management screen. The Contents tab for folderish objects; for non-folderish objects it is usually the Edit tab.
manage_owner	The method used for the Ownership tab. Allows changes to object ownership.
propertysheets/ Book_description/manage	The property management interface. Each property sheet in your ZClass will have its own manage method.

Because you need a view that will allow you to edit the properties of the book instances, select propertysheets/Book_description/manage, the method for managing the property sheet for this ZClass (see Figure 9-20).

4. Click Add.

Zope now creates a management tab called Properties, which appears in the tab bar when you click an object in your ZClass (visible in Figure 9-25 on page 176). Clicking this tab calls the method propertysheets/Book_description/ manage for the book instance, allowing you to change its properties.

By default, the BookClass has a Contents view that calls the Python method manage_main. This view and the manage_main method are inherited from the ObjectManager base class we selected for BookClass. Zope uses the manage_main method to display the contents of the object in the management screen.

Table 9-1 (page 167) shows the views Zope automatically creates when you select certain base classes.

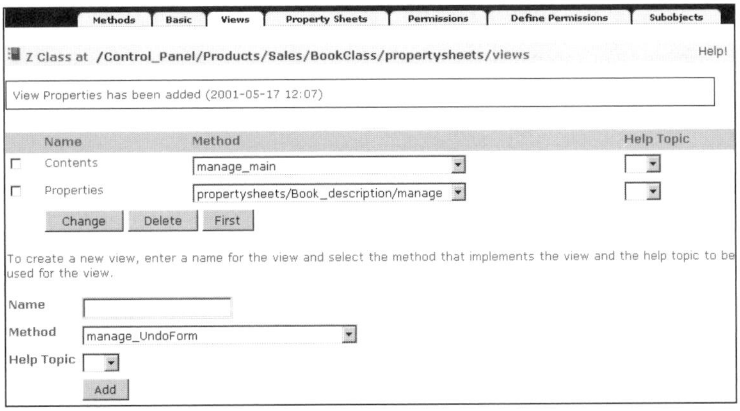

Figure 9-20: Management screen after creating the view

9.3.9 Creating Help Topics

You can create help topics for each view that will be available for the various views you specify for the ZClass. Suppose you want to be able to access help text by clicking a Help button as soon as you click a book—something like the setup in Figure 9-21.

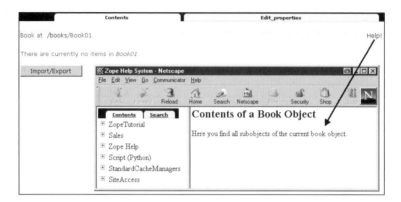

Figure 9-21: Function of the Help object

To create the following help topics, open the path Product at /Control_Panel/Products/Sales and click Help (Sales).

1. From the add menu, select Add Help Topic.
2. In the Id field, enter the word Content, and in the Title field, enter Contents of a Book Object.
3. Click Add. (See Figure 9-22.) Edit this object's contents by clicking Contents (Contents of a Book Object). You can now enter some help text to be displayed when you click the Help button, as in Figure 9-23.

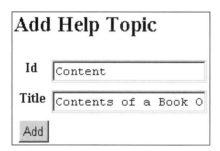

Figure 9-22: Creating a help topic in the Help object

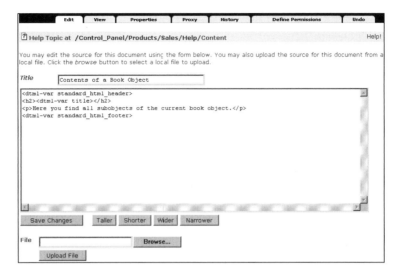

Figure 9-23: Editing the Contents help topic

9.3.9.1 Assigning the Help Topic to a View

But wait: We still need to assign the Contents help topic to the Contents view that displays the contents of a book, as shown in Figure 9-24. To do so, return to the Views tab of the BookClass ZClass; select the Content help topic from the pull-down menu in the Help Topic column for the Contents view, then click Change.

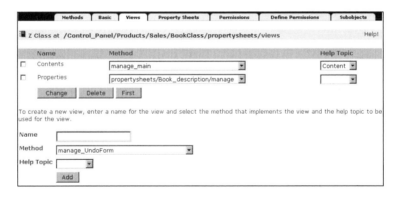

Figure 9-24: Assigning a help topic to a view

Now, with Contents properly assigned, when you create a book object called "Book" in the Books folder and then click it, the Contents view is called up, and a Help button appears that displays the contents of your help topic when you click it (see Figure 9-25).

9.3.9.2 Changing the Sequence of Views

To change the sequence of the views, currently Contents/Properties, select the checkbox of the view you want first and then click First. This sequence indicates how the buttons are arranged on the tab bar that appears when you click an object in the class.

The sequence in Figure 9-25 shows the management screen that appears when you click a Book class instance.

Figure 9-25: Management screen with the available views for Book

This management screen displays the contents of the Book object (using the function manage_main, which you already assigned to the Contents view). The Book object contains no other objects.

NOTE *Do not confuse the contents of an object with its properties; the object owns the properties, but the properties themselves are not the object. (See for yourself by clicking the Properties tab.)*

9.3.10 Editing Properties

Use the Properties tab to edit the values of properties for a book object instance. Changes you make to properties in one instance will not affect other instances of the class. This allows each Book object derived from our BookClass ZClass to have individual property value assignments.

Summary

Let's briefly summarize what we have accomplished. We have

- Created a simple Zope product.
- Created a ZClass in this Zope product.
- Established properties for the ZClass.
- Created views for the ZClass.

In Chapter 10, you will learn how to use your ZClass and how to enhance your Zope product with useful functions.

10

WORKING WITH THE ZCLASS

This chapter continues the overview of Zope classes (ZClasses) begun in Chapter 9 and continues the development of our Zope product, Sales, to demonstrate the key ways in which you can use ZClasses in an application.

10.1 Modifying the Constructor Methods

In Chapter 9, you created a basic ZClass. In this chapter, you will modify the constructor methods created by Zope (discussed in section 9.3.3), because the default versions contain only the bare minimum of code needed to create instances of our BookClass ZClass.

10.1.1 Modifying DTML Methods

The four objects created by Zope when you created your ZClass include two DTML methods (BookClass_add and BookClass_addForm), known as constructor methods. Zope uses these methods to create an instance of our ZClass in which we can code the actions needed to properly initialize our Book objects.

The default constructor form (BookClass_addForm) only contains an input box for the id of a new Book instance. The default constructor (BookClass_add) simply creates a Book object in the current folder (or folderish object) and sets that object's id to the value supplied in the constructor form. The other properties of the new Book object, which you created in section 9.3.7, are left to their default values. We need to modify both of these methods so that the other property values can be specified when a Book instance is created.

Let's start by modifying the constructor form, BookClass_addForm. At present, it looks like Listing 10-1.

Listing 10-1: The DTML method BookClass_addForm that Zope created when we created the ZClass BookClass

```
<HTML>
<HEAD><TITLE>Add Book</TITLE></HEAD>
<BODY BGCOLOR="#FFFFFF" LINK="#000099" VLINK="#555555">
<H2>Add b</H2>
<form action="BookClass_add"><table>
<tr><th>Id</th>
    <td><input type=text name=id></td>
</tr>
<tr><td></td>
<td><input type=submit value="Add"></td></tr>
</table>
</form>
</body>
</html>
```

Currently, this method displays the form shown in Figure 10-1.

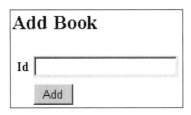

Figure 10-1: This input form appears after calling up the default DTML method BookClass_addForm

The screen shown in Figure 10-1 is used to enter the property values for a new Book instance. We need to add input fields for the other properties we created in our BookClass (see section 9.3.7 for information on the properties), so let's change BookClass_addForm as shown in Listing 10-2.

Listing 10-2: The modified DTML method BookClass_addForm used as an input form for creating a new book instance

```
<HTML>
<HEAD><TITLE>Create Book</TITLE></HEAD>
<BODY BGCOLOR="#FFFFFF" LINK="#000099" VLINK="#555555">
<H2>Create Book</H2>
<form action="BookClass_add"><table>
<tr><th>Book Id</th>
    <td><input type=text name=id size="60"></td>
</tr>
<tr><th>Title</th>
    <td><input type=text name=title size="60"></td>
</tr>
<tr><th>Author</th>
    <td><input type=text name=author size="60"></td>
</tr>
<tr><th>Published by</th>
    <td><input type=text name=publisher size="60"></td>
</tr>
<tr><th>Year of Publication</th>
<td><input type=text name=year_of_publication
size="60"></td>
</tr>
<tr><th>Genre</th>
<td><select name="genre">
        <dtml-in name="book_genre">
           <option value="<dtml-var sequence-item>">
                <dtml-var sequence-item></option>
        </dtml-in>
      </select>
</td>
</tr>
<tr><th>Price</th>
    <td><input type=text name=price size="60"></td>
</tr>
<tr><th>Delivery Time</th>
    <td><input type=text name=delivery_time size="60"></td>
</tr>
<tr><td></td><td><input type=submit value="Create">
</td></tr>
</table>
</form>
</body>
</html>
```

NOTE *When creating your constructor form, make sure that the name and capitalization of each input box matches exactly its respective property in the ZClass.*

Figure 10-2 shows our new constructor form:

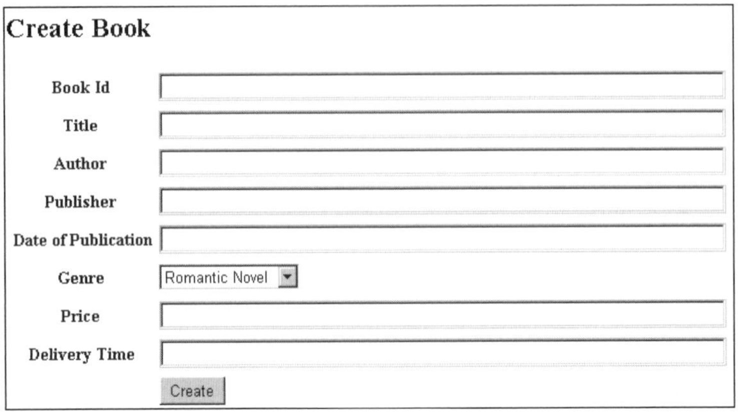

Figure 10-2: Modified BookClass_addForm Input form

Let's take a closer look at the code for our new form. Note that the line

```
<form action="BookClass_add">
```

causes the form to call the other DTML constructor method BookClass_add (created by Zope) when the form is submitted, passing it the values from the input boxes. The BookClass_add method then creates a Book instance based on the form values.

Unfortunately, the default code in the BookClass_add method does not set the property values for the new Book instance supplied by our new form. Instead, we must modify BookClass_add to store the form's values in their respective properties in the new Book instance. So, let's change BookClass_add as follows.

1. Remove all comments and <dtml-comment> tags except for

```
<dtml-call "propertysheets.Basic.manage_editProperties(REQUEST)">
```

You will need to make some changes to this tag in Step 3.

This line creates an instance of our BookClass ZClass (using the built-in method createInObjectManager). Using dtml-with, it places the new instance at the top of the DTML namespace so that we can perform further operations on the new instance.

2. Edit the line

```
<dtml-call "propertysheets.Basic.manage_editProperties(REQUEST)">
```

to read

```
<dtml-call "propertysheets.Book_description.manage_editProperties(REQUEST)">
```

This line calls the built-in method manage_editProperties on our Book_Description property sheet, passing it the REQUEST object containing all values entered in the form. This method sets the property values of the new Book instance to those specified on the input form (BookClass_addForm).

3. Insert the lines

```
<dtml-if NoRedir>
<dtml-else>
```

between the lines

```
<dtml-with>
```

and

```
<dtml-if DestinationURL>
```

The last lines of code, namely

```
<dtml-if DestinationURL>
<dtml-call
    "RESPONSE.redirect(DestinationURL+'/manage_workspace')">
<dtml-else>
    <dtml-call "RESPONSE.redirect(URL2+'/manage_workspace')">
</dtml-if>
```

will send you to the correct management screen when you create a book using the folder's add menu. From there, you will be redirected to the Contents view of the folder where you created the book. However, should you want to create your book instance using DTML code, you do not need to perform this redirection—because you'll use your own DTML methods instead of the built-in Zope management screens. In the modified constructor method, you'll specify which screen is to be displayed after you create a book.

4. To close the <dtml-else> tag from Step 3, go to the line

```
</dtml-if>
```

and insert the following lines after it:

```
</dtml-if>
</dtml-with>
```

5. Click Save Changes. The DTML method BookClass_add should now look like Listing 10-3.

Listing 10-3: BookClass_add after changes have been made

```
<HTML>
<HEAD><TITLE>Add BookClass</TITLE></HEAD>
<BODY BGCOLOR="#FFFFFF" LINK="#000099" VLINK="#555555">
<dtml-with "BookClass.createInObjectManager(REQUEST['id'], REQUEST)">
<dtml-call "propertysheets.Book_description.manage_editProperties(REQUEST)">
<dtml-if NoRedir>
    <dtml-return name="this">
<dtml-else>
<dtml-if DestinationURL>
<dtml-call
    "RESPONSE.redirect(DestinationURL+'/manage_workspace')">
<dtml-else>
    <dtml-call "RESPONSE.redirect(URL2+'/manage_workspace')">
</dtml-if>
</dtml-if>
</dtml-with>
</body>
</html>
```

The last nine lines of Listing 10-3 redirect you to the folder manage_work-space, where you will find yourself once you have created the object. For example, if you create a book with an id B01931 in the folder Books, you will find yourself back in the folder Books when you are finished.

NOTE *If you try to view this method inside the product, you will get a Zope error. To test it, you must call it from the add form (BookClass_addForm).*

10.1.2 Creating Objects with ZClasses

Before we test our ZClass, we need to create a folder to contain our Book instances. Here's how:

1. Open the root folder and create a folder by selecting Folder from the add menu.

2. Enter Books in the Id field, remove both check marks from the checkboxes, and click Add.

3. Open your new folder and select Book from the add menu (our ZClass meta type specified in section 9.3.2).

4. The input form from the DTML method BookClass_addForm appears. Enter the data for a book and click Create, as shown in Figure 10-3.

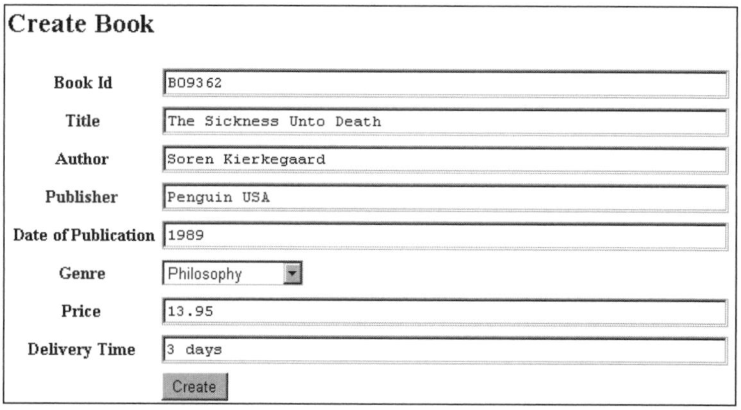

```
Create Book

Book Id              B09362

Title                The Sickness Unto Death

Author               Soren Kierkegaard

Publisher            Penguin USA

Date of Publication  1989

Genre                Philosophy      ▼

Price                13.95

Delivery Time        3 days

                     [ Create ]
```

Figure 10-3: Creating a Book object

You should now see the object B09362 in the Books folder, as shown in Figure 10-4.

Figure 10-4: Management screen after you create the object B09362

5. Create another book with the following details:

Book Id:	B19381
Title:	Dead Zone
Author:	Stephen King
Publisher:	Viking
Year of Publication:	1987
Genre:	Thriller
Price:	35.00
Delivery Time:	2 Days

You have now created two objects with the ZClass BookClass, simply by selecting Book from the add menu in the Books folder.

10.1.3 The Book Class Factory

If you're wondering how Zope knows to use the ZClass BookClass when you select Book from the Available Objects menu, take a look at the object BookClass_factory (shown in Figure 10-5), which was also automatically created by Zope when you created the ZClass.

As shown in Figure 10-5, we specify in the factory that the DTML method BookClass_addForm is to be called when Book is selected from the add menu. (The field Add list name contains Book, because that is the meta type in your ZClass.)

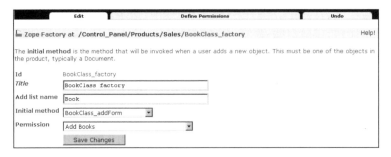

Figure 10-5: The BookClass_factory object's management screen

NOTE *In order for your ZClass to work correctly, make sure that the Add list name in the factory is always exactly the same as the meta type value in the basic tab of your ZClass. (See section 9.3.4.2 for more information.)*

10.2 Running the Store

In this sample web application—the bookstore scenario—our goals are

- To use an administration interface to manage all books on sale.
- To offer our books for sale to visitors.

To do so, we need

- An administration page, admin_html. Steps to create this element are explained in section 10.3.
- An index page, index_html, where customers can view and order items. Steps to create this element are explained in section 10.4.

These two DTML methods, admin_html and index_html, are very similar except that when visitors arrive through index_html, they cannot add, edit, or delete objects. Changes of this nature can be made only by the page administrator using admin_html.

10.3 Two Ways to Edit Your Book Objects

When editing the book objects you create, you can either work in the management screen for the Books folder or create a custom administration interface. It is much easier to manage all objects from a single administration interface, but we'll discuss both approaches here.

10.3.1 Working in the Books Folder with the Management Screen

Open the management screen (as shown in Figure 10-4), then add, delete, or edit a book as follows:

1. **Add:** Create a new book instance by selecting Book from the add menu. Pressing Add calls the method BookClass_addForm.

2. **Delete:** Delete a book by activating the checkbox to the left of the object and then clicking Delete.

3. **Edit:** Click a book to access the following views: Contents and Properties.

Try experimenting a little here by creating additional books, editing a book's properties (using the Properties view), and deleting some books. You can see that the books behave much like the built-in Zope objects (for example, DTML documents or files).

10.3.2 Working with an Administration Interface

Figure 10-6 shows an administration interface for managing book objects, which you can use to create new book objects, edit book data, and delete books. You can also create a page to sell the book objects you create using a DTML method.

10.3.2.1 Creating admin_html

To create admin_html in the Books folder, follow these steps:

1. Select DTML Method from the pull-down menu.

2. In the Id field, enter admin_html and click Add and Edit.

3. A field opens that contains the minimum code necessary for the method. Delete this code and enter the DTML code for the method admin_html as shown in Listing 10-4.

Listing 10-4: The DTML method admin_html

```
1:     <dtml-var standard_html_header>
2:     <table border=0 cellpadding=2 cellspacing=4 width="80%">
3:     <tr width="100%" bgcolor="#44BBCC">
4:         <th>Title</th>
5:         <th>Book Id</th>
6:         <th>Author</th>
7:         <th>Publisher</th>
8:         <th>Year of Publication</th>
9:         <th>Genre</th>
10:        <th>Price</th>
11:        <th>Delivery Time</th>
12:        <th>Last Modified</th>
13:     </tr>
14:     <dtml-in expr="objectValues(['Book'])" sort=title>
```

(continued on next page)

```
15:             <tr width="100%" bgcolor="#88DDBB">
16:                 <td><dtml-var name="title"></td>
17:                 <td><dtml-var name="id"></td>
18:                 <td><dtml-var name="author"></td>
19:                 <td><dtml-var name="publisher"></td>
20:                 <td><dtml-var name="year_of_publication"></td>
21:                 <td><dtml-var name="genre"></td>
22:                 <td><dtml-var name="price"></td>
23:                 <td><dtml-var name="delivery_time"></td>
24:                 <td><dtml-var name="bobobase_modification_time"
25:                         fmt="%d/%m/%Y - %H:%M"></td>
26:                 <td><FORM ACTION="<dtml-var
27:                     name="sequence-item" url/EditForm_html">
28:                     <input type=submit value="Edit Book">
29:                 </FORM>
30:                 <FORM action="DeleteConfirm_html">
31:                 <input type=hidden name="id"
32:                         value="<dtml-var name="id">">
33:                 <input type=submit value="Delete Book">
34:                 </FORM>
35:             </td></tr>
36:     </dtml-in>
37:     </table>
38:     <form action="CreateForm_html">
39:     <input type=submit value="Create a New Book">
40:     </form>
41:     <dtml-var standard_html_footer>
```

This method creates a page on which all Book instances in the folder are arranged in a table sorted by title. Each row of the table contains the property values of a Book instance and two buttons: Edit Book and Delete Book. Use the Create New Book button at the bottom of the table to add new book instances to the folder.

The resulting DTML method admin_html displays a screen like the one shown in Figure 10-6.

Title	Book Id	Author	Publisher	Year of Publication	Genre	Price	Delivery Time	Last Modified	
A Man in Full	B16630	Tom Wolfe	Jonathan Cape	1998	Mystery	19.99	5 days	26/06/ 2001 - 20:56	Edit Book / Delete Book
The Sickness Unto Death	B09362	Soren Kierkegaard	Penguin USA	1989	Philosophy	13.95	3 days	26/06/ 2001 - 21:01	Edit Book / Delete Book

Create a New Book

Figure 10-6: Administration page admin_html after you create two books

Let's take a closer look at the code for admin_html.

First, a table is opened and a row of column headings is created (Lines 2–13). Then Line 14 is used to loop through the Books in the folder.

Folderish objects (with an ObjectManager base class) have the built-in method objectValues, which returns a list of the objects contained in the folder. Because the admin_html method is not folderish (and therefore lacks the object-Values method), it acquires the method from the folder it is called in. To specify a folder, we could use dot notation in the expression, as in:

```
expr="books.objectValues(['Book'])"
```

DTML documents act differently from DTML methods in this regard. DTML documents do have a method objectValues, which always returns an empty list. If admin_html were a DTML document, we would need to write the expression using the dot notation as above.

An optional argument, which filters the meta types of the objects returned, can be passed to objectValues. This argument value is a list of the meta type strings for the desired objects. If the argument is omitted, all objects in the folder are returned. In our application, we are only interested in objects with the meta type Book, so we pass this value to the method. Putting it in square brackets makes it a list with a single item; in fact, when specifying a single meta type as above, a simple string value can be passed and the square brackets omitted. The dtml-in tag is then used to iterate through the Book instances returned by objectValues.

Once inside the in loop (lines 15–25), the property values from each Book instance are inserted into a new table row. In the last column of the table (Lines 26–35), two forms are inserted to create the Edit Book and Delete Book action buttons. The following code on Lines 26 and 27 requires explanation:

```
<td><FORM ACTION="<dtml-var
    name="sequence-item" url>/EditForm_html">
```

In this form tag, the action URL is set to the URL of the current Book instance followed by /EditForm_html (a DTML method we will define in the next section).

The URL attribute of dtml-var inserts the full absolute URL path of any Zope object. By calling it after the Book instance in the URL, Zope places the Book instance at the top of the namespace stack, thus allowing easy access (via acquisition) to the Book properties from within the EditForm_html method. This is a powerful technique that takes advantage of the fact that DTML methods can act like methods of any object you call them on. In this case we are calling the Edit-Form_html method on a book instance. This method will display the book's properties in a form so that the values can be edited.

The second form (Line 30) calls another DTML method, DeleteConfirm_html, which we define below. It deletes a Book object when we pass its id using a hidden form field (Line 31); the form, table row, and the in loop are then closed (Lines 34–36). A third form (Lines 38–40), added below the table, creates new book instances; its action calls a third DTML method CreateForm_html—which we also define below.

NOTE *The admin_html method can be located above or inside the Books folder in the folder hierarchy. To call admin_html on several different folders containing Books, put it above these folders in the Zope hierarchy. Remember, if a method called for an object is not found inside that object, Zope uses acquisition to search upward through the folder hierarchy to find it.*

10.3.3 Admin_html DTML Methods

As noted above, the admin_html method calls three DTML methods: Create-Form_html, EditForm_html, and DeleteConfirm_html. We will create these now and then take a closer look at each.

10.3.3.1 CreateForm_html

CreateForm_html is called when you click Create New Article on the admin_html management screen. To create the DTML CreateForm_html, delete the code automatically generated by Zope and then create a new CreateForm_html method, as shown in Listing 10-5.

Listing 10-5: CreateForm_html, which is used as an input form for a new book

```
1:      <dtml-var standard_html_header>
2:      <h2 align="center">Create Book</h2>
3:      <form action="CreateInstance_html">
4:      <table border=2 cellpadding=0 cellspacing=2
5:           align="center" valign="center" width=50% height=50%>
6:          <tr><th>Book Id</th>
7:              <td><input type=text name=id size="60"></td>
8:          </tr>
9:          <tr><th>Title</th>
10:             <td><input type=text name=title size="60"></td>
11:         </tr>
12:         <tr><th>Author</th>
13:             <td><input type=text name=author size="60"></td>
14:         </tr>
15:         <tr><th>Published by</th>
16:             <td><input type=text name=publisher size="60"></td>
17:         </tr>
18:         <tr><th>Year of Publication</th>
19:             <td><input type=text name=year_of_publication
20:                     size="60"></td>
21:         </tr>
22:         <tr><th>Genre</th>
23:             <td> <SELECT NAME="genre">
24:             <dtml-in book_genre>
```

(continued on next page)

```
25:                    <OPTION VALUE="<dtml-var name="sequence-item">">
26:                        <dtml-var name="sequence-item">
27:                    </OPTION>
28:              </dtml-in>
29:              </SELECT></td>
30:          </tr>
31:          <tr><th>Price</th>
32:              <td><input type=text name=price size="60"></td>
33:          </tr>
34:          <tr><th>Delivery Time</th>
35:              <td><input type=text name=delivery_time
36:                      size="60"></td>
37:          </tr>
38:          <tr><th> </th>
39:              <td><input name="create" type=submit value="Create">
40:                 
41:              <input name="cancel" type=submit value="Cancel"></td>
42:          </tr>
43:      </table>
44:      </form>
45:      <dtml-var standard_html_footer>
```

CreateForm_html displays the management screen shown in Figure 10-7 and is very similar to the BookClass_addForm method we adapted in Section 10.1.1.

Compare the methods in Listing 10-2 and in Listing 10-5. The screen in Figure 10-7 is used for the administration interface and uses the DTML Method admin_html.

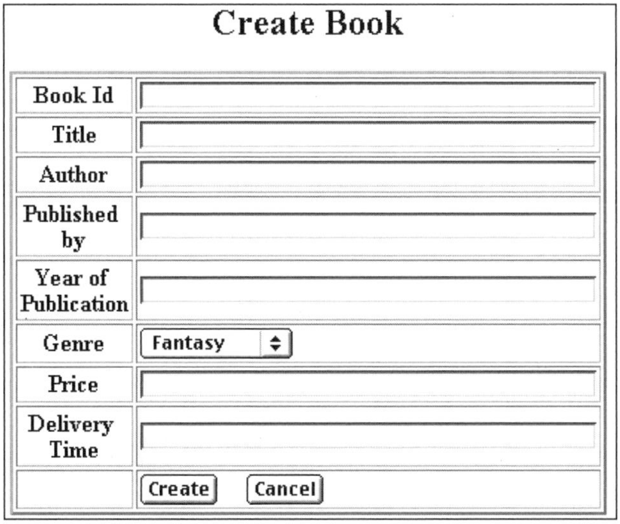

Create Book

Book Id	
Title	
Author	
Published by	
Year of Publication	
Genre	Fantasy ⇕
Price	
Delivery Time	
	Create Cancel

Figure 10-7: The page created by CreateForm_html

CreateInstance_html

CreateForm_html calls the DTML method CreateInstance_html to create a book instance using the specified id value. CreateInstance_html is shown in Listing 10-6.

Listing 10-6: The DTML method CreateInstance_html, which creates a new book instance

```
1:      <dtml-if name="create">
2:          <dtml-let NoRedir="1">
3:              <dtml-with expr="manage_addProduct['Sales']">
4:                  <dtml-call name="BookClass_add">
5:              </dtml-with>
6:          </dtml-let>
7:      </dtml-if>
8:      <dtml-call expr="RESPONSE.redirect('admin_html')">
```

Let's examine this code more closely. First, the name create is tested using dtml-if (Line 1). This determines whether the user pressed the Create button in the CreateBook_html form (see Line 39 of listing 10-5). If the user instead pressed the Cancel button, the code inside the dtml-if would not be executed because the name create would not be submitted from the form.

Assuming the Create button was clicked, Line 2 sets a variable named "NoRedir" to 1 using dtml-let. This value is checked by our modified BookClass_add constructor to suppress the default redirection to the management screen (see Listing 10-3). In this case we want to redirect to our own management screen (admin_html).

We then use dtml-with (Line 3) to put our Sales product on the namespace so that we can access the constructor BookClass_add contained in it. BookClass_add is then called using dtml-call (Line 4), which creates a new Book instance in the current folder. The values from the CreateBook_html form along with the variable NoRedir are passed to the constructor because we call it by name. (If we called it in an expression, these values would need to be passed explicitly as arguments to BookClass_add.) Next, the dtml-with, dtml-let, and dtml-if are closed (Lines 5–7).

Finally, we redirect the user back to the admin_html page, which will redraw showing the new Book instance just created. If the user clicks cancel on the CreateBook_html form, this is the only line executed, and no book instance is created.

10.3.3.2 EditForm_html

EditForm_html displays a form in which you can enter new values for an object's defined properties, such as a book's title, author, publisher, and so on. The DTML for EditForm_html is shown in Listing 10-7.

Listing 10-7: The DTML method EditForm_html

....

```
<dtml-var standard_html_header>
<FORM ACTION="Edit_html">
<h2 align="center">
     Edit Book <em>"<dtml-var name="id">"</em>
</h2>
<table border=2 cellpadding=0 cellspacing=2
       align="center" valign="center" width=50% height=50%>
     <tr><th>Title</th>
          <td><input type=text name="title"
                     value="<dtml-var name="title">" size="60"></td>
     </tr>
     <tr><th>Author</th>
          <td><input type=text name=author
                     value="<dtml-var name="author">" size="60"></td>
     </tr>
     <tr><th>Publisher</th>
          <td><input type=text name=publisher
                      value="<dtml-var name="publisher">" size="60"></td>
     </tr>
     <tr><th>Year of Publication</th>
          <td><input type=text name=year_of_publication
                     value="<dtml-var name="year_of_publication">"
                     size="60"></td>
     </tr>
     <tr><th>Genre</th>
          <td><SELECT NAME="genre">
          <dtml-in book_genre>
               <dtml-if "_['sequence-item'] == genre">
                    <OPTION VALUE="<dtml-var sequence-item>" selected>
                         <dtml-var sequence-item>
               <dtml-else>
                    <OPTION VALUE="<dtml-var sequence-item>">
                         <dtml-var sequence-item>
               </dtml-if>
               </OPTION>
           </dtml-in>
          </SELECT></td>
     </tr>
     <tr><th>Price</th>
          <td><input type=text name=price
                 value="<dtml-var name="price">" size="60"></td>
     </tr>
     <tr><th>Delivery Time</th>
          <td><input type=text name=delivery_time
```

(continued on next page)

```
                    value="<dtml-var name="delivery_time">" size="60"></td>
        </tr>
        <tr><th> </th>
            <td><input name="save" type=submit value="Save Changes">
                 
            <input name="cancel" type=submit value="Cancel"></td>
        </tr>
</table>
</FORM>
<dtml-var standard_html_footer>
```

EditForm_html is very similar to CreateForm_html, except that it already contains the object's property values prepopulated in the form's input fields. The input fields in the code get their values from `<dtml-var name="title">`, `<dtml-var name="author">`, and so on, so that they are filled when the form is rendered with the real values "The Sickness Unto Death," "Soren Kierkegaard," and so on, all relating to the Book instance being edited (Book id: B09362 in our example). This feature saves you from having to enter all of the property values again if you want to change only one.

EditForm_html creates the management screen shown in Figure 10-8.

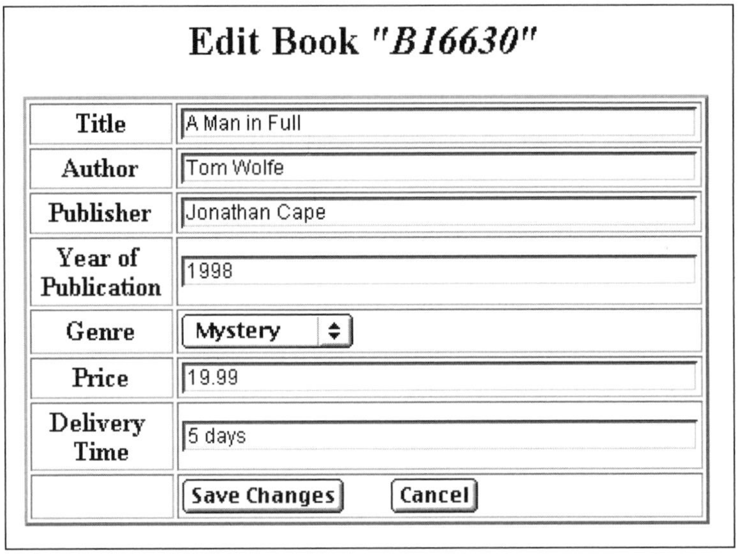

Edit Book "B16630"

Title	A Man in Full
Author	Tom Wolfe
Publisher	Jonathan Cape
Year of Publication	1998
Genre	Mystery
Price	19.99
Delivery Time	5 days
	Save Changes Cancel

Figure 10-8: This page is generated by the DTML method EditForm_html

10.3.3.3 Edit_html

EditForm_html calls a DTML method called Edit_html when the form is submitted, which sets the property values of the Book instance to the values entered on the form. Use the code in Listing 10-8 to create the Edit_html DTML method.

Listing 10-8: The DTML method Edit_html changes a book's properties

```
1:    <dtml-if name="save">
2:    <dtml-call expr="propertysheets.Book_description.manage_changeProperties(REQUEST)">
3:    </dtml-if>
4:    <dtml-call expr="RESPONSE.redirect(URL2 + '/admin_html')">
```

This code is similar to part of the code used in the BookClass_add constructor method we modified in Section 10.1.1. It works by first checking to see if the Save button on the form was pressed, by using dtml-if to see if the name save is in the namespace (Line 1). If so, it calls the built-in method manage_changeProperties on the Book_description property sheet of the Book instance being edited (Line 2). Because this method is called in the context of this Book instance (by calling it after the URL of the Book), the book is at the top of the namespace. The built-in manage_changeProperties method changes the Book's property values to those passed in REQUEST from EditForm_html.

Finally we redirect back up to the admin_html page. URL2 returns the URL of the folder containing the book instance, which is up two levels from this method call. For example, if the URL used to call Edit_html is

```
http://localhost:8080/Books/B09362/Edit_html
```

the value of URL2 is

```
http://localhost:8080/Books
```

—that is, the same path with the last two objects removed from the right. In our expression we add /admin_html to this, which results in the following URL:

```
http://localhost:8080/Books/admin_html
```

which is the URL of our custom management screen for the Books folder.

10.3.3.4 DeleteConfirm_html

Now we'll work on the DeleteConfirm_html method, which confirms that the Book instance selected on the form should be deleted. If you click Delete in DeleteConfirm_html, a second method, Delete_html, is called to perform the deletion. Pressing Cancel simply returns you to the admin_html page.

Figure 10-9 shows the confirmation form generated by DeleteConfirm_html:

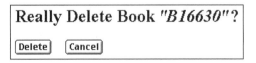

Figure 10-9: This page is generated by the DTML method DeleteConfirm_html

To create DeleteConfirm_html, create the DTML method DeleteConfirm_html using the code in Listing 10-9.

Listing 10-9: The DTML method DeleteConfirm_html

```
1:    <dtml-var standard_html_header>
2:    <H2>Really Delete Book <em>&quot;
3:        <dtml-var expr="REQUEST.id">&quot;</em>?</h2>
4:    <form action="Delete_html">
5:    <input type=hidden name="id" value="<dtml-var expr="REQUEST.id">">
6:    <input type=submit name="delete" value="Delete">
7:       
8:    <input type=submit name="cancel" value="Cancel"
9:    </form>
10:   <dtml-var standard_html_footer>
```

DeleteConfirm_html is a simple form with two buttons, Delete and Cancel. The id of the Book instance to be deleted is passed to the Delete_html action method using a hidden field (Line 5). Delete_html passes this value to the appropriate Zope method to delete the instance.

Let's create the DTML method Delete_html by entering the code shown in Listing 10-10.

Listing 10-10: The DTML method Delete_html, which you can use to delete books

```
1:    <dtml-if name="delete">
2:        <dtml-call expr="manage_delObjects(ids=[REQUEST.id])">
3:    </dtml-if>
4:    <dtml-call expr="RESPONSE.redirect('admin_html')">
```

Here again we first check a for a name in our namespace. In this case, we check for delete (Line 1), which tells the method whether the user clicked Delete in the DeleteConfirm_html. If so, the built-in method manage_delObjects is called on the current folder, passing it an argument named ids (Line 3). The method expects a list of string values in its ids argument containing the ids of the objects to be deleted from the folder. We have one object to delete, the Book instance, so its id, passed from the form in REQUEST, is made into a list by placing square brackets around it and is passed as the value for ids. Finally, we redirect the user back to the admin_html page (Line 4), which will show that the Book instance was deleted.

At this point, you should have created the following DTML methods in the Books folder:

admin_html   The main administrative page, which displays the Book instances and allows you to edit, delete, and create new instances.

CreateForm_html   The form used to specify the property values for a new Book instance.

CreateInstance_html   The method called by CreateForm_html that creates the new Book instance and sets its property values.

EditForm_html	The form used to view and edit the property values of an existing Book instance.
Edit_html	The method called by EditForm_html that sets the property values of the Book instance to the new values specified on the form.
DeleteConfirm_html	A form used to confirm the deletion of a selected Book instance.
Delete_html	The method called by DeleteConfirm_html that actually deletes a selected Book instance.

The Books folder's contents should now look like Figure 10-10.

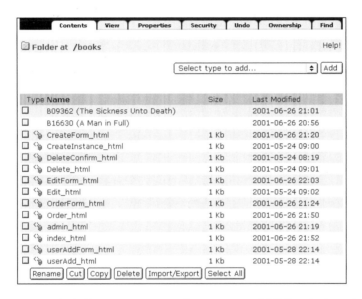

Figure 10-10: Management screen after you create all DTML methods needed to manage your books

Congratulations! You have now established the basic framework for managing your books. The only things missing are the DTML methods necessary to allow customers to order your books.

10.4   Selling Your Books

To make it easy for people to order books from your site, you'll create a DTML method called index_html, plus the DTML methods OrderForm_html and Order_html, which index_html needs to complete its ordering mechanism. The index_html method looks like the DTML method admin_html, except that the visitor does not see the Edit Book and Delete Book buttons or the Last Modified field. Instead, the visitor's page contains a button called To Order Form, which opens the DTML method OrderForm_html.

10.4.1 Creating index_html

To create the index_html method, do the following: In the Books folder, create the DTML method index_html and enter the code shown in Listing 10-11.

Listing 10-11: The DTML method index_html gives visitors to your site an overview of all available books

```
1:   <dtml-var standard_html_header>
2:   <table border=0 cellpadding=2 cellspacing=4 width="90%" align="center">
3:   <tr width="100%" bgcolor="#44BBCC">
4:       <th>Title</th>
5:       <th>Book Id</th>
6:       <th>Author</th>
7:       <th>Publisher</th>
8:       <th>Year of Publication</th>
9:       <th>Genre</th>
10:       <th>Price</th>
11:       <th>Delivery Time</th>
12:       <th>Photo</th>
13:   </tr>
14:   <dtml-in expr="objectValues(['Book'])" sort=Title>
15:       <tr width="100%" bgcolor="#88DDBB">
16:           <td><dtml-var name="title"></td>
17:           <td><dtml-var name="id"></td>
18:           <td><dtml-var name="author"></td>
19:           <td><dtml-var name="publisher"></td>
20:           <td><dtml-var name="year_of_publication"></td>
21:           <td><dtml-var name="genre"></td>
22:           <td><dtml-var name="price"></td>
23:           <td><dtml-var name="delivery_time"></td>
24:           <td><dtml-in expr="objectValues(['Image'])">
25:                   <dtml-var name="sequence-item">
26:           <dtml-else>
27:                       No Photo Available
28:           </dtml-in></td>
29:       </tr>
30:   </dtml-in>
31:   </table>
32:   <center>
33:   <form action="OrderForm_html">
34:   <input type=submit value="Go To Order Form">
35:   </form>
36:   </center>
37:   <dtml-var standard_html_footer>
```

Let's look at Lines 24 through 28 in detail, which insert available photos for the Book. Because a Book instance is a folderish object, its images can be contained inside the Book instance itself.

To display images, we use a dtml-in loop on the value returned by the method objectValues (Line 24). Remember that this method returns a list of the objects contained by a folder or folderish object, and that the first dtml-in (Line 14), which loops through the Book objects in the books folder, places each Book instance at the top of the namespace in turn. This means that our second dtml-in (Line 24) calls objectValues on the Book instance, whereas the first dtml-in (Line 14) calls objectValues on the books folder (or whichever folder this method is being called for).

NOTE *As you can see in this example, the namespace has as much to do with the behavior of your DTML code as anything else. To avoid many logic errors and bugs in DTML code, pay close attention to the current state of the namespace stack.*

When this code is rendered, the DTML method index_html displays the screen shown in Figure 10-11.

Title	Book Id	Author	Publisher	Year of Publication	Genre	Price	Delivery Time	Photo
The Sickness Unto Death	B09362	Soren Kierkegaard	Penguin USA	1989	Philosophy	13.95	3 days	No Photo Available
A Man in Full	B16630	Tom Wolfe	Jonathan Cape	1998	Mystery	19.99	5 days	No Photo Available

Go To Order Form

Figure 10-11: The page generated by the DTML method index_html

10.4.2 Creating the DTML Methods for Ordering Books

Let's now create the DTML methods needed for ordering books. You will need the following:

- A DTML method called OrderForm_html that presents customers with an order form they can use to select books and enter personal information such as their name and email address.
- A DTML method called Order_html that enters the articles selected by the customer and their personal information, and emails this information to you.

10.4.2.1 Creating OrderForm_html

Create the DTML method OrderForm_html in the Books folder, then enter the code shown in Listing 10-12.

Listing 10-12: The DTML method OrderForm_html

```
<dtml-var standard_html_header>
<form action="Order_html">
<h2 align="center">Order Form</h2>
<table border=0 cellpadding=2 cellspacing=4 width="100%">
<tr bgcolor="#FFBB88"><th>Last Name, First Name:</th>
    <td><input name=name size=40></td>
</tr>
<tr bgcolor="#FFBB88"><th>Address:</th>
    <td><input name=address size=40></td>
</tr>
<tr bgcolor="#FFBB88"><th>Telephone:</th>
    <td><input name=telephone size=40></td>
</tr>
<tr bgcolor="#FFBB88"><th>Fax:</th>
    <td><input name=fax size=40></td>
</tr>
<tr bgcolor="#FFBB88"><th>Email:</th>
    <td><input name=email size=40></td>
</tr>
<tr bgcolor="#FFBB88"><th> </th><td> </td></tr>
<tr bgcolor="#FFBB88">
    <th>Select the books<br>
        you want to order.</th>
    <td><SELECT MULTIPLE size=20 NAME="order:list">
        <dtml-in expr="objectValues(['Book'])" sort=Title>
            <OPTION VALUE="<dtml-var name="id">">
            <dtml-var name="author"> - "<dtml-var name="title">" -
            Price: <dtml-var name="price"></OPTION>
        </dtml-in>
    </SELECT></td></tr>
    <tr><th> </th>
        <td><input type=submit value="Order Now"></td>
    </tr>
</table>
<dtml-var standard_html_footer>
```

When rendered, this DTML method displays the screen shown in Figure 10-12.

Creating Order_html

Finally, you create the DTML method Order_html to email the order information to you by entering the code shown in Listing 10-13.

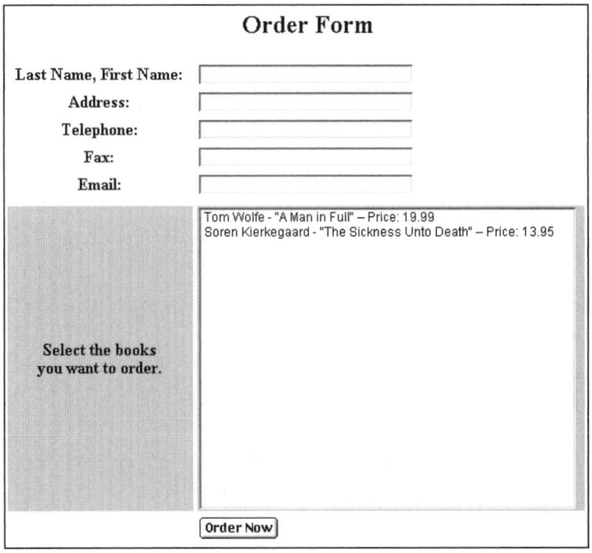

Figure 10-12: This page is generated by OrderForm_html; select multiple books by holding down CTRL and clicking in the list box

Listing 10-13: The DTML method Order_html

```
1:    <dtml-var standard_html_header>
2:    <dtml-sendmail mailhost="MailHost">
3:    To: myName@mycompany.com
4:    From: <dtml-var name="email">
5:    Subject: Order
6:    Name: <dtml-var name="name">
7:    Address: <dtml-var name="address">
8:    Telephone: <dtml-var name="telephone">
9:    Fax: <dtml-var name="fax">
10:    Email: <dtml-var name="email">
11:    Order:
12:    <dtml-in name="order">
13:    <dtml-with expr="_.getitem(_['sequence-item'])">
14:    _____
15:    Author: <dtml-var name="author">
16:    Title: <dtml-var name="title">
17:    Book Id: <dtml-var name="sequence-item">
18:    Price: <dtml-var name="price">
19:    _____
20:    </dtml-with>
21:    </dtml-in>
22:    </dtml-sendmail>
23:    <center>
```

(continued on next page)

```
24:    <p>Thank you for your order!</p>
25:    <p><form action=index_html>
26:    <input type=submit value="Okay">
27:    </form></p>
28:    </center>
29:    <dtml-var standard_html_footer>
```

This page uses dtml-sendmail to email you the customer's order using information from the OrderForm_html form to fill the body of the email.

One special case is the order variable submitted from the following select list in OrderForm_html:

```
<td><SELECT MULTIPLE size=20 NAME="order:list">
```

This form field differs from the rest because it has ":list" at the end of it, which tells Zope to convert the value submitted from the browser into a list. In this case, this is a list of the Book ids selected by the user. Because the value for order is a list, we can use dtml-in to iterate it (Line 12) and look up the information about the Books selected (Line 13). (The lookup is necessary because only the id values for the books are passed from the form to the Order_html method.)

To retrieve the other properties of each Book, we use dtml-with with the getitem method of the underscore namespace variable. Using the value of sequence-item as its argument (which contains the id of each Book ordered), _.getitem returns the Book instance, and dtml-with puts the instance at the top of the namespace. Inside the dtml-with block (Lines 14–19), simple dtml-var tags insert the property values of each selected Book instance.

10.4.3 Sending the Order

To email the customer's order to you, we add a mail host to the Books folder to specify the mail server responsible for sending the email. The mail host's management screen is shown in Figure 10-13.

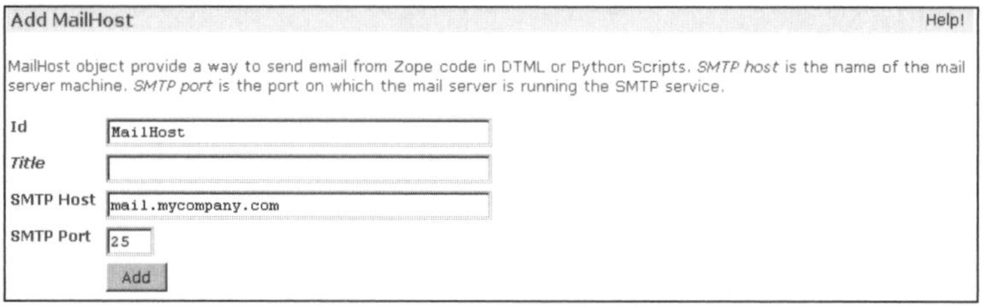

Figure 10-13: Management screen for defining a mail host

To create a mail host for use with our example, choose Mail Host from the books folder's add menu and set the id to MailHost. Enter a title to describe this object if you wish, then enter the Internet name of the SMTP server you will use to deliver your mail. (If you don't know this information, check with your system administrator or check the configuration of your own email software). Then click on Add.

10.5 Ideas for Expanding Your Zope Product

Now that you have created and worked with your first ZClass and Zope product, you should be able to create additional ones. Here are some ideas for expanding your Zope product:

- Expand the product range and create additional ZClasses in your Sales product, such as a class for creating CD-ROM objects.
- Extend the custom administrative interface to allow you to add or remove product photos.
- Make your application even easier for customers to use by allowing them to order directly from the customer screen (index_html) by creating an additional ZClass called Orders to gather the data for an order.

Summary

This chapter has given you a more detailed overview of Zope classes and, we hope, encouraged you to create your own products using ZClasses. Although the Zope product Sales is only one example of how you can use ZClasses, it demonstrates the basics of how to use Zope classes to create an application.

11

THE ZCATALOG

You use the *ZCatalog* product, part of the standard Zope installation, to arrange objects in Zope according to your own indexes. ZCatalogs allow you to index and then search for objects based on the values of the indexed attributes of those objects. These attributes can be the content of documents, the values of properties, even the values returned by Python scripts and methods. In this chapter, we look at how to create a new ZCatalog and examine the individual components of a ZCatalog.

11.1 Creating a ZCatalog

To create a new ZCatalog, open the folder's add menu and select ZCatalog. The screen shown in Figure 11-1 appears.

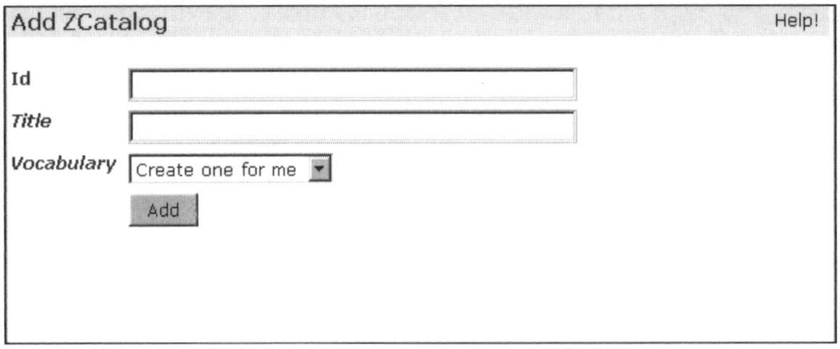

Figure 11-1: Screen for creating a new ZCatalog

As with all Zope objects, you must specify an id for the ZCatalog object; you may enter a title if you wish.

11.1.1 Choosing a Vocabulary

A *vocabulary* is a list of searchable words culled from objects cataloged in the ZCatalog. As objects are indexed in the Catalog using a TextIndex (see section 11.2.5.1), the text from the object is split into words and stored in the vocabulary in a manner that allows the catalog to quickly find which words are contained in which objects. When you create a ZCatalog, you may select an existing vocabulary or create a new one (see section 11.5, "The Vocabulary"). To do the latter, select the Create one for me option from the Vocabulary list, which will automatically create a vocabulary object inside your new ZCatalog to store the word list.

This option allows you to share a vocabulary among several ZCatalogs—an important feature if you have several ZCatalogs that contain TextIndexes, because it is more efficient for them to share a single vocabulary than for each to have a separate one. To share a vocabulary between ZCatalogs, create a vocabulary object (using the add menu) in a folder that's at or above the location of your ZCatalogs in the Zope hierarchy; then choose this vocabulary when you create each ZCatalog.

11.1.2 Globbing

If you create a vocabulary independently of a ZCatalog, you have the option to enable *globbing*, which allows you to use wildcard characters (such as asterisks [*] and question marks [?]) in your ZCatalog searches to match partial words. Generally, you will want to enable globbing to give you greater search capabilities, but you can save memory and disk space by disabling it.

NOTE   *Vocabularies created for you by ZCatalog automatically have globbing enabled.*

11.2   The ZCatalog Screens

You are probably already familiar with several of the ZCatalog's tabs common to other objects (shown in Figure 11-2), including Content, Properties, View, Find, Security, Undo, and Ownership. But Figure 11-2 also shows five new tabs: *Catalog, Indexes, Metadata, Find Objects,* and *Advanced*—which will be explained in sections 11.2.2 through 11.2.6.

Figure 11-2: The tab bar in a ZCatalog

11.2.1 Contents Screen

Because ZCatalogs are folderish objects, you can create objects in a ZCatalog using the ZCatalog Contents screen (Figure 11-3). For example, you could store objects to be cataloged by the ZCatalog or the ZCatalog's search and report pages (see section 11.3, "Z Search Interface").

NOTE *Cataloged objects do not need to be physically contained in the ZCatalog. In fact, they can be scattered about in many different folders throughout the Zope hierarchy (which is often the case). This ability to bring together and search objects throughout your Zope application is one of the ZCatalog's greatest strengths.*

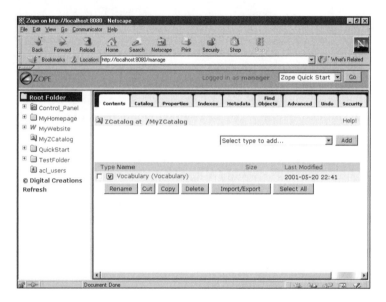

Figure 11-3: A ZCatalog Contents screen

11.2.2 The Catalog Screen

The Catalog management screen, shown in Figure 11-4, contains a list of all objects currently cataloged in the ZCatalog. You can determine which objects are cataloged by specifying the appropriate criteria on the Find Objects screen. By default, it will find and catalog all objects at or below the ZCatalog object.

You may choose to manually catalog objects using Find Objects or to allow instances of ZClasses that have the base class CatalogAware to catalog themselves automatically when they are created. These objects are called *catalog aware objects.*

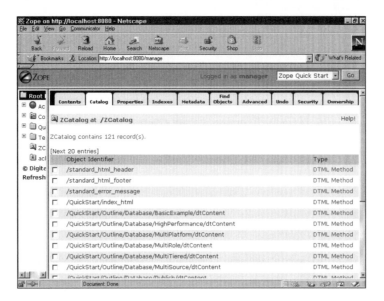

Figure 11-4: Catalog management screen for a ZCatalog

The cataloged objects are displayed in groups of 20 per page. Click the Next 20 entries or Previous 20 entries links to move forward or back through the list of cataloged objects.

11.2.2.1 The Remove and Update Buttons

The two buttons above and below the list, Remove and Update, relate only to the cataloged objects you've selected via their checkboxes. The Remove button removes the index and metadata entries for all selected objects from the ZCatalog, but does not actually delete the objects themselves. Removed objects are no longer searchable through the ZCatalog.

NOTE *If you delete a cataloged object from Zope, its entry in the ZCatalog is removed only if it is a catalog aware object. For all other objects, you must manually remove the entry from the ZCatalog on this screen.*

The Update button reindexes the selected objects and updates their metadata values. When you modify the content or properties of an indexed object, you must update it to keep the ZCatalog indexes and metadata in sync. Even catalog aware objects do not reindex themselves automatically when they are modified.

NOTE *You can update all cataloged objects at once using the advanced screen (see section 11.2.6.1 for more information).*

11.2.3 The Find Objects Screen

The Find Objects screen (shown in Figure 11-5) lets you search for the objects you want to catalog and index. Use it to find and index new objects. Find Objects

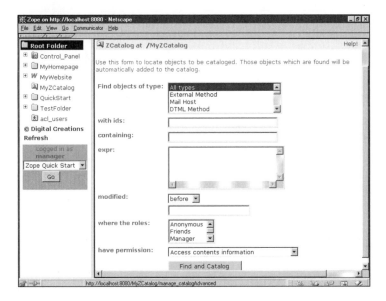

Figure 11-5: Find Objects screen for a ZCatalog

retains existing cataloged objects, so make sure the ZCatalog is empty first (see Catalog Maintenance in section 11.2.6.1) if you do not want to keep the existing entries. Here are the criteria for Find Objects:

11.2.3.1 Find objects of type:
This is a list of all available object meta types.

11.2.3.2 with ids:
Here you can specify the specific ids (separated by spaces) for each object to catalog.

11.2.3.3 containing:
Use this field to enter words, characters, and phrases that objects must contain to be cataloged. You can also enter DTML commands, such as

```
<dtml-var name="sequence-item">
```

to find and catalog DTML objects that contain that command.

11.2.3.4 expr:
Use this field to specify expressions that must be true for the objects to be cataloged. For example, you can use the following query to search for all objects larger than 1K:

```
get_size()>1024
```

Another option here is to check property values. If, for example, several objects all have the property Price, you can find those objects whose Price is $19.95 as follows:

```
Price==19.95
```

11.2.3.5 modified:

This field consists of two parts: a list from which you can select either before or after (today's date), and a field in which you can enter the time and date in one of the following formats:

```
2000/09/30
2000/09/30 15:00
2000/09/30 15:00:38.00 GMT+2
```

11.2.3.6 where the roles:

This criterion and the next one (have permission) belong together. Here you can select from the list of roles assigned to the permission in the *have permission list*. The ZCatalog then searches for objects whose selected roles have the relevant permission.

11.2.3.7 have permission:

From this list you can select a permission that the roles in the *where the roles list* must have. The ZCatalog then finds and catalogs all objects whose roles have the specified permission.

Figure 11-6 shows an example of a completed Find Objects form. In this example, we are searching for all objects (All types) that have the id index_html and that contain <dtml-var title_or_id>. The objects must have been edited after 16:50 on August 28, 2000 (2000/08/28 16:50:00.00). In addition, the objects must have the permission Change DTML Methods for the Anonymous role.

11.2.4 Metadata Screen

ZCatalog metadata is a cache of specific attribute values (from properties and methods) of the cataloged objects, created when they were cataloged. Use the Metadata screen (see Figure 11-7) to manage the metadata for the cataloged objects. When the ZCatalog searches for objects to index, Zope saves all specified attributes of the cataloged objects to a table. The values are saved only if the object's attribute name exactly matches the metadata element name specified in this screen.

Metadata will optimize the performance of ZCatalog queries when many results are returned, because it allows you to work with the cached attribute values of many objects rather than looking up or deriving these values individually when generating a report. Use metadata sparingly, however, because it will greatly increase the size of your Zope database if you catalog many objects and cache many of their attributes as metadata. Attribute values not stored as metadata can still be looked up from the original objects as well (see section 11.4.2 below). This can also be beneficial if an object's attribute values change often, because metadata values are not automatically updated when an object changes.

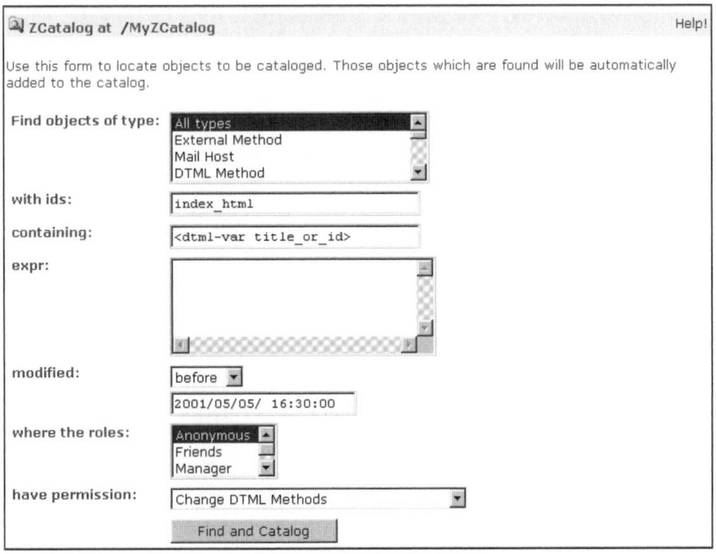

Figure 11-6: Example of a Find Objects form

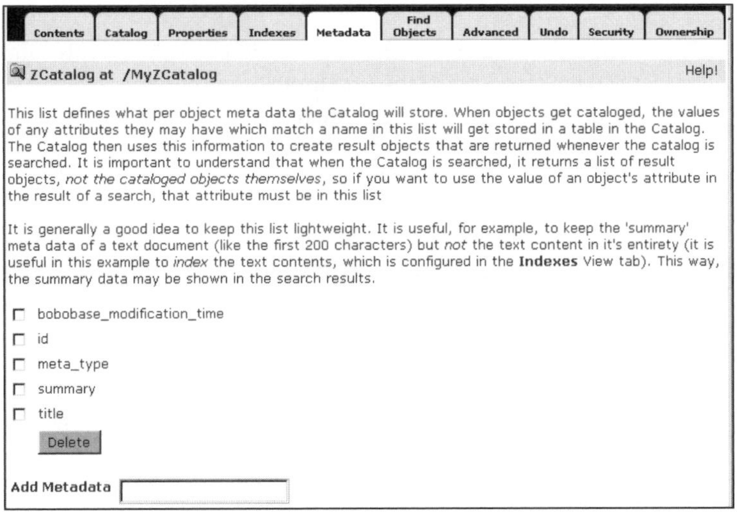

Figure 11-7: Metadata Screen

11.2.4.1 Default ZCatalog Metadata Attributes

When you create a new ZCatalog, several common metadata attributes are specified by default. These elements are

- title
- id
- summary
- meta_type
- bobobase_modification_time

The attributes title, id, meta_type, and bobobase_modification_time already exist for all objects in Zope; you do not need to create them yourself. You do, however, need to create the *summary* attribute for an object.

The summary attribute is provided for CatalogAware objects; it returns the first 200 characters of a DTML document or method instead of the complete text, which saves storage space and can be used as a teaser paragraph. You can use teasers, for example, to display several summaries of many articles on one page.

Metadata elements are automatically included in the results page generated with the Z Search Interface (see section 11.3) for the ZCatalog.

11.2.5 Indexes Screen

Use the Indexes screen (see Figure 11-8) to delete or create new searchable ZCatalog indexes.

Indexes indicate which of the object's attributes (property or method values) are searchable in the ZCatalog. There are three types of indexes:

11.2.5.1 Text index

This index splits text into individual words and is frequently called a "full-text search." When you search the text index, the results are sorted according to the number of word matches; the more instances of the search term found in the

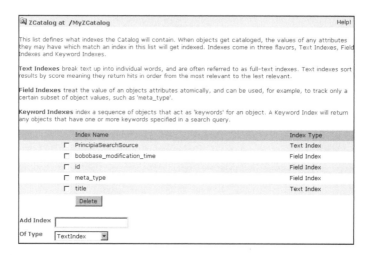

Figure 11-8: Index screen for a ZCatalog

object, the higher up in the list the object will be.

Text indexes also support simple boolean search expressions (using "and," "or," and "and not") and partial word matching using wildcards: "?" matches any single character and "*" matches any substring of characters. To use wildcards, the ZCatalog's vocabulary object must have globbing support enabled (see Section 11.1.2 for details). Built-in automatic support matches multiple word forms, so that a search for the word "walk" will also match "walks" and "walking" in the cataloged object.

Text indexes are used on text or string attributes that will contain multiple words or long passages of text. They also can be useful for single-word values if wildcard and multiple-word form matching is important.

NOTE *When text is indexed in a text index, all punctuation, capitalization, and numeric data in the text are ignored.*

11.2.5.2 Field index

A field index is a simple index that searches against the entire value of an attribute. With a field index, you can find objects by exactly matching the indexed value or by specifying a range that it must fall between (see section 11.4.3.2 for more on range searching). Field indexes are ideal for indexing numeric or date/time data. They are also useful for indexing short string values that should be matched exactly, such as an object's meta_type attribute.

11.2.5.3 Keyword index

A keyword index allows you to search a list of values, such as a lines or tokens property. To match against a keyword index, you must match only one element of the indexed value list.

As its name implies, keyword indexes are useful for keyword searches. They are also useful as a way to express one-to-many relationships between objects. For example, you can use a lines property in an object to store the ids of related objects, then create an index on the property and use it to find objects related to one another.

11.2.6 Advanced Screen

The Advanced screen is divided into two sections: Catalog Maintenance and Subtransactions, as shown in Figure 11-9.

11.2.6.1 Catalog Maintenance

Two buttons appear in the top section of the Advanced ZCatalog screen: Update Catalog and Clear Catalog.

Update Catalog reindexes all objects that are currently indexed in the ZCatalog and updates the metadata table. It also removes the entries for any indexed objects that have been deleted but not removed from the catalog. Use it when you have added new indexes or metadata elements to your catalog to populate their values from the objects in the catalog.

The Clear Catalog button removes all cataloged objects from the ZCatalog. After using it, you can use the Find Objects tab to repopulate the ZCatalog.

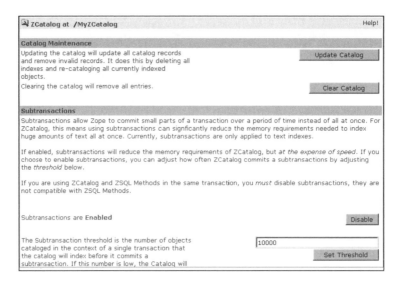

Figure 11-9: Advanced screen for a ZCatalog

11.2.6.2 Subtransactions

The bottom section of the maintenance screen is used for managing the use of subtransactions by the ZCatalog. If subtransactions are enabled in a ZCatalog, the ZCatalog indexes objects incrementally rather than all at once. This value lets you control the memory usage of ZCatalog while objects are being indexed.

The subtransaction intervals used by a ZCatalog to index objects are defined using a *threshold value*. The threshold value also determines how many words are to be indexed when there is only one instance. The higher the threshold value, the faster the indexing will take place. However, if the value is set high, the ZCatalog will require more memory. The lower the value, the less memory will be used, although indexing will take longer.

In general you should leave subtransactions enabled with the default threshold value of 10,000, which means a maximum of 10,000 field values or words of text will be held in memory before being commited to the ZODB. If you find that Zope uses excessive amounts of memory during indexing operations, you can lower the threshold value to decrease the memory required. Or, if memory is plentiful and indexing speed is most important, you can increase the threshold value or disable subtransactions entirely.

NOTE *If you are using ZCatalog together with Z SQL methods, you must disable subtransactions, because they are not compatible with Z SQL methods.*

11.3 Z Search Interface

You need two pages to search a ZCatalog: one to receive the search query, and another to display the search results. Using the Z Search Interface option in the folder's add menu, you can easily create standardized search and results pages, which can then be adapted to your needs. Figure 11-10 shows the form for creating both pages.

To save time, create the search interface pages after you have defined all the metadata and indexes in your catalog, because these will be used to create the search and results pages. If you add metadata or indexes later, you will need to modify the pages manually.

Figure 11-10 shows the form used to create a Z Search Interface. Following the figure is an explanation of the fields on this form.

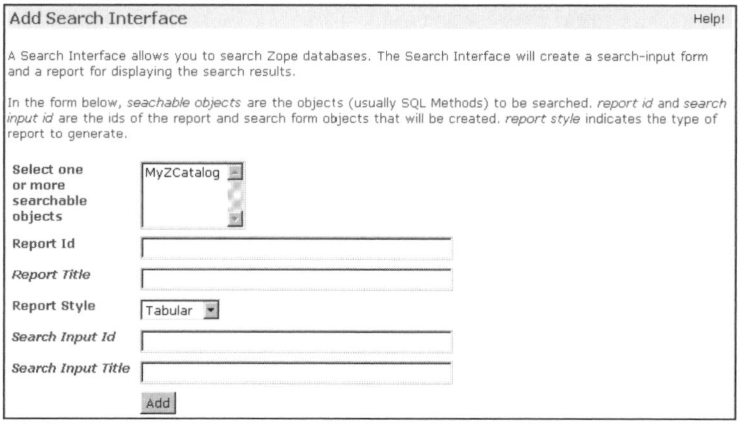

Figure 11-10: Form for creating a search and results page

Select one or more searchable objects:
This list contains all searchable objects (ZCatalogs, Z SQL methods) that can be acquired from the current folder (that is, those in the folder's namespace stack). You can select one or more searchable objects from this list.

Report Id and Report Title:
These are the id and title of the results page to be created.

Report Style:
This offers two options for presenting the results of a search: in tables or as records. The former displays each object found on a row of a table, with each metadata element in its own column. The latter displays the metadata of each object on a line separated by commas.

Search Input Id and Search Input Title:
Use these fields to specify the id and title for the search page, which is a form for users to provide the criteria with which to search the ZCatalog.

11.3.1 The Search Page

The search page consists of a simple HTML form arranged in a table, as shown in Listing 11-1. The individual cells in the table are automatically created when you create the search page, according to the objects to be searched using this form.

Listing 11-1: Standard search page for a simple ZCatalog

```
<dtml-var standard_html_header>
<form action="report_html" method="get">
<h2><dtml-var document_title></h2>
Enter query parameters:<br><table>
<tr><th>Title</th>
    <td><input name="title"
            width=30 value=""></td></tr>
<tr><th>Meta type</th>
    <td><input name="meta_type"
            width=30 value=""></td></tr>
<tr><th>Id</th>
    <td><input name="id"
            width=30 value=""></td></tr>
<tr><th>Summary</th>
    <td><input name="summary"
            width=30 value=""></td></tr>
<tr><th>Bobobase modification time</th>
    <td><input name="bobobase_modification_time"
            width=30 value=""></td></tr>
<tr><td colspan=2 align=center>
<input type="SUBMIT" name="SUBMIT" value="Submit Query">
</td></tr>
</table>
</form>
<dtml-var standard_html_footer>
```

If the search page is created to search ZCatalogs, the form input fields are created based on the indexes defined in the selected ZCatalog. If you specify several ZCatalogs as searchable, the indexes are taken from all the ZCatalogs, arranged according to ZCatalog, and used to create a form. The search form for the various ZCatalogs is listed as shown in Figure 11-11.

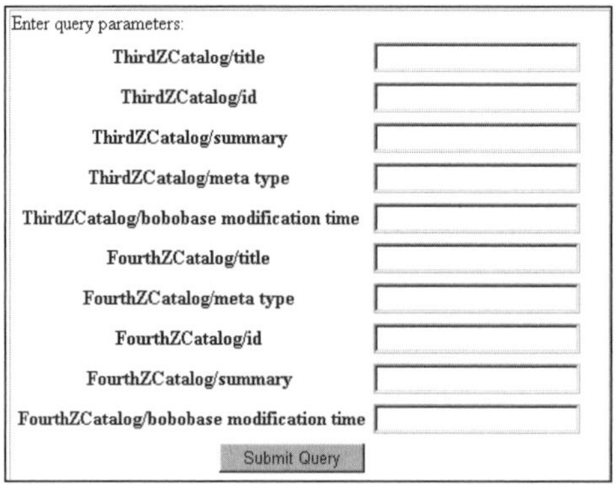

Figure 11-11: Search page for two ZCatalogs (ThirdZCatalog and FourthZCatalog)

You can modify this form as needed. For example, if to provide an interface to search only some of the indexes, you could simply delete the unecessary ones from the form. Conversely, if you later add an index to the catalog, you can make it searchable by adding an input field to the search form with the same name as the index.

If you also select one or more Z SQL methods, the arguments for the Z SQL methods are used to construct the table, as shown in Figure 11-12.

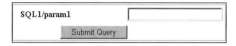

Figure 11-12: Example of a search field for a Z SQL method

NOTE *If all search fields on the form are left blank, the results page will display all of the objects indexed in the ZCatalog.*

11.3.2 The Results Page

As mentioned under "Report Style" above, Zope offers two ways to display the results page: as a table or in records. Figure 11-13 shows an example of a table report, and Figure 11-14 shows an example of a records report.

Title	Id	Summary	Meta type	Bobobase modification time	Data record id
	ThirdZCatalog		ZCatalog	2000/09/11 11:09:24.65 GMT+2	0
Vocabulary	Vocabulary		Vocabulary	2000/09/11 11:09:24.65 GMT+2	1
User Folder	acl_users		User Folder	2000/09/11 11:09:33.21 GMT+2	2
	index_html		DTML Method	2000/09/11 11:09:41.12 GMT+2	3

Figure 11-13: Search results presented as a table

, ThirdZCatalog, , ZCatalog, 2000/09/11 11:09:24.65 GMT+2, 0

Vocabulary, Vocabulary, , Vocabulary, 2000/09/11 11:09:24.65 GMT+2, 1

User Folder, acl_users, , User Folder, 2000/09/11 11:09:33.21 GMT+2, 2

, index_html, , DTML Method, 2000/09/11 11:09:41.12 GMT+2, 3

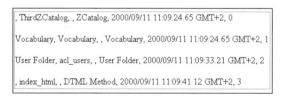

Figure 11-14: Search results presented as records

If the search and results pages apply to more than one searchable object, the corresponding results are displayed beneath each other and separated by a line, as shown in Figure 11-15.

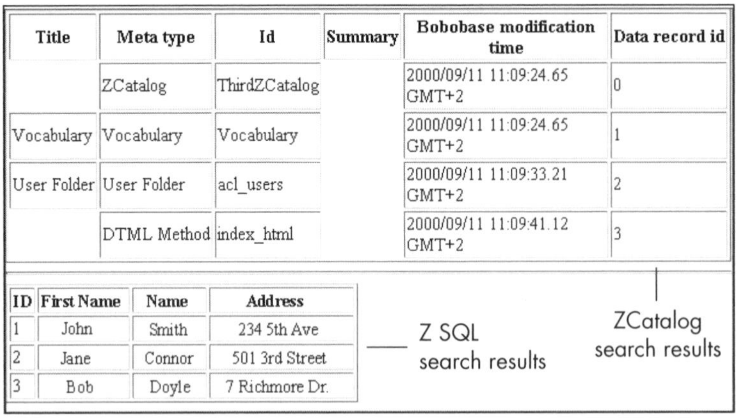

Title	Meta type	Id	Summary	Bobobase modification time	Data record id
	ZCatalog	ThirdZCatalog		2000/09/11 11:09:24.65 GMT+2	0
Vocabulary	Vocabulary	Vocabulary		2000/09/11 11:09:24.65 GMT+2	1
User Folder	User Folder	acl_users		2000/09/11 11:09:33.21 GMT+2	2
	DTML Method	index_html		2000/09/11 11:09:41.12 GMT+2	3

ID	First Name	Name	Address
1	John	Smith	234 5th Ave
2	Jane	Connor	501 3rd Street
3	Bob	Doyle	7 Richmore Dr.

Z SQL search results — ZCatalog search results

Figure 11-15: Search results for a ZCatalog and a Z SQL method

11.3.2.1 Batch Size

The standard generated results page shows 50 results per selected ZCatalog or Z SQL method. In other words, the standard batch size is 50. If there are more than 50 results, Next and Previous links appear, which allow you to navigate the results (as shown in Figure 11-16).

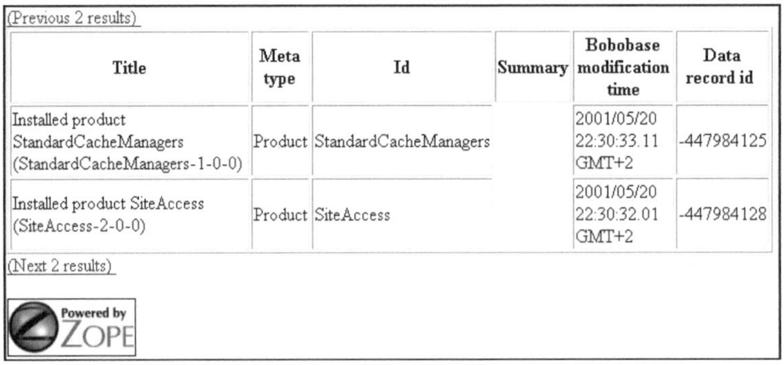

(Previous 2 results)

Title	Meta type	Id	Summary	Bobobase modification time	Data record id
Installed product StandardCacheManagers (StandardCacheManagers-1-0-0)	Product	StandardCacheManagers		2001/05/20 22:30:33.11 GMT+2	-447984125
Installed product SiteAccess (SiteAccess-2-0-0)	Product	SiteAccess		2001/05/20 22:30:32.01 GMT+2	-447984128

(Next 2 results)

Powered by ZOPE

Figure 11-16: Results page with two displayed results and Previous and Next links

To change the number of results displayed, simply replace the batch size number of 50 with the number of results that you want displayed in the following line of the report DTML method (and in other lines if there is more than one searchable object):

```
<dtml-in ZCatalog size=50 start=query_start>
```

If you have several searchable objects, you may need to change the batch navigation logic by renaming the query_start variable for each (for example, to query_start1, query_start2, and so on). The query_start variable determines the starting point for each batch displayed. Creating separate ones will prevent the next 50 results being displayed for each searchable object when you want to display them for only one object.

Remember to change the variables in all relevant locations in the source code. The other locations in addition to size in the in-tag include the lines where the Previous and Next links are created.

Figure 11-17 demonstrates a modified report page with different batch sizes for multiple search results.

(Previous 2 results)

Title	Meta type	Id	Summary	Bobobase modification time	Data record id
DateTime	Help Topic	DateTime.py		2001/05/28 23:44:23.84 GMT+2	-447984247
Cache manager associations	Help Topic	CacheManager-associate.stx		2001/05/28 23:44:23.84 GMT+2	-447984246

(Next 2 results)

(Previous 5 results)

Title	Id	Summary	Meta type	Bobobase modification time	Data record id
	index_html		DTML Method	2001/01/20 22:39:14.2876 GMT+1	-1872825419
	index_html		DTML Document	2001/05/27 13:20:23 GMT+2	-1872825418
	login_html		DTML Method	2001/05/27 13:24:51.75 GMT+2	-1872825417
	search_html		DTML Method	2001/05/28 23:44:28.79 GMT+2	-1872825416
	report_html		DTML Method	2001/05/29 00:07:53.67 GMT+2	-1872825415

(Next 5 results)

Powered by ZOPE

Figure 11-17: Two ZCatalog results with different batch sizes (2 and 5)

11.4   ZCatalog Queries

Although the Z Search interface is useful for quickly creating a simple user interface for searching a Zope site's contents, it is often inadequate for specialized queries. To increase your flexibility, let's look at how to use a ZCatalog to customize a Z Search Interface to better suit your needs.

11.4.1 Querying ZCatalogs from a Form

The code generated by the Z Search Interface is simply a query of a ZCatalog from values specified on a form. A ZCatalog is a callable object, like a method, and when called it returns results based on the search criteria passed to it. When you call a ZCatalog by name, form values in the REQUEST object are automatically passed as query criteria. By modifying the search form, you can control the search criteria passed to the catalog.

For example, let's create a simple search form, queryForm and a simple report queryReport. In our example, there is a ZCatalog named "Catalog" with the attribute title as both an index and metadata element.

Listing 11-2 shows the DTML code for queryForm, a simple HTML form with a single input field.

Listing 11-2: Code for queryForm DTML document

```
<dtml-var standard_html_header>
<form action="queryReport">
<p>Title: <input type="text" name="title" size="40"></p>
<p><input type="submit"></p>
</form>
<dtml-var standard_html_footer>
```

Listing 11-3 shows the code for queryReport, which lists the titles of the cataloged objects found, based on the title entry made in queryForm.

Listing 11-3: Code for queryReport DTML Document

```
<dtml-var standard_html_header>
<dtml-in name="Catalog">
    <dtml-var name="title"><br>
</dtml-in>
<dtml-var standard_html_footer>
```

The most important line of code in queryReport is the dtml-in statement on the second line. This statement calls the Catalog by name, passing it any values submitted from the form. If the user types words into the title field of the form and submits it, these words are used as search criteria against the title text index in the Catalog.

11.4.2 Catalog Brains

When a ZCatalog is called, as in our simple example queryForm, it does not return the actual objects matched by the query criteria. It instead creates a sequence of *brain* objects that contain the cached metadata values of the matched objects along with several methods that can be put to various uses. It is very important to understand that when you are working with Catalog results, you are not working with the actual objects found, only their metadata. You can, however, explicitly access the actual objects if you need to.

Table 11-1 lists the methods available on the brain objects (that is, result items) returned from a ZCatalog query. Each of these methods is directly available inside of a dtml-in loop that iterates over the ZCatalog results (such as in queryForm above), because dtml-in puts each result item at the top of the namespace in turn as it steps through the result sequence.

The two most useful methods listed in Table 11-1 are getURL and getObject. The former can be used to easily create links in your results page to each object found; the latter to access any additional object attributes—such as properties and methods—that you may need in addition to the metadata cached in the ZCatalog.

NOTE *Calling getObject on many result objects can slow your ZCatalog searches. Use it sparingly and with small batch sizes when using dtml-in.*

Table 11-1: ZCatalog Brain Methods

ZCatalog Brain Method	Description
has_key(key)	Returns true if the result item has a metadata element named "key."
getPath()	Returns the physical path of the result item in your Zope hierarchy.
getURL()	Returns the absolute URL of the result item (which may differ from getPath() if you are using virtual hosting).
getObject()	Returns the actual Zope object corresponding to the ZCatalog result.
getRID()	Returns the ZCatalog's internal record id for the result item, which is the same as the data_record_id_ variable returned by ZCatalog. This can be used to uniquely identify results more easily.

Let's enhance our queryReport page (Listing 11-4) using the getURL method above, which will allow us to construct a link to each object returned by the query.

Listing 11-4: Enhanced queryReport DTML document

```
<dtml-var standard_html_header>
<dtml-in name="Catalog">
    <a href="<dtml-var name="getURL">">
        <dtml-var name="title">
</a><br>
</dtml-in>
<dtml-var standard_html_footer>
```

By adding the anchor tag to the queryReport code and using the getURL method of the ZCatalog brain to insert the object's URL in the href attribute, each search result now links to the object found by the query.

11.4.3 Querying ZCatalogs Directly

To query a ZCatalog directly, we call the ZCatalog using an expression and explicitly pass it the query criteria as arguments. The argument names match the indexes you wish to query against, and the values contain the query criteria for each named index. You can supply criteria for as few or as many indexes as you wish. (You can also use other arguments to control the sort order of the result items returned by the ZCatalog.)

Let's create some sample queries on a ZCatalog containing the indexes shown in Table 11-2 (which are the defaults created by Zope).

Table 11-2: ZCatalog Indexes

ZCatalog Indexes	Index Type
PrincipiaSearchSource	TextIndex
bobobase_modification_time	FieldIndex
id	FieldIndex
meta_type	FieldIndex
title	TextIndex

11.4.3.1 Basic Field Index Queries

Field Indexes can be used to find objects whose attributes match the values you specify. To match objects with a field index, we simply pass arguments with the name of each index we want to match, followed by the value desired. For example, to find all cataloged objects with the meta_type value 'DTML Document' and the id value 'index_html', you would use the following ZCatalog query expression:

```
expr="Catalog(id='index_html', meta_type='DTML Document')"
```

When you pass multiple indexes, they are "anded" together to form the search query, meaning that all criteria must be matched for the object to be returned in a result. To expand the search to match multiple values of an indexed attribute simultaneously, pass the desired values in a list to the index you are matching against. For example, to expand the above search to include DTML Document objects, use this expression:

```
expr="Catalog(id='index_html', meta_type=['DTML Document', 'DTML Method'])"
```

When you use the above expression, a meta_type value of DTML Document or DTML Method, along with an id value of index_html, would satisfy the search criteria for an object.

NOTE *Keyword indexes work the same way, except that the search value needs to match only one item of the keyword indexed list attribute (such as a lines or tokens property).*

11.4.3.2 Range Queries on Field Indexes

It's a more complex process to match a field index against a range than it is to match it against an exact value. To match a range, we must specify two arguments for the index, the desired range value(s) and range usage. The range value(s) are passed in an argument matching the name of the field index. The usage argument uses the field index name followed by _usage. The three usage values that control how the range matching is performed against the index are shown in Table 11-3.

Table 11-3: Usage values for range matching

Range usage value	Description
range:min	Matches indexed values equal to or greater than the range value.
range:max	Matches indexed values less than or equal to the range value.
range:min:max	Matches indexed values between a specified minimum and maximum value.

For example, let's consider how we would query our ZCatalog by date, using the bobobase_modification_time index to find objects based on their modified date and time.

For our first example, let's find all cataloged objects modified in the last 30 days. This could be used in our bookstore application to find recently added or modified Book instances.

```
expr="Catalog(bobobase_modification_time=ZopeTime()-30,
          bobobase_modification_time_usage='range:min')"
```

In the first argument, which matches the index name, we pass the value of the current Zope system date and time minus 30, which calculates the date 30 days prior to today as our search value. The second usage argument instructs the ZCatalog to return objects whose date is equal to or greater than the search value.

By simply changing the usage value, we could find all object that have not been modified for at least 30 days, as follows:

```
expr="Catalog(bobobase_modification_time=ZopeTime()-30,
          bobobase_modification_time_usage='range:max')"
```

To match values that fall between two values (a minimum and maximum), you must pass a list containing at least two items as the search value. The item of the list with the smallest value is treated as the minimum search value and the item with the largest value as the maximum search value. For example, to find all cataloged objects modified yesterday, we could use the following expression:

```
expr="Catalog(bobobase_modification_time=[(ZopeTime()-1).earliestTime(),
                               (ZopeTime()-1).latestTime()],
          bobobase_modification_time_usage='range:min:max')"
```

(ZopeTime()-1) returns the date and time exactly 24 hours ago as a Date-Time object. To determine the starting and ending time of the previous day for use as our maximum and minimum values, we use the earliestTime() and latestTime() method respectively of the DateTime object. These are passed in a two-item list as the search value. We then use the range:min:max usage value to instruct the ZCatalog to perform the bounded query.

11.4.3.3 Sorting the Results Using Field Indexes

Field indexes are also useful for sorting resulting objects efficiently. Although the dtml-in tag allows you to sort a sequence using the sort="..." attribute, this sorting occurs in RAM, which requires all of the ZCatalog search results to be loaded into memory regardless of whether they are displayed in the current batch. Normally only those results displayed are actually loaded into memory.

To sort results efficiently using a field index, pass a *sort_on* argument to the ZCatalog, with its value set to the name of the field index to sort by. You can also specify an optional second *sort_order* argument to determine whether the sort order is ascending or descending. This sorting occurs when the query is performed, thus avoiding the memory and performance penalties of the dtml-in sort attribute.

Let's extend the earlier example that returned objects modified in the last 30 days. To return the results sorted by modified date with the most recently modified object appearing first, use this expression:

```
expr="Catalog(bobobase_modification_time=ZopeTime()-30,
              bobobase_modification_time_usage='range:min',
              sort_on='bobobase_modification_time',
              sort_order='descending')"
```

NOTE *Because sort_on can be used only with field indexes, you will still need to use the dtml-in sort option to sort by other attribute values, like an object's title. To sort using the dtml-in sort option, the desired attribute must be a metadata element of the ZCatalog.*

11.4.3.4 Text Index Queries

Text index query arguments are coded like exact field index queries, except that the value represents a query string rather than an exact value to match. This query string allows simple boolean searching and partial word-match functionality on large quantities of indexed text (see section 11.2.5.1 for more details).

Our example ZCatalog has two text indexes: title and PrincipiaSearchSource. The former is the title property of the object, the latter is the body text of the document or object. To find cataloged objects whose titles contain the words "event" and "calendar," you could use the following expression.

```
expr="Catalog(title='event and calendar')"
```

As we discussed with field indexes, if multiple indexes are included, all the search criteria must be satisfied on an object for it to be returned.

NOTE *You can simultaneously search field, text, and keyword indexes in a single expression by combining the other techniques described above in section 11.4.3.*

11.4.3.5 ZCatalog Query Limitations

Although it is easy to create "and" queries that match criteria from multiple indexes and return objects satisfying all of them, it is difficult to perform "or" queries across multiple indexes. For example, you cannot use a simple query to return objects where the search criteria match either the title or PrincipiaSearchSource indexes.

There are two ways to overcome this limitation. The first is to perform each query separately and combine the results into a single result set. The second is to create a new method attribute of the object or a script that programmatically combines the contents of the attributes, then index against this combined value.

Let's explore the first option: combining search result sets, which you can do simply by adding the results of ZCatalog queries using the plus (+) operator. For example, to return all objects containing the word "victory" in either their title or body text, do the following:

```
expr="Catalog(title='victory') + Catalog(PrincipiaSearchSource='victory')"
```

Although this approach will get us what we want, it has one slight problem: Objects containing the search word in both attributes will be returned twice by our expression, which is not usually the desired result.

The second approach, to create method or script that combines the attribute values, is somewhat more complex and involves writing Python code, but it does solve the duplicate results problem. The sample Python script shown in Listing 11-5, text_content, can be created in Zope's root folder, so that it can be acquired by all of the cataloged objects.

Listing 11-5: text_content Python Script

```
return context.title + '\n' + context.PrincipiaSearchSource()
```

This script returns the object's title, followed by a line break (\n) and the body text returned by the PrincipiaSearchSource method of the object. If, after creating the script, you create a TextIndex called "text_content" in your ZCatalog and update it (using the advanced tab); the ZCatalog will call this method for all cataloged objects and index the result. After doing this, you can perform the desired query using the following expression:

```
expr="Catalog(text_content='victory')"
```

(We will discuss Python in more detail in Chapters 13 through 15.)

NOTE *You cannot use a DTML method as the source for an index, because the ZCatalog expects the attributes to be simple values, properties, or Python methods/scripts that do not require arguments.*

11.5 The Vocabulary

When you create a new ZCatalog, you are asked whether you also want to create a new vocabulary or use an existing one. A vocabulary contains words (normal text, DTML, and HTML tags) found in the objects cataloged in the corresponding ZCatalog.

11.5.1 The Vocabulary Screen

The Vocabulary screen, the Vocabulary object's main screen, contains a list of all words found in the attributes of cataloged objects that are text indexed. The batch size of this list, that is, the number of words displayed, is 20 words per page.

DTML and HTML tags are stored in the vocabulary without angle brackets, and DTML tags are stored as single words without hyphens. For example, say you have a ZCatalog named "MyZCatalog" that contains only one object: the DTML document index_html with the source text shown in Listing 11-6.

Listing 11-6: index_html source text

```
<dtml-var id>
<hr>
<a href="../index_html">Back</a>
hey, you!
hello
hi there
many hellos!
```

Figure 11-18 shows the words generated in the vocabulary from this source text.

11.5.2 Searching the Vocabulary

You can use the Query screen's short form, consisting of an input field and a Submit button, to search the vocabulary. If a vocabulary is created using globbing (see section 11.1.2 for details), you can search it using wildcards (such as * or ?). For example, if you were to search the vocabulary shown in Figure 11-18, the results of the following queries would be as shown:

he*	['hey', 'hello']
hellos	['hello']
hello	['hello']
h?l*	['hello']
*y	['hey','many']

NOTE *The globbing option is chosen only when the vocabulary object is created. You cannot change the globbing option after the fact. To change the globbing option, you would need to delete the original vocabulary, create a new one with the same id, and update all the ZCatalogs that share the vocabulary (using the Advanced screen of the ZCatalogs).*

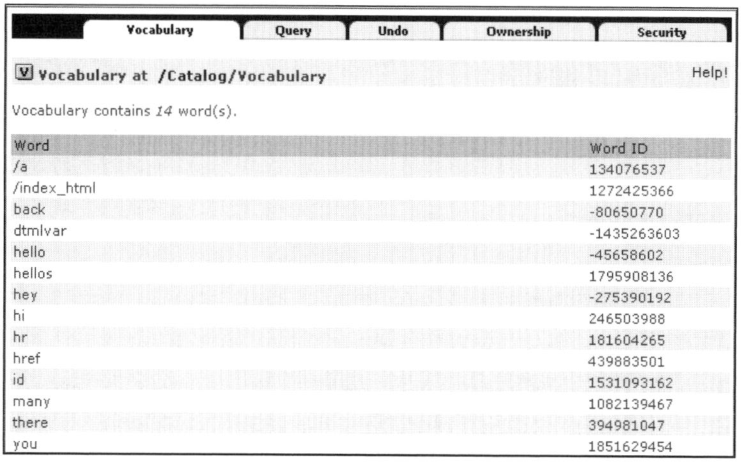

Word	Word ID
/a	134076537
/index_html	1272425366
back	-80650770
dtmlvar	-1435263603
hello	-45658602
hellos	1795908136
hey	-275390192
hi	246503988
hr	181604265
href	439883501
id	1531093162
many	1082139467
there	394981047
you	1851629454

Figure 11-18: Vocabulary example

11.5.3 Expanding the Vocabulary: The insert() and manage_insert() Methods

You can expand a vocabulary using the insert() and manage_insert() methods.

11.5.3.1 The insert() Method

You can enter new words into a vocabulary yourself using the vocabulary object's insert() method. Using this method, you can, for example, insert the word "catalog" using DTML (assuming that the vocabulary has the id Vocabulary):

```
<dtml-call "Vocabulary.insert('Catalog')">
```

11.5.3.2 The manage_insert() Method

You can also enter new words in a vocabulary with the manage_insert() method, using the URL of the vocabulary, as follows:

```
http://localhost:8080/Vocabulary/manage_insert?word=Catalog
```

As you can see, the parameter shown for this method—that is, the word to be added—is named "word." If your addition is actually several words and you want to include it in the vocabulary using the URL, enter it like this:

```
http://localhost:8080/Vocabulary/manage_insert?word=My+Catalog
```

To insert new words using a form, insert the input value using the url_quote_plus option of dtml-var (see Appendix A).

11.5.4 ZCatalog with Special Characters

The ZCatalog supplied by with Zope cannot index words with foreign characters correctly—for example, German umlauts or Japanese Kanji characters—to enable searches for them. However, there are several replacement ZCatalog splitters to handle indexing foreign character sets.

One such splitter patch is the Voodoo Kludge Splitter, which lets you map special characters so that they are indexed properly in ZCatalog vocabulary. You can download this product at

```
http://www.zope.org/Members/kslee/VoodooKludgeSplitter
```

NOTE *Unfortunately this Splitter is slower than the one delivered with Zope and, as a result, updates take longer. You should, therefore, consider whether you want improved speed or special characters.*

Summary

This chapter has explored how to use ZCatalogs to index and search Zope objects and examined the strengths and weaknesses of ZCatalog and how to use it effectively and efficiently. Armed with this knowledge, you should be able to construct search engines for your Zope website to facilitate a site search or other more specific object query functionality.

Chapter 12 will explore how to connect Zope to external relational database systems.

12

ZOPE AND MYSQL

Most complex Internet applications have a database backend, and Zope is no exception: The ZODB (Zope object database) is at your disposal.

However, you may have certain applications that house data more efficiently in a traditional relational database, or you may use an existing database that needs to be connected to Zope. How can you decide which is best?

12.1   ZODB or External Database?

Consider the advantages of using an external SQL database to store your application's data:

- The relational database model easily allows for complex data relationships and rules that would be more difficult to create in the ZODB.

- Storage and retrieval of large numbers of small data quanta are fast and efficient. Many databases can quickly and efficiently query tables containing millions of records.

- You gain the enormous flexibility of SQL as a query language and can leverage the knowledge of other experienced database programmers who may not know Zope.

- You can place Zope and the database server on separate computers for enhanced performance and security.

- Programs other than Zope will be able to directly access data in the database.

- You can access and manipulate existing databases in your organization through Zope without "reinventing the wheel."

- You can more readily separate the data from the code in your application.

Consider also the disadvantages of using an external database:

- Having a separate database is more complex and requires more planning, development time, and maintenance.

- Additional database software and/or hardware may be more costly.

- Hierarchical data models do not always map well onto relational databases, whereas they map directly to the ZODB.

- The storage and retrieval of large data quanta (such as file or image data) are often less efficient in a database than in the ZODB.

- You must be able to program and debug at both the database level and the Zope level.

- You lose the versioning and undo capabilities that you would have with data stored in the ZODB.

- You may need to create additional interfaces through Zope to administer your database.

For each application, you will need to weigh whether the ZODB or an external database is the right option. If you find that you need to use an external database system in your application, your first task will be to learn how to connect it to Zope.

12.2 RDMBS

Relational databases are the industry standard way to store and retrieve large quantities of tabular data. These systems consist of server programs, which are database backends (or engines) that respond to commands from client programs, including Zope. These commands are given in the SQL language, an accepted standard database query language.

There are essentially two types of *relational database management system (RDBMS)*: commercial and open source. Following are some of the most important examples of each:

Commercial RDMBS

Oracle	http://www.oracle.com	A widely used, robust commercial database.
Sybase	http://www.sybase.com	A successful commercial database platform.

Open Source RDBMS

MySQL	http://www.mysql.com	A fast and increasingly sophisticated open source database engine. Commonly used for web applications because of its query performance.

Open Source RDBMS (cont'd.)

PostgreSQL	http://www.postgresql.org	Perhaps the most sophisticated open-source database system. Tailored toward sophisticated multi-user applications. Better suited for write-intensive applications than MySQL.
Interbase	http://www.intebase.com	A robust open source database from Borland. Not as widely used as MySQL and PostgreSQL, but growing in popularity.
ODBC	http://www.odbc.com	Not a database itself, but a standard interface that allows you to connect to nearly any database available (such as MS SQL Server or even MS Access).

This chapter will not attempt to turn you into a database or SQL specialist. In fact, if you're like most web programmers, you will probably leave the relational modeling and the database programming to someone else. Instead, we'll focus on how to connect your programmed database to Zope using the open-source database MySQL as an example. MySQL is widely used for web applications because it is simple and its high read performance is well suited to the web.

12.3   The MySQL Database

Before attempting to work with MySQL under Zope, be sure that you have a MySQL server (version 3.22.32 or higher) running on your computer. (Please refer to the documentation included with MySQL to install and run the database server.) Once it is running, you will log in to the database server and create a database for use in Zope.

12.3.1 Starting MySQL Monitor

The MySQL monitor is a command line program that allows you to access and administer MySQL databases. At a shell prompt (DOS prompt for Windows users), enter the following command to run the MySQL monitor:

```
shell> mysql -h host -u user -p
Enter password: ********
```

You'll need to enter the host parameter if the MySQL server is running on a different computer. For the user parameter, enter the username you use on the MySQL server. Once you have logged on, the following text appears:

```
Welcome to the MySQL monitor.  Commands end with ; or \g.
Your MySQL connection id is 459 to server version: 3.22.20a-log

Type 'help' for help.

mysql>
```

The mysql prompt (mysql>) now appears so that you can enter SQL statements. The command

```
mysql> help
```

will call up a list of all available options.
To log off the MySQL server, enter the command

```
mysql> quit
```

or press CTRL-D.

12.3.2 Creating a Database with MySQL Monitor

First, you'll create a database called "myDB," in which you will then store user data, with the following steps:

1. Run the MySQL monitor as described above.
2. Create a new database and name it myDB with the following command:

```
mysql> CREATE DATABASE myDB;
```

3. Select this database (you have to do this each time you start a new MySQL session) by entering

```
mysql> USE myDB;
```

In response, you should see

```
Database changed
```

You have now created and selected the database myDB. Before you can add data to it, you need to create the appropriate tables in the database to hold your data. Define tables by specifying a table name and information about the table's fields including field names, data types, and other data rules. Each field defines a single column of the table. Data in tables is stored as records; each record is a single row of the table with specific values specified for each field.

NOTE *To display all available databases, enter* SHOW Databases; *at the prompt.*

12.3.3 Creating the User Data Table with MySQL Monitor

You can create data tables in a database using either the MySQL monitor or using Zope. Because you have not yet connected Zope with myDB, use the MySQL monitor to create the tables. (Section 12.3.5, "Establishing a Z MySQL Connection in Zope," discusses how to create tables in the MySQL database from within Zope, without the MySQL monitor.)

User data will be stored in a table called "user," which should contain these fields:

userid	zipcode
firstname	city
lastname	telephone
address	

To create the user table, enter the following SQL statement:

```
CREATE TABLE user (
    userid      INT(12) NOT NULL,
    firstname   CHAR(20) NOT NULL,
    lastname    CHAR(20) NOT NULL,
    address     CHAR(20) NOT NULL,
    zipcode     INT(5) NOT NULL,
    city        CHAR(20) NOT NULL,
    telephone   CHAR(15) NOT NULL,
    PRIMARY KEY(userid)
);
```

The above SQL code creates the table user using the CREATE TABLE SQL statement. Lines 2–8 specify the fields in the table. The first column of each line is the field name, the second column is the data type, and the last column describes any constraints on the field. The last line specifies that the field userid is the record's primary key—that is, its unique identifier. No two user records can have the same primary key value.

Now enter the command

```
mysql> show tables;
```

to see whether the user table has been created properly. If it has, you should see the following:

```
+-------------------+
| Tables in myDB    |
+-------------------+
| user              |
+-------------------+
1 row in set (0.00 sec)
```

Table 12-1: Database Adapter Required Files

File	Description
ZMySQLDA-2.0.6.tar.gz (or newer). (Download from http://www.zope.org/ Members/adustman/Products/ZMySQLDA)	The database adapter.
MySQL-python-0.3.5.tar.gz (or newer). (Download from http://www.zope.org/ Members/adustman/Products/MySQLdb)	The MySQL database module, containing more up-to-date drivers than those supplied with the database adapter.

12.3.4 Installing the Database Adapter ZMySQLDA

Before Zope can communicate with the myDB database, you must connect to the MySQL server using a database adapter, which is the interface between myDB and Zope. We'll install the database adapter ZMySQLDA.

Before you begin your installation, download the files listed in Table 12-1, which include ZMySQLDA, the database adapter itself, and the latest MySQL drivers.

To install ZMySQLDA under Linux, do the following:

1. Unpack the ZMySQLDA archive in the top directory of your Zope installation. For example, if you installed Zope in the directory Zope-2.3, extract the archive into that directory. Extracting the archive creates a folder named "Zope-Directory/lib/python/Products/ZMySQLDA."

2. Unpack the MySQL drivers in the directory Zope-Directory/lib/python/ Products. To do so, follow the installation instructions included with the product.

3. Restart Zope to make the changes take effect.

12.3.5 Establishing a Z MySQL Connection in Zope

Now that we've installed the database adapter on our Linux machine, we can establish a connection between the MySQL database and Zope. To do so, open the root directory and select Z MySQL database connection from the folder's add menu. You should see the management screen shown in Figure 12-1.

NOTE *Create the database connection object in a folder where it can be acquired by any Z SQL methods you might create. The root folder is often a good choice.*

12.3.5.1 Database Connection String

In the Database Connection String field, enter information about your database using the following syntax:

```
<DatabaseName[@Host]> <Username> <Password>
```

For the purposes of our example, enter the information shown in Figure 12-2.

NOTE *Because the database and the Zope server are both on the same computer in this example, we've omitted the parameter [@Host]. Substitute the username and password appropriate for your database server.*

Congratulations! You have just established a connection between Zope and your MySQL database, and you now have immediate access to your myDB database from within Zope.

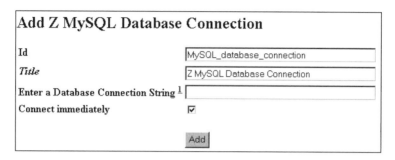

Figure 12-1: Creating a Z MySQL database connection

Figure 12-2: The Database Connection String

12.3.5.2 Checking the Database Connection Status

To check the status of your database connection, click MySQL_database_connection. You should see a screen like the one shown in Figure 12-3.

To close the connection at any time, click Close Database Connection; to reopen it, click Open Database Connection. On the Properties tab, you can change the Title and Database Connection String parameters for the database.

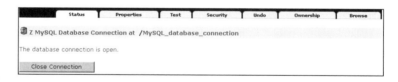

Figure 12-3: Database status screen

12.3.6 Testing SQL Queries to Your Database

To test your database, formulate a query for the database to determine what data records are contained in the user table. To do this, send the following SQL statement to the database:

```
select * from user
```

When you click the Test tab, you should see a screen like the one shown in Figure 12-4.

In the Query text field, enter the following SQL command (as shown in Figure 12-4):

```
select * from user
```

Using this screen, you can submit SQL statements to your MySQL database from within Zope without having to switch to the MySQL Monitor.

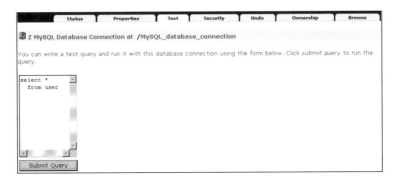

Figure 12-4: Sending and testing SQL queries to the database

You can formulate various SQL statements in the Query field to query the database (as above), create a new table, or enter new data. And, now that your database is connected to Zope, you can create the same table you created in Section 12.3.3 in the MySQL Monitor using the Zope interface by entering the SQL statement for creating the user table in the Query field.

12.4 Filling Tables with User Data Using Zope

Before you can fill the user table with data, you must create the objects listed in Table 12-2 in Zope. Place them in a folder called "Methods."

Table 12-2: Objects for Creating Users

Object Name	Function
userAddForm_html	Input form for the user data.
userAdd_html	Transfers the input values to the SQL method userInsert_sql and reports the result to the user.
userInsert_sql	SQL method that writes the input values in the database.

As mentioned earlier, you can formulate SQL queries in the Query field, including queries to fill the user table with data. However, if you want web site users, who do not have access to the Zope management screen, to be able to access and use the database, you must create a separate input form for the fields last name, city, address, and so on.

12.4.1 The userAddForm_html Method

Use the code in Listing 12-1 to create the input form userAddForm_html.

Listing 12-1: userAddForm_html

```
<dtml-var standard_html_header>
<form action="userAdd_html">
<input type=hidden name=userid value="<dtml-var name="ZopeTime">">
<table border=0 cellpadding=2 cellspacing=2 bgcolor="#BBAAAA">
<tr><th align=left>First name:</th>
    <td><input type=text name=firstname size="40"></td>
</tr>
<tr><th align=left>Last name:</th>
    <td><input type=text name=lastname size="40"></td>
</tr><tr><th align=left>Address:</th>
    <td><input type=text name=address size="40"></td>
</tr>
<tr><th align=left>City:</th>
    <td><input type=text name=city size="40"></td>
</tr>
<tr><th align=left>ZIP code:</th>
    <td><input type=text name=zipcode size="40"></td>
</tr>
<tr><th align=left>Phone:</th>
    <td><input type=text name=telephone size="40"></td>
</tr>
<tr><td colspan="2" align="center">
    <input type=submit name="create" value="Create">
    <input type=submit name="cancel" value="Cancel"></td>
</tr>
</table>
</form>
<dtml-var standard_html_footer>
```

As you can see at the beginning of Listing 12-1, the DTML method user-Add_html is called when this form is submitted. The userAdd_html method will execute the Z SQL method that inserts the new user record. The variable userid (in the third line) receives as its value a string formed from the current system time, down to milliseconds. This ensures that the userid will be unique (which it must be, given that it's the primary key of the user table), because the system time is never the same value twice.

You now need to create a DTML method called userAdd_html, which will pass the values to the Z SQL method userInsert_sql and inform you that a user has been successfully created in the user database. Then, because this DTML method cannot write data to the database, you will create a Z SQL method for writing the input values (see section 12.4.3).

12.4.2 The userAdd_html Method

Enter the code shown in Listing 12-2 to create the DTML method userAdd_html.

Listing 12-2: userAdd_html

```
1:    <dtml-var standard_html_header>
2:    <dtml-if name="create">
3:    <dtml-try>
4:        <dtml-call name="userInsert_sql">
5:        The user <dtml-var name="firstname">
6:        <dtml-var name="lastname">
7:        was successfully added to the database.
8:    <dtml-except>
9:        Sorry, the user was not added to the database
10:       because an error occurred.
11:   </dtml-try>
12:   <center>
13:   <form action="<dtml-var name="URL1">">
14:       <input type="submit" name="userAddForm_html:method"
15:       value="Create Another User">
16:       <input type="submit" name="index_html:method" value="Done">
17:   </form>
18:   </center>
19:   <dtml-else>
20:   <dtml-call expr="RESPONSE.redirect('index_html')">
21:   </dtml-if>
22:   <dtml-var standard_html_footer>
```

Let's take a closer look at how this code works when the userAddForm_html form is submitted:

First, see if the user clicked on the Create button using dtml-if (Line 2). If so, open a dtml-try block (Line 3) in which you call the Z SQL method userInsert_sql (Line 4); because this Z SQL method returns no results, execute it using dtml-call. A message for the user is then inserted if the method executes successfully (Lines 5–7). If there is an error inserting the user record, the dtml-except block (Lines 8–10) inserts an error message for the user.

Following the dtml-try block, insert a form with two buttons to allow the user to either create another user record or return to the index_html method (Lines 13–17). This requires you to create a form with two potential action methods: user-AddForm_html and index_html. To accomplish this, use a Zope feature called *method marshaling*. First, set the action of the form to the folder containing the action methods—which, in this case, is the same folder containing this method (userAdd_html). To do this, use the built-in variable URL1 to insert the URL of the containing folder (Line 13). Then create a Submit button (Lines 14–15) to send the user back to the userAddForm_html to enter another user. To do this, set the name attribute of the submit button like so: name="userAddForm_html:method". The :method suffix at the end of the button's name tells Zope to call the method with that name when the form is submitted, in this case userAddForm_html. The same technique is used to create the second Submit button (Line 16)—except that this button's name tells Zope to go to index_html instead.

Below the form is a dtml-else block (Lines 19–21) that is executed if the user clicks the Cancel button on the userAddForm_html form. The code executed (Line 20) simply directs the user back to index_html without executing the Z SQL method, so no user is created.

12.4.3 The userInsert_sql Method

Now you'll create an Z SQL method userInsert_sql.

NOTE *You can create an SQL method only if the database connection is active.*

1. From the folder's add menu, select Z SQL Method. The management screen shown in Figure 12-5 appears.

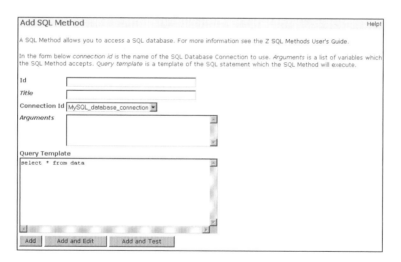

Figure 12-5: Creating an SQL insert method

2. For the id, enter userInsert_sql.
3. In the Connection Id field, select MySQL_database_connection.
4. In the Arguments field, enter all values to be passed to this SQL method, as follows (be sure to leave one space between each of the individual arguments):

```
userid firstname lastname address zipcode city telephone
```

5. In the Query field, enter the following SQL statements:

```
INSERT INTO user
      (userid,firstname,lastname,address,zipcode,city,telephone)
VALUES
('<dtml-var name="userid" sql_quote>',
'<dtml-var name="firstname" sql_quote>',
'<dtml-var name="lastname" sql_quote>',
'<dtml-var name="address" sql_quote>',
'<dtml-var name="zipcode" sql_quote>',
'<dtml-var name="city" sql_quote>',
'<dtml-var name="telephone" sql_quote>')
```

6. Click Add and Edit. You should see the screen shown in Figure 12-6.

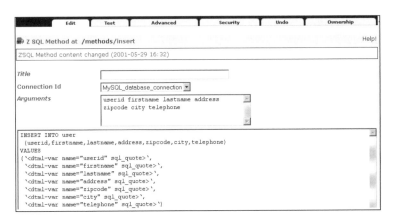

Figure 12-6: The Z SQL method userInsert_sql

NOTE *The sql_quote attribute of dtml-var used above prevents characters significant to SQL, such as the single quote (') or semi-colon (;), from causing errors if they are submitted from the form. Otherwise the last name "O'Connell" could not be successfully submitted, for instance.*

12.4.4 Testing Your SQL Methods

To test your SQL methods, click Change and Test. You should see the form shown in Figure 12-7, where you can enter the values for your user and then write them to the user table to test the Z SQL method.

If the test above succeeds, you can now test your custom create user form, as follows:

1. View the DTML document userAddForm_html and enter the data as shown in Figure 12-8.

2. Click Create.

The data from the form is sent to the userAdd_html method, which in turn calls the Z SQL method just created (userInsert_sql) to insert the data into the user table of the MySQL database, as shown in Figure 12-9.

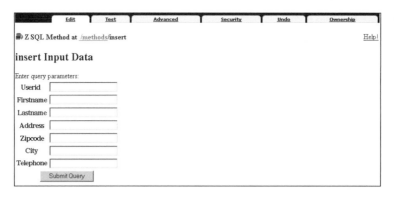

Figure 12-7: Testing the SQL insert method

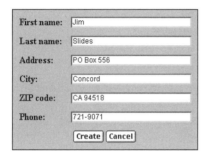

Figure 12-8: Creating a user

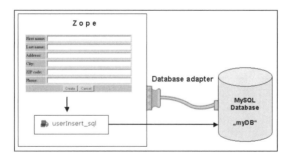

Figure 12-9: Communication between Zope and myDB

Sending data from an html form to the database through Zope actually involves several steps:

1. The form is completed and submitted by the client to Zope.

2. Zope encapsulates the form values in the REQUEST object and calls the object that is the target of the form's action URL.

3. The form's target object then calls a Z SQL method, which creates an SQL statement to send to the database backend.

4. The Z SQL statement sends the SQL statement to the database backend using a database adapter.

5. The backend database executes the SQL statement and returns the results (if any) to Zope via the database adapter.

6. The Z SQL method receives the results from the database adapter and returns them to the form's target object.

7. The form's target object displays the results or takes action based on them.

12.5 Querying the Database Using Zope

Let's now create a search screen with which you can perform a query to request information from the database. To do so, you'll need the following:

- Z SQL methods that contain the SQL query code to perform the search
- A Search interface that uses this Z SQL method and formats its output
- An input form for entering the search criteria

12.5.1 Creating SQL Methods for Searching

First, create the Z SQL method search_lastnames (shown in Figure 12-10) to query the user table by last name.

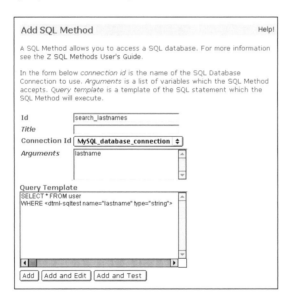

Figure 12-10: Z SQL method search_lastnames

12.5.2 The sqltest Tag

The sqltest DTML tag is a special tag that can only be used in Z SQL methods. The sqltest tag inserts an SQL comparison expression between a table's column and a value supplied as an argument. The column name, lastname in this example, is used in the sqltest tag:

```
<dtml-sqltest name="lastname" type="string">
```

The argument name with which the column is to be compared is also called "lastname." All arguments used as variables in Z SQL methods must be specified explicitly in the Arguments field of the method. Assuming the value "Slides" was supplied as the value of the lastname argument, the above sqltest tag would insert the following text into the SQL statement:

```
lastname='Slides'
```

To create the Z SQL method search_firstnames, use the same approach. The general syntax is

```
<dtml-sqltest name="variablename" column="columnname" type="datatype" optional>
```

To create an SQL method to search for first names, assuming an argument "name" enter the following code into the Z SQL method:

```
SELECT * FROM user
WHERE <dtml-sqltest name="name" column="firstname" type="nb">
```

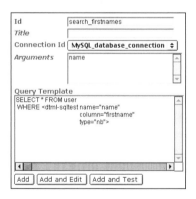

Figure 12-11: SQL search_firstnames method

Figure 12-11 shows the completed search_firstnames Z SQL method. Table 12-3 lists the attributes of the sqltest tag.

Table 12-3: Attributes of the sqltest Tag

Attribute	Description
name	Name of the variable to be written in the table.
column	Name of the column in the table.
multiple	A flag that indicates whether several values can be used.
optional	A flag that indicates whether the test is optional. If the test is optional and no value exists for a variable or if an invalid empty string is used, no operations are performed.
op	Parameter indicating the comparison operation. The standard value is =. The following comparison operations can be used: = > < <> >= <= Others may also be available for your database, consult your database documentation for details.
type	The data type of the variable to be inserted, such as string, int, float, nb. (nb stands for nonblank and represents a string longer than 0 characters.)

12.5.3 The sqlvar Tag

The sql-var tag is another DTML tag that is used only in Z SQL methods. This tag is used to ensure that certain value types, such as string, are correctly interpreted in the SQL text. Data values are converted (if possible), strings are properly quoted, special characters are escaped (as with the sql_quote option of dtml-var), and numeric values are passed according to the conventions of your database. Use sqlvar in place of dtml-var in your Z SQL methods.

The syntax to use is

```
<dtml-sqlvar name="name" type="datatype" optional>
```

Table 12-4 lists the attributes of the sqlvar tag.

Table 12-4: Attributes of the sqlvar Tag

Attribute	Description
name	Name of the variable to be written to the table.
type	The data type of the variable to be inserted, such as string, int, float, nb. (nb stands for nonblank and represents a string that has a length greater than 0 characters.)
optional	Inserts nothing if the value is omitted or cannot be successfully converted to the type specified. If this attribute were omitted, a Zope error would occur.

12.6 Creating a Search Interface

Although you certainly may, you do not need to create your own database search interface manually. Zope provides you with a search interface to reduce some of the workload for you. To create a search interface with Zope's help, follow these steps:

1. Select Z Search Interface from the folder's add menu, then enter the values shown in Figure 12-12.

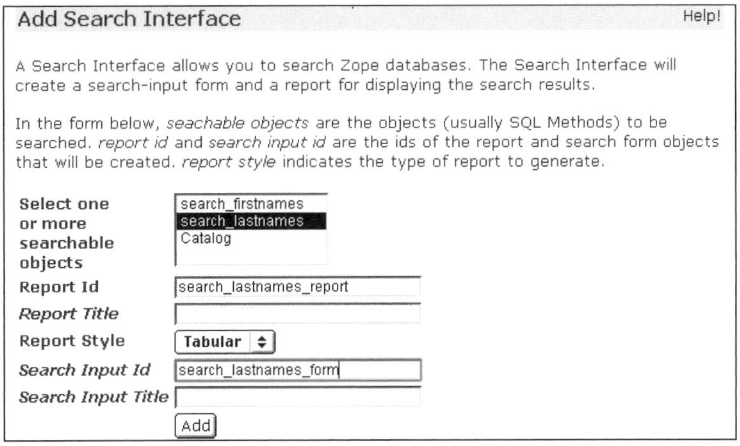

Figure 12-12: Creating a search interface

2. The top field contains a list of all available SQL methods (and other searchable objects like ZCatalogs). From this list, select the methods you want your search interface to access. For this example, select the SQL method search_lastnames.

3. In the Report Id field, enter `search_lastnames_report`.

4. In the Search Input Id field, enter `search_lastnames_form`.

5. Click Add to have Zope create the DTML method searchinterface.

12.6.1 Creating an Input Screen for the Search

Suppose you want to search the user table in your myDB database for records by last name. The search screen should look like Figure 12-13.

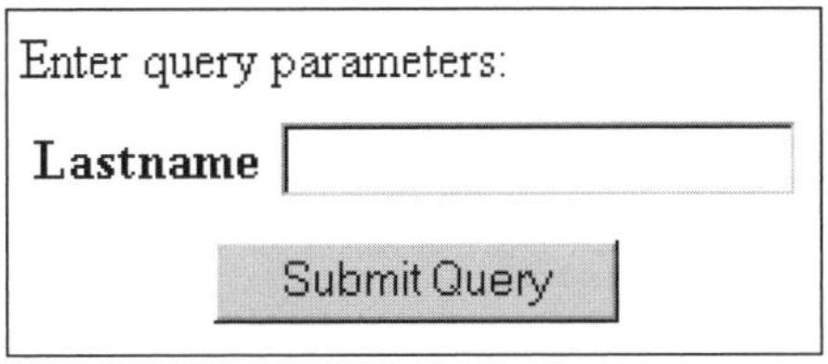

Figure 12-13: Search screen for search_lastnames_form

Figure 12-14 shows the relationships among the DTML methods search_lastnames_form and search_lastnames_report and the Z SQL method search_lastnames.

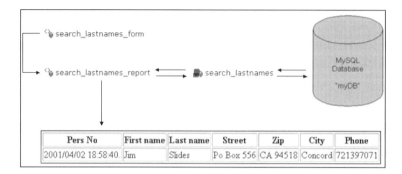

Figure 12-14: Interrelationship of the DTML and SQL methods

To summarize this process,

1. The user uses search_lastnames_form to submit the lastname value to the method search_lastnames_report.

2. The search_lastnames_report calls the Z SQL method search_lastnames, which creates an SQL statement that is sent to the MySQL database through the database adapter.

3. The search_lastnames method returns the matching records to search_lastnames_report, which creates a table to display them to the user. This table is returned as the report web page.

Listing 12-4 shows the code for the DTML method search_lastnames_form. In search_lastnames_form, the DTML method searchinterface (Z Search Interface) is called as soon as you click the Submit Query button, as shown in bold.

Listing 12-4: search_lastnames_form

```
<dtml-var standard_html_header>
<table>
<tr><th valign=top>Last name:</th>
<td><form action="search_lastnames_report">
    <input type=text name=lastname>
    <input type="submit" value=" Go ">
</form></td>
</tr>
</table>
<dtml-var standard_html_footer>
```

Now, if you run search_lastnames_form and enter Slides in the last name field, you'll see the output shown in Figure 12-15.

Userid	Firstname	Lastname	Address	Zipcode	City
2001/04/02 18:58:40.	Jim	Slides	Po Box 556	CA 94518	Concord

Figure 12-15: Search results

To add more search fields to the search screen shown in Figure 12-13, do the following:

- Expand the DTML method search_lastnames_form with additional input fields.
- Create additional SQL methods like search_lastnames.
- Create new Z Search Interfaces for the newly created SQL methods (for example, search_address, search_city, and so on).

For more information on working with ZSQL and MySQL, visit:

http://zope.org/Documentation/Guides/ZSQL

http://mysql.com

Summary

You should now know how and why to use external databases with Zope and how to combine the data manipulation and query capabilities of an SQL database with Zope's web publishing functionality. With this knowledge, you will be able to create completely data-driven Zope applications.

Chapter 13 discusses more about the Python language and how to use it to extend and enhance Zope and other applications.

13

PROGRAMMING ZOPE: PYTHON IN A JIFFY

As discussed in Chapter 1, Zope is written mostly in the Python programming language. Therefore, to take full advantage of Zope, you must at least be familiar with Python's basic characteristics—not just to use DTML's expression syntax, but also to create Python scripts and external methods, to use Python products, and to debug effectively. With a good grasp of Python, you will also be able to modify and expand Zope to suit your needs.

Zope lets you use Python code in three ways:

- In Python scripts
- In external methods
- In products

Python scripts, new to Zope 2.3 and higher, allow you to write Python code through the web much like DTML. Although you will not have access to all Python modules and functions (for security reasons), Python scripts are an excellent way to code business logic that would be difficult or cumbersome in DTML. They are also excellent for writing instance methods for your custom ZClasses. (Chapter 14 discusses Python scripts in more detail and offers some examples.)

External methods are interfaces to external files (modules) that contain Python methods. This means that you can write your own Python methods externally (which can call other methods in Zope or other Python modules) and expose them to your Zope application using external method objects. (Section 14.2 takes a detailed look at external methods.)

Sections 13.1 through 13.4 will look at elements of Python's syntax, then section 13.5 will discuss how to use Python to create classes and methods. Finally, we'll apply our knowledge using a simple program example.

13.1 Data Types

To truly master Python, consult a good Python book (O'Reilly's *Learning Python*[1] or New Riders' *Python Essential Reference*[2]).

This section discusses the data types supported by Python and offers several simple examples, with each example accompanied by the corresponding result (the relevant screen output).

NOTE *The results shown in this section derive from output produced if you run the examples in Zope (for example, by calling them from within DTML). If you try to test these examples in a pure Python environment, you may encounter differences.*

Python supports the following basic data types:

- Numeric
- Sequential
- None

Python numeric types can be further divided into:

- Integer values
- Long-integer values
- Floating-point numbers
- Octal and hexadecimal numbers
- Complex numbers

Python sequential types include the following data types:

- Strings
- Lists
- Tuples
- Dictionaries

---

[1] Lutz, Mark and David Ascher. *Learning Python*. California: O'Reilly & Associates, 1999. ISBN: 1-56592-464-9.

[2] Beazley, David M. *Python Essential Reference*. 2nd ed. Indiana: New Riders Publishing, 2001. ISBN: 0735710910.

13.1.1 Numeric Types

Numeric data of various kinds can be stored and manipulated in Python. These types range from simple integers to complex numbers.

13.1.1.1 Integer Values

Integer values are whole numbers between –2147483647 and 2147483647. If you use numbers outside this range, or if you use expressions with results outside this range, an error message will appear.

Integer numbers cannot begin with zero or they will be interpreted as octal numbers.

Example	Result of Evaluation
123	123
–3456	–3456
2147483647	2147483647
2147483648	Zope error

13.1.1.2 Long-Integer Values

Long-integers are also whole numbers. However, unlike integers, they can grow to unlimited size, as long as their size does not exceed the amount of memory in the computer. A long-integer value is produced by adding a lowercase or uppercase letter L ("l" or "L") to the number, thus allowing you to use whole numbers of any size as well as expressions whose evaluation can then grow to an unlimited size.

Example	Result of Evaluation
99999999999L	99999999999L
2147483648L	2147483648L
9 * 999999999l	8999999991l

13.1.1.3 Floating-Point Numbers

Floating-point numbers are positive and negative real numbers that use a period (.) to indicate the number of decimal places. In the case of larger values, you can use scientific notation by inserting either an "e" or an "E."

Example	Result of Evaluation
–3.14	–3.14
3.14e–1	10.314
3.14e+10	3.1400000000.0
4E5	400000.0
4.0e+210	4e+210
–0.005	–0.005

13.1.1.4 Octal and Hexadecimal Numbers

In addition to decimal numbers, you can use octal and hexadecimal numbers (base-8 and base-16 numbers) in expressions. Octal numbers begin with zero (0); hexadecimal numbers begin with 0X or 0x.

Example	Result of Evaluation
010	8
05	5
0x10	10
0X15	21
0X2F	47

13.1.1.5 Complex Numbers

Complex numbers have a real and an imaginary component. In Python, a complex number looks like this: Real Part+Imaginary Part. The number is followed by the letter "J" or "j." This "J" or "j" must be preceded by a value; otherwise, Python will interpret it as a variable.

Example	Result of Evaluation
6+6j	(6+6j)
6.9+0j	(6.9+0j)
1j	1j

13.1.2 Sequential Types

Python supports four *sequential data types,* including various collections of objects. The individual elements of these data types are indexed, meaning that each element has a position number. In Python, this numbering starts at zero, and the first element in a sequence is always index 0. You can use the built-in Python function *len* to determine the number of elements in a sequence.

Elements in a sequence are accessed by index; you can also access a subsection of a sequence using a technique called *slicing*. The table below illustrates the syntax used to access elements and slices of a Python sequence.

Example	Result of Evaluation
s[0]	First element of sequence
s[1]	Second element of sequence
s[−1]	Last element of sequence
s[0:3]	First three elements of sequence
len(s)	Number of elements in sequence

13.1.2.1 Strings

Strings are sequences of characters that form a chain or string. A string can consist of several characters, one character, or no characters and can essentially contain anything that can be converted to text in some way.

Strings are enclosed in either single or double quotation marks; an empty string is produced by two adjacent quotation marks. Python also supports multiline strings that are enclosed in three single or double quotation marks and are called *triple quoted strings*.

NOTE *You must use single quotation marks to use strings in DTML.*

Example	Result of Evaluation
' '	There is no screen output because the string is empty.
'DTML'	DTML
'hgz%dd@'	hgz%dd@
"DTML"	DTML
"""Multiple Lines"""	Multiple Lines

13.1.2.2 Lists

A *list* is an indexed collection of objects of various data types used to form a sequence. Unlike strings, lists can contain other objects, which may include floating-point numbers or even other lists, in addition to characters. Lists are like arrays in other languages except that lists are not fixed in size and their elements are not a fixed data type.

A list is enclosed in square brackets, with the individual elements separated by commas.

There are several methods available to list objects, including *append* and *insert*. These methods are used to add new items to the end or middle of a list.

The table below shows the syntax used in Python to create and manipulate lists.

Example	Result of Evaluation
[ ]	There is no screen output because the list is empty.
[1,3,'Zope',5.3]	[1,3,'Zope',5.3]
[12,['Internet', 'Intranet']]	[12,['Internet', 'Intranet']]
l = [2,4,6,8] l.append(10)	[2,4,6,8,10]
l = [2,3,4] l.insert(0, 1)	[1,2,3,4]

13.1.2.3 Tuples

A *tuple* is an indexed collection of elements, much like a list, used to form an object. Unlike lists, however, the sequence of the individual elements in a tuple cannot be changed, and new elements cannot be appended or inserted. Tuples are used when you need to store a sequence that should not be modified by other parts of the program. The tuple is enclosed in parentheses, with the elements separated by commas, as shown in the following table.

Example	Result of Evaluation
()	The empty tuple.
('Easter', 'bunny')	('Easter', 'bunny')
(1, 2, 3)	(1,2,3)
('uno',)	('uno',)

13.1.2.4 Dictionaries

Dictionaries are an unordered collection of key and value pairs—essentially, a list of keys, each of which has been assigned a value. These keys can be numeric constants, strings, tuples, and a number of constant objects. Dictionaries can be nested (that is, contain other dictionaries), and they may also contain lists and tuples as their values.

A dictionary is enclosed in curly brackets (also called "braces") with its elements separated by commas and its keys separated from their values with a colon, as follows:

```
{Key1:Value1, Key2:Value2, Key3:Value3, and so on}
```

A dictionary is like a simple word list containing a word (the key) and its corresponding value. For example,

```
{'house':'Haus', 'lawnmower':'Rasenmähermann', 'graveyard':'Friedhof'}
```

New keys and corresponding values can be directly assigned into a dictionary. You can use the keys method of a dictionary to return a list of the dictionary's keys. The table below shows how Python dictionaries are created and manipulated:

Example	Result of Evaluation
`{ }`	The dictionary is empty, and nothing is output to the screen.
`{'Goethe':1, 'Schiller':2, 3:4}`	`{'Goethe':1, 'Schiller':2, 3:4}`
`{1:'ugh', 2:{'inter':'net'} }`	`{1:'ugh', 2:{'inter':'net'} }`
`d = {1:'fair', 2:'good'}` `d[3] = 'excellent'`	`{1:'fair', 2:'good', 3:'excellent'}`
`d = {1:'one', 2:'two', 3:'three'}`	`(The order is arbitrary.)`
`d.keys()`	`[2,3,1]`

13.1.3 None

The data type None has one value only, None, which denotes an empty object. It is used as a placeholder for variables and is an implicit return value for methods for which no return value has been defined.

13.2 Operators

Table 13-1 lists the operators that can be used in Python along with brief examples of each. The operators are arranged according to the data type with which they are used.

Table 13-1: Operators

Operator	Function	Example	Evaluation
Boolean Operators			
<	Less than	`5 < 10`	1 (true)
<=	Less than or equal to	`5 <= 5`	1
>	Greater than	`5 > 10`	0 (false)
>=	Greater than or equal to	`5 >= 5`	1
==	Equal to (same value)	`3 == 3`	1
!=	Not equal (like <>)	`3 != 3`	0
is	Same objects	`Object1 is Object2`	1
is not	Different objects	`Object1 is not Object2`	0
not	False?	`not 1`	0

(continued on next page)

Table 13-1: Operators (continued)

Operator	Function	Example	Evaluation
or	Or	1 or 0	1
and	And	1 and 0	0
Operators for Strings, Lists, and Tuples			
in	Contained in	1 in [1,2]	1
not in	Not contained in	3 not in [1,2]	1
for ... in ...:	Count loop	for x in [1,2]: print 'hello'	hello hello
+	Concatenation	"he" + "llo"	hello
*	Repetition	2 * "You"	You You
X[i]	Indexing; returns element from X to position i+1	x="hello" x[1]	e
X[i:j]	Slicing; returns subelement from I+1 to j from X	x="hello" x[0:3]	hel
len(s)	Length	len("hello")	5
X.sort()	Sort a list	l=[8,6,5,3] l.sort()	[3,5,6,8]
min(s)	Smallest element	min([6,4,2,5])	2
max(s)	Largest element	max([6,4,2,5])	6
Operators for Dictionaries (Sample Dictionary Used: stats= {"inning":7, "home":3, "visitor":2}			
d[k]	Indexing by key	stats["home"]	3
d[k]=x	Change or create value pairs	stats["out"]=2	no output
del d[k]	Delete a value pair by key	del stats["out"]	no output
d.keys()	The keys of the dictionary as a list	stats.keys()	["visitor", "inning", "home"]
len(d)	Number of value pairs	len(stats)	3

(continued on next page)

Table 13-1: Operators (continued)

Operator	Function	Example	Evaluation
Numeric Operators for Integer and Long-Integer Values, Floating-Point, and Complex Numbers			
+	Addition	1+1	2
–	Subtraction	1–1	0
*	Multiplication	12*6	72
/	Division	12/6	2
%	Remainder	12%6	0
–x	Negative sign	x=12 –x	–12
+x	Identity	+x	12
|	Bit or	12 | 6	14
&	Bit and	12 & 6	4
^	Bit exclusive or	12 ^ 6	10
<<	Bit shift left	12 << 6	768
>>	Bit shift right	12 >> 6	0
x ** y	Power y to base x	12 ** 6	2985984
abs(x)	Absolute value of x	abs(-12)	12
int(x)	Convert x to an integer value	int(12.6)	12
long(x)	Convert x to a long-integer value	long(12.6)	12L
float(x)	Convert x to a floating-point number	float(12)	12.0
complex(re, im)	Convert to a complex number	complex(4,3)	(4+3j)
divmod(x,y)	Return the whole number part and the whole number remainder of a tuple	divmod(12,5)	(2,2)
pow(x,y)	Power y to base x	pow(12, 6)	2985984

13.3 Variables and Assignments

User-defined variables begin with a letter or an underscore (_) and can be followed by any desired combination of letters, numbers, or underscores. Variable names cannot contain any special characters, with the exception of underscores, and they cannot be the same as any of the reserved words listed below.

NOTE *Python is case sensitive and differentiates between uppercase and lowercase letters. For example, Python considers "Price" and "price" to be different variable names.*

Python's Reserved Words

and	elif	global	or
assert	else	if	pass
break	except	import	print
class	exec	in	raise
continue	finally	is	return
def	for	lambda	try
del	from	not	while

Variables are assigned using the equal-sign assignment (=) operator. An indicator (variable name) that appears on the left side of the operator is assigned the value on the right; for example:

```
x=42
a=['Item1', 'Item2', 'Item3']
_hgf78={1: 'Value1', 2: 'Value2'}
lengths=(1, 3, 5)
x, y=12, 43   =>   x=12   y=43
```

13.4 Indention

One of Python's unique features is that blocks of related instructions are indicated by indentation. Unlike other programming languages, such as Java or C, Python does not use brackets or similar elements to identify the start and end of code blocks. Thus, instructions in the same block must be on the same indent level. A line of code beginning a block, such as a method definition or a looping statement, ends with a colon (:). See Listing 13-1 for an example.

Listing 13-1: Sample f() method showing indention

```
1    def f():
2        for i in [1,2,3,4,5]:
3            j=i+1
4            print j
5        return "All done. Bye Bye."
```

In the method definition shown above, Lines 2 and 5 belong to the method body, and Lines 3 and 4 belong to the for-loop body.

13.5   Classes and Methods

The following section will show how to define a class with your own attributes and methods and how to derive (or instantiate) objects. The principle of inheritance will also be introduced.

13.5.1 Example: Creating a Class

A class definition is preceded by the class keyword, as follows:

```
class animal:
```

The class definition can then be followed by a constructor method: __init__() (two underscores on each side). The constructor method is called every time an instance of the class is created and is often used to set up the new instance in an initial state. For example, instance variables can be initialized in a constructor method and, if necessary, used to set up an initial value, as shown in Listing 13-2. The def statement defines a Python method.

Listing 13-2: The Animal class with the constructor method __init__()

```
1 class animal:
2     Animal Class
3     def __init__(self, age, gender):
4         """Constructor Method"""
5         self.age=age
6         self.gender=gender
7         self.awake=1
```

The constructor method shown in Listing 13-2 says that an age and a gender must be provided for each instance of the Animal class (Lines 3, 5, and 6). In addition, each animal is automatically regarded as awake (Line 7).

The first argument of the constructor, self, is where Python passes the current instance of the class to the method. When the method needs to examine or manipulate the current instance of the class, you use the self argument as in Lines 5 through 7, where we assign three new attributes to the instance. The self argument is placed first in the argument list of the method; Python automatically passes this argument to a method when it is called.

Lines 2 and 4 contain a special comment called a *doc string*, which describes the class and method. A doc string should appear immediately after a class or def statement. A triple-quoted string is normally used (as in Line 4 above) so that a multiline doc string can be specified if necessary. The doc string is mandatory for a class's method to be accessible from Zope, and if it is not included, an error message appears if you attempt to call it from Zope.

Listing 13-3 could be used as more methods for the Animal class.

Listing 13-3: The sleep() and wakeUp() methods for the Animal class

```
1        def sleep(self):
2               The animal is sleeping
3               self.awake=0
4               print 'ZZZZZZ'
5        def wakeUp(self):
6               The animal is awake
7               self.awake=1
8               print 'The animal is awake'
```

At this point, we can't do very much with the Animal class except to create Animal objects that have a name and a gender and that are either awake or sleeping. This is simply not a detailed enough description of the real animal world.

13.5.1.1 Creating Subclasses

To better represent the real animal world, we must create additional classes, known as subclasses, based on the Animal class. These subclasses assume all of the attributes of the Animal class (including name, gender, awake, __init__, sleep, and wakeup) through *inheritance,* and can add their own attributes.

NOTE *Subclasses inherit the attributes of their base class and expand upon them. Instances of different subclasses share particular attributes because they inherit them from the same base class.*

Let's create two subclasses as an example: the Reptile class and the Bird class. Objects in both classes inherit the same basic attributes from the Animal class and will also have other, new attributes, such as fly and swim.

NOTE *Subclasses are defined like base classes except that the name of the base class appears in parentheses after the class description.*

The Reptile class is defined as shown in Listing 13-4.

Listing 13-4: The Reptile class: a subclass of the Animal class

```
class reptile(animal):
    """Reptiles"""
    def swim(self):
        """The reptile swims"""
        if self.awake:
            print 'paddle paddle splish splash'
```

The Bird class is defined as shown in Listing 13-5.

Listing 13-5: The Bird class: a subclass of the Animal class

```
class bird(animal):
    """Bird"""
    def fly(self):
        """The bird flies"""
        if self.awake:
            print 'flap flap flutter flip'
```

13.5.1.2 Creating an Instance

To instantiate a class instance, we call the class like a function and assign the result to a variable (here, Hedwig and Dundee). This variable then becomes the object instance:

```
Hedwig=bird(1, 'female')
Dundee=reptile(4, 'male')
```

Now that we have created the instances, we can use the methods of both subclasses on the two objects. The following illustrates the methods in Python's interactive mode, which can be entered by entering python at a command prompt:

```
>>Hedwig.fly()
flap flap flutter flip
>>Dundee.sleep()
ZZZZZZ
>>Dundee.swim()
>>Dundee.wakeUp()
The animal is awake
>>Dundee.swim()
paddle paddle splish splash
>>Hedwig.sleep()
ZZZZZZ
```

To call a method on an object, we use *point notation*, wherein the relevant object is specified first, followed by a period, and then, on the right, by the desired method name. The following scheme is the result:

```
Object.Method()
```

NOTE *Make sure that the method is immediately followed by two parentheses when you wish to call it, even if no arguments are passed.*

Hedwig and Dundee are instances of different base classes: bird and crocodile. Both classes, however, have the same base class: animal. Both instances then have all of the attributes: methods (like __init__ and sleep) and instance variables (like age and gender) of the animal class. In addition to these attributes, Hedwig has the attributes of the bird class (the fly method) and Dundee has the attributes of the crocodile class (the swim method). This allows us to define code once that is to be shared by all animal subclasses. If we add to or modify the animal class in the future, all instances of any subclasses would automatically inherit the change.

Summary

You now have the basic knowledge required to explore using Python to extend your applications and Zope itself. By better understanding Python, you greatly enhance your ability to understand and leverage the inner workings of the Zope core.

In the chapters that follow, we will put Python to work for us in example applications and products.

14

SCRIPTING ZOPE WITH PYTHON

Zope provides two facilities to integrate Python functions directly into the Zope environment: Zope Python scripts and external methods. Using the techniques introduced in this chapter, you can code complex business logic and functionality directly in Python that you can directly access from other Zope objects, such as DTML documents and methods.

14.1   Zope Python Scripts

Zope Python scripts are a feature of Zope version 2.3 and newer. They allow you to include Python code directly inside Zope through the management screen, just like DTML. Although there are some restrictions on the built-in functions and Python modules you can access, Python scripts are an extremely powerful way to code complex business logic for your Zope application.

Some of the things you *cannot* do with Python scripts include accessing files on the file system, calling system programs, importing arbitrary modules, and calling restricted Python methods in the Zope core. To do these things you still need to use an external method or Python product (described in section 14.2 and Chapter 15). You can, however, call any other unrestricted methods or objects, perform complex calculations or data manipulation, and import select Python modules.

14.1.1 Creating Python Scripts

You create a Python script as you do other Zope objects by using the folder's add menu; in the menu, select Script (Python). On the form that appears, specify an id, an optional title, and an optional file containing the Python code to be uploaded into the script. Then click on the Add button to create the script object, as shown in Figure 14-1.

Figure 14-1: Add Python script screen

Once you have created your script, you should see the management screen shown in Figure 14-2.

The first three management screen tabs—Edit, Bindings, and Test—are specific to Python scripts.

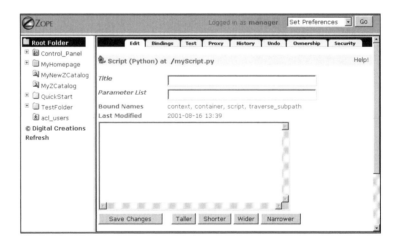

Figure 14-2: Python script management screen

14.1.2 Edit Management Screen

This management screen is similar to the edit screens of DTML documents and methods. Python scripts also have an additional *Parameter List* property under the title that allows you to specify the arguments needed to call the method (if any). The parameter list is a comma-separated list of argument names that must be passed to your script. These arguments are the input values for your script to process.

Use the large edit window to enter the Python code for your script. You do not need to write a def statement for your function here because it is automatically created for you by Zope; enter only the body code of the script.

14.1.3 Bindings Management Screen

The Bindings management screen lets you manage the bound variable names of your script, which contain special values automatically passed to your script by Zope. These variable names are used to access the Zope environment from your script. In this screen, you can edit the names of these values, examine their current settings, or remove a bound variable completely by clearing its name.

Figure 14-3 shows the Bindings management screen for a Python script:

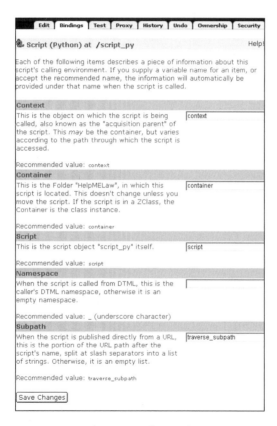

Figure 14-3: Bindings screen for a Python script

Below is a description of each bound variable available to your script:

context   This variable is the object that the script is called on. Python scripts, like DTML methods, can act like methods of any object. Because context is a Zope object, the rules of acquisition apply, and you can access other objects or attributes that are in the acquisition path of context as well. For example, entering context.REQUEST will return the REQUEST object via acquisition.

container   This variable is the folderish object that contains the script; its value never changes unless the script is moved. Use this variable to access other methods and attributes from the container (including objects in the acquisition path). If the script is called directly via its absolute URL, this value will be the same as context's.

script   This variable is the script object itself. You can use it within your script to access attribute values of the script.

namespace   This variable is used to access the DTML namespace if the script is called from DTML. It is not bound to a variable name by default; if you need it, it is generally bound to the underscore (_) variable, though you can pick any name that you like.

subpath   This variable is used to pass data provided in the URL path to the script. By default it is bound to the variable name traverse_subpath. If the script is called directly via a URL, this variable will contain a list of any additional path names following the name of the script in the URL. For example, if you have a Python script named "pythonScript" in your root folder, the client browser will request the following URL:

```
http://localhost:8080/pythonScript/python/is/great
```

Although this URL does not point to a real object, because Python scripts are not folderish, Zope passes the subpath following the script name in the traverse_subpath variable. In this case, the value of traverse_subpath in your script would be:

```
['python', 'is', 'great']
```

You can use the subpath data to pass parameter data to Python scripts via the URL without using the CGI query notation.

14.1.4 Test Management Screen

This screen allows you to test your Python script by giving it values for any parameters you have specified. If you are not using the script as a method for other objects, you can use this screen as a debugging tool. If your script relies on specific context values, however, it will not be as useful.

14.1.5 Importing Modules into Python Scripts

Select Python modules, functions and classes provided with Zope are available for use in Zope Python scripts. The standard Python modules (string, math, and random) may be imported directly into Python scripts.

A suite of functions has been packaged with Zope for safe use in Pythons scripts. To access them, place the following import statement at the top of your Python script:

```
import Products.PythonScripts.standard
```

This import statement gives you access to the following functions:

Function	Description	Example	Result
html_quote(value)	Replaces characters signifcant to HTML with their corresponding HTML entities.	html_quote('>>Click Here<<')	>>Click Here<<
url_quote(value)	Escapes characters significant in URLs.	url_quote('spaced out')	spaced%20out
url_quote_plus (value)	Like url_quote, but substitutes + for spaces. Used for CGI variable values.	url_quote('spaced out')	spaced+out
newline_to_br (value)	Replaces newline characters in a string with HTML tags.	newline_to_br("""Home on the range""")	Home on the range
structured_text (value)	Renders a string containing structured text into HTML.	structured_text('_This_ *is* **structured text**.')	<u>This</u> is structured text.
whole_dollars (value)	Formats a number as a whole dollar amount.	whole_dollars(4.5)	$4
dollars_and_cents (value)	Formats a number as dollars and cents.	dollars_and_cents(4.5)	$4.50
thousand_commas (value)	Formats a large number with commas at every thousands place.	thousand_commas(1000000L)	1,000,000

14.1.6 Calling Python Scripts from DTML

Python scripts can be called with any DTML tag that uses the name or expr attributes. Normally, however, you will use dtml-var or dtml-call to execute a Python script: dtml-var if the script returns a value to be inserted, and dtml-call if no insertion is desired or no value is returned by the script. If the Python script has no parameters in its parameter list you can call it using the name="..." notation as shown here:

```
<dtml-var name="pythonScript">
```

If you specified a variable name for the namespace binding (see section 14.1.3 above), Zope will automatically pass any parameter values implicitly from the namespace when you call the Python script by name.

You can also use an expression to call a Python script with no parameter as shown:

```
<dtml-var expr="pythonScript()">
```

However, if a parameter list was specified for the script, and you want to pass it values explicitly, the expr="…" notation must be used, with the parameter argument values placed between the parenthesis as follows:

```
<dtml-var expr="pythonScript(arg1, arg2,…)">
```

In the above examples, the context-bound variable in the script would be set to whatever object is at the top of the DTML namespace. To specify a different object as the context, use the dot notation when calling the script, which makes the script act as a method of the object specified. For example:

```
<dtml-call expr="myObject.pythonScript(arg1, arg2,…)">
```

In the above example, the context variable would be bound to myObject when the script executes.

NOTE *For the above example to work, pythonScript must be in the acquisition path of myObject so that myObject can acquire pythonScript from its namespace.*

14.1.7 Example: Creating a Zope Python Script

Because Python scripts are often used to perform calculations, you may need to create a script to return the sum of a list of numbers. Although you could code this in DTML, Python is far easier and more readable.

Begin by creating a Python script by choosing Script (Python) from the folder's add menu. Type total for the id and click Add. You should have a new, blank Python script. For the Parameter List, enter the word list, which tells Zope that your script will take a single parameter, "list", the list of numbers you are totaling. Next, enter the code from Listing 14-1 into your script body, taking care to indent the code as shown:

Listing 14-1: The total Python script

```
1:    total = 0
2:    for item in list:
3:        total = total + item
4:    return total
```

Take a quick look at this code. First, we set the variable total to zero (Line 1), which will be used to accumulate the total of the list items. Next, we begin a for loop (Line 2), which sets the variable item to each element of list in turn and executes the code in the indented block (Line 3). (This code block simply adds each item to the total.) In Line 4, we use the Python return statement to exit the script returning the value of total to the caller.

Once you have entered the code for this script, click on Save Changes. Your screen should look like Figure 14-4.

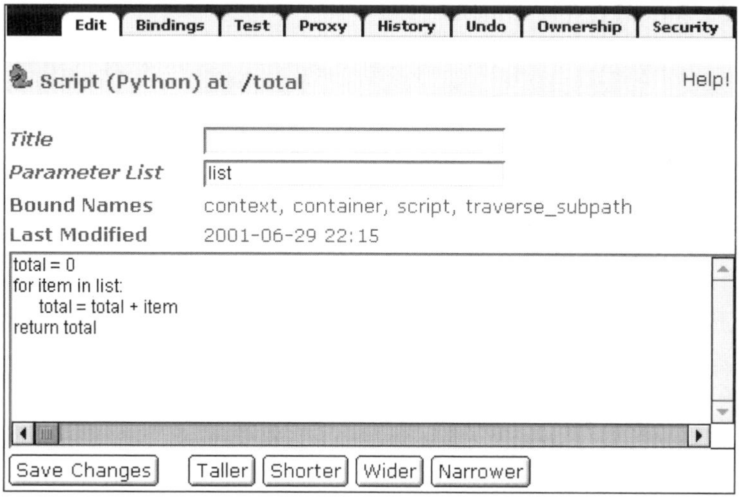

| Edit | Bindings | Test | Proxy | History | Undo | Ownership | Security |

🐍 Script (Python) at /total   Help!

Title	
Parameter List	list
Bound Names	context, container, script, traverse_subpath
Last Modified	2001-06-29 22:15

```
total = 0
for item in list:
    total = total + item
return total
```

[Save Changes]   [Taller] [Shorter] [Wider] [Narrower]

Figure 14-4: The total Python script

14.1.8 Using the Script from DTML

The following code could be used to add the numbers 10, 21, 35, 6, and 14:

```
<dtml-var expr="total([10, 21, 35, 6, 14])">
```

The result of processing this code would be

```
86
```

As an exercise, you might try creating a form that allows the user to submit a list of numbers with an action that would call the total Python script and display the result. Here's a hint: If you create multiple input fields on a form with the same name and suffix it with :int:list, Zope will automatically convert the values to integers and combine the contents of these fields into a list. For example, the input form code could look something like the following:

```
<input type="text" name="values:int:list"><br>
<input type="text" name="values:int:list"><br>
<input type="text" name="values:int:list"><br>
...
```

When submitted, this code would create a list of integers named "values" in the REQUEST object that could then be passed directly to the total script.

14.2 External Methods

External methods interface with external files (modules) that contain Python methods. These files must have the extension .py and must be located in the Extensions directory of your Zope installation.

External methods allow you to extend the full power of Python into Zope because, when you use them, you are not restricted to specific modules and functions as you are when using only Python scripts. However, you cannot edit external methods from within Zope, so you must be able to write files into your Zope installation directory to create external methods.

NOTE *Be careful to code your external methods to avoid creating security holes in your server that can be exploited through the web.*

14.2.1 Creating External Methods

If you do not have an Extensions directory in your Zope installation directory, create one now; you'll then create the external method objects using the Zope management screen. These external method objects expose the external Python code so that they can be called from within Zope.

The following explanation assumes that you are in the folder in Zope where you want to create the external method object. On the folder's add menu, you will find the entry for creating external methods as shown in Figure 14-5.

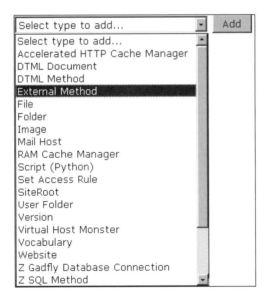

Figure 14-5: The add objects menu

Figure 14-6 shows the add external method form:

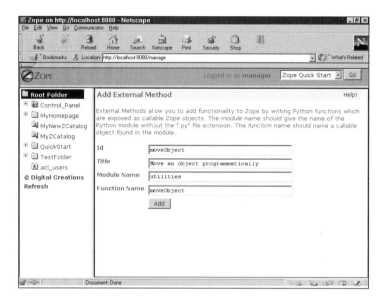

Figure 14-6: Creating an external method

NOTE

Make sure that the file you create containing the Python method code is in the Extensions directory (and that it has the file extension .py) before you create the external method object, or Zope will not be able to find the file to link to the object.

Zope requires the following information when creating external methods:

Id
As with all objects in Zope, an external method needs an id for it to be accessed in Zope.

Title
As with all objects in Zope, a title is not essential for an external method. It is, however, advisable to enter one to provide a brief description of the object.

Function name
You must enter the name of the Python method you want to access with this external method.

Python module file
Enter the name of the Python file that contains your methods. Make sure that you enter the name *without* the file extension (.py). Otherwise, because Zope automatically adds the extension, Zope will search for a file ending with .py.py.

Once you have completed the form and clicked Add, you are returned to the Contents screen of the current folder, where you should see the external method you just created.

14.2.2 Accessing Python Methods with DTML

You can access Python methods created in this way using the following DTML command:

```
<dtml-var expr="Name_of_External_Method(arg1, arg2,...)">
```

Here, arg1, arg2, and so on are arguments that your Python method may need. If your method requires no arguments, you can call it with nothing between the parenthesis, but you cannot omit them entirely. The DTML command below shows how to call an external method that takes no arguments:

```
<dtml-var expr="Name_of_External_Method()">
```

14.2.3 Example: Creating an External Method

As an example, let's create an external method that will move an object from one folder to another programmatically (like cut and paste). Because we will need to access internal Zope methods and attributes that cannot be accessed from DTML and Python scripts, we'll code this in an external method. Listing 14-2 contains the Python code for the moveObject external method; save this code to a file named "utilities.py" in your Zope Extensions directory:

Listing 14-2: moveObject External Method

```
1:    def moveObject(id, fromFolder, toFolder):
2:        """Move an object from folder to folder programmatically"""
3:        object = fromFolder[id]
4:        toFolder._setObject(id, object.aq_base)
5:        fromFolder.manage_delObjects([id])
```

In Line 1 of Listing 14-2, the def statement defines the method and specifies the arguments it needs. The method takes three arguments: id (the id of the object being moved), fromFolder (the folder containing the object), and toFolder (the folder to move the object into). The next line (Line 2) is a doc string used to more clearly describe the method's function.

In the body of the method, the first thing to do is to retrieve the object to be moved (given that the method started with just its id) and store it in a variable. Because folderish objects in Zope act like dictionaries, with the keys being the ids of subordinate objects, the dictionary lookup syntax is used to retrieve the object from fromFolder given its id (Line 3) and then store it in the variable named "object."

Once the object has been retrieved, it is put into toFolder (Line 4). Folderish objects use the method _setObject for this purpose, which takes two arguments: the id of the object and the object itself.

NOTE *Zope methods named with a leading underscore are called "private methods" and cannot be called from DTML or Python scripts. Private methods can, however, be accessed from external methods such as this one.*

Take a closer look at Line 4 of this method. Notice in the second argument of _setObject that we are accessing the attribute aq_base of object, a special, restricted acquisition attribute that bears explanation.

Remember that Zope objects support acquisition so that you can retrieve attributes that lie above an object in the Zope hierarchy. This is still true of Zope objects used in external Python code. When you retrieve the object from its original folder (fromFolder) in Line 3, it comes with the acquisition path that includes this folder; this is called the acquisition wrapper. Because you are moving the object to a different folder, this acquisition path is no longer valid, so you must strip it from the object.

All objects that support acquisition (essentially, all objects stored in Zope) have the restricted attribute aq_base, which returns the object stripped of its acquisition wrapper. _setObject will give the object a new acquisition path in the context of the new folder it is moved to (toFolder). Like _setObject, aq_base can be accessed only from external Python code (because it also strips the acquired security settings from the object).

Once you have the object in its new folder, you need only remove it from the original folder. Do so by calling the manage_delObjects method of fromFolder and passing it the id of the object.

NOTE *Because of the way Python handles objects, this call does not really fully delete the object—it just removes its old reference from the original folder.*

14.2.4 Creating an External Method Object in Zope

You can now create an external method object using the Zope management screen to establish the connection to the method in your file utilities.py. Add an external method object to your root folder in Zope with the following parameters:

Id	moveObject
Title	Move an object programmatically.
Function name	moveObject
Python module file	utilities

Here, moveObject is the name of the external method object, which is also the name of the Python method in your code (although these may often be the same name, they need not be). The name of the Python module where the method moveObject() is stored in the Extensions directory is "utilities." Figure 14-7 shows the form for creating the external method.

With this external method, you can now use DTML to move an object within Zope. Because your method returns no result, you would use dtml-call to execute it. For example, to move an object named "package1" from a folder named "hold" to a folder named "shipped," use this line of DTML code:

```
<dtml-call expr="moveObject('package1', hold, shipped)">
```

```
Add External Method                                          Help!

External Methods allow you to add functionality to Zope by writing Python
functions which are exposed as callable Zope objects. The module name
should give the name of the Python module without the ".py" file extension.
The function name should name a callable object found in the module.

Id              moveObject
Title           move an object from folder to folder
Module Name     utilites
Function Name   moveObject
                 Add
```

Figure 14-7: Creating the external method moveObject

14.2.5 Summary of Creating External Methods

To create and use external methods, do the following:

1. Create the Python module to contain the method using a text editor and save
    it in Zope's Extensions directory.
2. Create the external method object that links to the Python method.
3. Call the external method from Zope using DTML or Python in a Python script.

14.3   Using External Methods to Change Roles and Permissions

Another, more comprehensive example of an external method applies to users,
roles, and permissions. You'll create the external method and then use it to activate various permissions for several roles while deactivating the Acquire permission settings? option for these permissions. (For a review of roles and permissions,
see Chapter 6.)

This method is useful when you want to switch off acquisition for certain permissions to assign different permissions to the roles (and consequently, to the
users with these roles) by setting them individually.

14.3.1 Changing Permissions for Multiple Roles

You can call external methods easily using a number of DTML commands. As a
result, you can save a lot of time and effort changing the permissions for different
objects by simply calling this external method repeatedly (according to the number of objects whose permissions you need to change) in a DTML method or
Python script instead of changing the individual permissions by hand.

To change multiple permissions simultaneously or to change several roles for
one object, pass the external method lists of roles and permissions to be changed
in the arguments permissions_list and roles_list. The code in Listing 14-3 permits
the external method to work with these lists.

Listing 14-3: The permission() method: external method for changing permissions (the roles and permissions to be changed are variable)

```
def permission(object, roles_list, permissions_list):
    Changes the distribution of permissions for the roles assigned to
    the object which are specified in roles_list
    old_permissions = object.permission_settings()
    new_permissions = []
    permissions_for_role = []
    for item in old_permissions:
        for item2 in permissions_list:
            if item['name'] == item2:
                permissions_for_role.append(item['name'])
        if item['name'] not in permissions_list:
            new_permissions.append(item['name'])
    object.manage_acquiredPermissions(new_permissions)
    for role in roles_list:
        object.manage_role(role, permissions_for_role)
```

The loop variables item and item2 pull the relevant element from the corresponding list.

Once you have created an external method object in Zope that links to this function, you can call it from DTML or Python scripts to call the Python function above. To do so, two lists must be passed: the list of roles to be changed and the list of permissions to be changed for this role. The DTML syntax required to do this is

```
<dtml-var "name_of_ext_method(['Role1','Role2'], ['Permission1','Permission2'])">
```

The permission() external method in the permissions.py file uses the following Python methods already present in Zope:

- permission_settings()
- manage_acquiredPermissions()
- manage_role()

NOTE *To see how these methods work, view the Role.py module in the lib/python/AccessControl directory.*

14.3.2 permission_settings()

To better understand the permission method, take a closer look at the results returned by permission_settings(). This method returns all permissions for the objects it is used on, presenting them as a list of dictionaries. Each element in the dictionary list has the following form:

```
{'acquire': 'CHECKED',
 'roles': [{'name': 'p0r0', 'checked': ''},
           {'name': 'p0r1', 'checked':''},
           {'name': 'p0r2', 'checked': 'CHECKED'},
           {'name': 'p0r3', 'checked': ''}],
 'name': 'Access contents information'}
```

The keys of each dictionary contain the following information:

'acquire'   This field is the string value 'CHECKED' if Acquire permission settings? is activated; otherwise, it is an empty string.

'roles'   This field contains a list of dictionaries. The value of 'name' is a combination of letters and numbers (p*a*r*b*). For example, 'p0r0' indicates the zero (first) permission (p = permission) of the zero role (r = role); the value is zero because Python starts counting from zero. If the value of 'checked' is 'CHECKED', the relevant role has full permission.

'name'   This is the name of the permission. As you can see in this example, the name of the permission corresponds to the value of *a* in the 'p*a*r*b*' values of the 'roles' field: 'Access contents information' is the first permission value, with an index of zero.

> **NOTE**   *The values* a *and* b *in the keys listed above indicate the position of the permissions and the roles as seen in the Security view of the object: from top to bottom for the Acquire permissions settings? list and from left to right for permissions.*

14.3.3 The Permission Method Step by Step

Take a closer look at the code for the permission method. First, it saves the object's current permission assignments and create two new empty lists:

```
old_permissions = object.permission_settings()
new_permissions = []
permissions_for_role = []
```

Next, it begins looping through the object's permission assignments:

```
for item in old_permissions:
```

Then, it iterates through the list of permissions to be changed that was passed in the argument permissions_list:

```
for item2 in permissions_list:
```

For each permission in permissions_list, it checks to see whether it matches the current element of the first for loop:

```
if item['name'] == item2:
```

If it does, the permission is stored in a list to be used later to set the permission for the roles

```
permissions_for_role.append(item['name'])
```

Next, it checks to see whether to deactivate the Acquire permission settings? option for the permission by checking to see if the current permission of the outer for loop was passed in the permission_list argument. If not, it adds the permission to a list to be deactivated, as follows:

```
if item['name'] not in permission_list:
new_permissions.append(item['name'])
```

This process is then repeated using the outer for…in… loop for the remaining elements in the current permission assignment list. Once the entire list has been used, the Acquire permission settings? option for the relevant permissions is deactivated for all permissions in the new_permissions list:

```
object.manage_acquiredPermissions(new_permissions)
```

Finally, the permissions for the roles are changed. To do this, each role in role_list is passed to the manage_role method of the object:

```
for role in role_list:
object.manage_role(role,permissions_for_role)
```

14.3.4 Using the permissions.py Method

Save the Python function code above to a file named "permissions.py" in the Zope Extensions directory. Create a folder named "Test," and in it create an external method object with the following details:

Id	setPermissions
Function name	permission
Python module file	permissions

NOTE *When you specify the Python module file, be sure to write* permissions, *not* permissions.py.

For example, to set all permissions on selected roles in the Test folder and deactivate Acquire permission settings?, create a Python script in the Test folder. This Python script takes no parameters. Once you enter the Python code shown in Listing 14-4 in the script, you can run it by clicking the Test tab. To see the result of executing the script, take a look at the Security screen of the Test folder.

Listing 14-4: Python script that uses setPermissions

```
1:    permissions_list = []
2:    for permission in container.permission_settings():
3:         permissions_list.append(permission['name'])
4:    container.setPermissions(container, ['Friends', 'Owner'], permissions_list)
```

Take a closer look at this script's code. First, we set the variable permissions_list to an empty list (Line 1). Then we open a for loop (Line 2) that steps through the results of calling the permission_settings() method on the container (Test). (It will be accumulating the permission names into this variable next.) (Recall from section 14.3.2 that this method returns a list of dictionaries that supply the permission information for the object.)

Each time through the loop, the variable permission is set to the next permission dictionary in the list. Each dictionary has a key name that contains the name of the permission. Inside the for loop, it appends each name to the permissions_list variable (Line 3).

Once the loop is completed, the permissions_list variable contains the names of all the permissions available for the Test folder. It then calls the external method setPermissions, passing it the roles Friends and Owner and the list of permissions gathered above. The external method grants every permission on Test to these two roles and deactivates the Acquire permission settings? option for every permission as well.

14.3.5 The createUser() Method

As a final example, you will create an external method to create users in the current folder. To do this, you first need to determine whether a User folder already exists in the specified folder. If no such folder exists, you must create one before you can add the new user, as shown in Listing 14-5.

Listing 14-5: The createUser() method

```
import AccessControl
def createUser(self, name, pwd, confirm, roles, domains, REQUEST, RESPONSE):
    Create a new user and an acl_user folder, if necessary
    in a specific folder """
    try:
        folder=AccessControl.User.UserFolder()
        self._setObject('acl_users',folder)
    except:
        pass
    self.acl_users._addUser(name, pwd, confirm, roles, domains, REQUEST)
    RESPONSE.redirect('index_html')
```

14.3.5.1 The try . . . except . . . Command

This method creates both a User folder and a user if no User folder exists. If a User folder exists, the method generates an error because only one acl_users User folder can exist in a folder at one time.

To prevent this error from being returned to the user, use the Python try...except... statement to create a conditional statement that will depend on whether an error message occurs (an exception). At first, assume that no User folder exists and it attempts to create one (the instructions are located between try and except commands). If an error occurs in these instructions, execution moves to the except statement. This method simply uses the pass statement here, which does nothing.

The following is a schematic representation of the try...except... command:

```
try:
        Create User Folder
except:
        Do nothing
```

Look first at the instructions for creating the User Folder. User Folder objects are instantiated from the UserFolder class of the User module in the AccessControl module. In the first line of the method, the command import AccessControl retrieves this module for use here. To traverse through the modules to the class, use the dot notation shown below:

```
folder=AccessControl.User.UserFolder()
```

This creates an instance of the UserFolder class and stores it in the variable: folder. Now, we have a User Folder instance, but still must put it into the Zope folder where the user is to be created. The next line does so using the folder's _setObject method, just as in the first external method: moveObject (section 14.2.3). The folder to use is passed in the self argument of the method. The following line puts the User Folder into the folder specified in self:

```
self._setObject('acl_users', folder)
```

The two arguments for _setObject are the id ('acl_users') and the object (the User Folder instance stored in folder). If an acl_users User Folder already exists in the folder self, an error will occur, which will cause execution to skip down to the except statement. If no acl_users existed previously, then this call will succeed and add one.

At this point in the code, we know we have an available User Folder. All that's left now is to add the user to it. The built-in _addUser() method of the User folder is used to do so. Because we created a User folder with the id acl_users, this method can be accessed from the folder specified in self as follows:

```
self.acl_users._addUser(name, pwd, confirm, roles, domains, REQUEST)
```

We have successfully added the User Folder (if necessary) and the new user to it. In the last line, we redirect the browser back to the index_html method, because there is no result to be returned.

```
RESPONSE.redirect('index_html')
```

Summary

You have now learned how to integrate Python code into Zope both internally in Python scripts and externally in external methods. With these tools, you can code complex operations that would be cumbersome in DTML and also utilize restricted features and functionality of Zope. You now have the knowledge to enhance your Zope applications through Python.

In Chapter 15 we will explore another way of extending Zope through Python, by using Python products.

15

ZOPE PRODUCTS

Although you can use the Zope management screen to create an application, doing so can be cumbersome if you need to use a lot of Python code either in external methods or scripts. In such cases, it makes much more sense to create a Zope *product* to store your application's classes, methods, and interface in Python and DTML files in the filesystem.

This approach has several advantages:

- You have complete access to all Zope and Python modules and use the numerous built-in Zope base classes to build your own objects.

- You can use text editors more suited to programming (such as emacs), instead of using a web browser.

- You can use versioning systems (such as CVS) to allow several programmers to work on the same product files simultaneously.

- You can conveniently distribute and install your Zope product on multiple Zope servers or even contribute it to the Zope community as open source software.

- Your code is insulated from content managers or others working in the Zope management screen who are not programmers, and you can tailor your product's management interface for them.

- Your data (in the ZODB) and your code (in the product) are kept separate, making it easier to upgrade or replace code without disturbing the data or vice versa.

Products are a powerful way to encapsulate Zope applications and object classes, but they often require more diligence, attention to detail, and knowledge of the Zope core than does coding in the Zope management screen. Although the development time may be longer for a product-based approach, the payoffs in terms of portability, reuseability, power, and control are often worth it. It is not uncommon, however, for applications to be prototyped through the web using only DTML and ZClasses (because of their rapid development time) and then ported to Python-based products for production.

To show you how to use Zope in conjunction with roles, permissions, and users, we will create a simple product called "Website." The key points we present focus on this particular sample product, but several more general points apply to all products.

Our sample product will allow you to create a website that will permit certain visitors to log in and create, edit, and delete users. It will not be particularly complex or demanding to write. Nevertheless, the structures you will create for this example are fundamental to the creation of all products and to handling Zope users, roles, and permissions programmatically.

15.1   A Tool for Creating Objects

Products are an important tool for creating custom objects in Zope. In a product, you can encapsulate all of the components needed to create and manage a website application, which is essentially Zope's main purpose.

Many products will enable a Zope manager to create instances of the product in Zope, which in our case is an actual website. And, of course, the manager can create multiple instances of the website if desired.

The manager sees the second-tier view of the product, in the Zope management screen. A normal site user sees the product in the third tier, which displays the product's top level user interface. The user is generally unaware of the product itself and does not see it directly; it fits in seamlessly with the rest of the Zope site. Only the product's added functionality is apparent to the user in the third tier.

NOTE   *Because products can usually be instantiated many times throughout a Zope application, they can often serve as a customizable framework that may be adapted to a user's requirements throughout the application.*

15.2   Constructing a Product

Products are coded externally to Zope, using text editors. All essential Python methods and objects needed for creating a product instance in Zope (DTML methods and so on) are created with a text editor and stored in the product directory. (DTML methods are created in the product directory as text files with the file extension .dtml.)

The following sections describe the various files needed to construct our sample Website Zope product.

15.2.1 Bootstrapping the Product

We need a mechanism that will provide us with an instance of the product—something that will actually create an instance for us. This mechanism must be included in our product so that the Zope manager using the product can create an instance using the Zope management screen.

Constructor methods coded in Python actually create the instance. These methods are registered for use by Zope but can also be used elsewhere in a product (see section 15.4.4 for more information on the main constructor method of the Website product).

Among other things, registering these methods causes the product to appear in the add menu of folderish objects, with a name that is the metatype we assign to our product's class. Our example will use the metatype "Website."

The product also provides a form that users complete when they choose the product's metatype from the add menu. When this form is submitted, the appropriate constructor method is called to create the product instance in the Zope folder.

To accomplish these operations, your product will include not only Python code and modules, but also DTML files for the forms, management, and user interface of your product, as well as additional files such as images, data, and configuration files. These ancillary files are often exposed to Zope via wrapper classes that, for example, can convert a DTML text file into a DTML method object (see section 15.4.3 for details).

As with all objects in Zope (and Python and object-oriented languages as a whole), a product is based on one or more classes that ensure that all essential elements are "inherited" by each instance of the product. This class defines, among other things, the methods each instance of the product requires to perform its functions. The methods in our sample product are addNewWebsiteUser(), editWebsiteUser() and deleteWebsiteUser().

For a product to create instances within Zope, a class must be assigned to it and associated with the appropriate methods and other elements, such as icons. In our example product, we also call this class "website" (see section 15.4.2.3, "Class Definitions").

15.2.2 Necessary Components

To create a working product, we must create the following components:

- A subdirectory for the product in lib/python/Products to contain the product's files. When you start the Zope server, Zope will search the Products directory and register all products it finds, including new or changed ones. (See section 15.4.1.)

- The product directory must contain an __init__.py file, which Zope executes at startup to initialize and register the product. If you create Python modules in additional subdirectories inside your product, each subdirectory must also have an __init__.py file. (See section 15.4.5.1 for more information.)

- Your product must include a way for users to create an instance of it in Zope, including an entry (which is the metatype) in the folder add menu, as well as a form in which the user can enter the basic data for the instance. To provide this functionality, include the proper product registration code in the product's __init__.py, provide a DTML file to create the add form, and code a constructor method in the product's main module. (See sections 15.4.3, 15.4.4, and 15.4.5.)

- Files created by the product for visitors in the third tier (including HTML, DTML, and normal text) are created using a text editor and stored in a dtml subdirectory of the product directory with the .dtml file extension.

- To ensure that Zope can access the product's interface, the .dtml files in the product directory must be integrated into Zope as DTML methods. Consequently, the product code must contain a Python method that adds .dtml files as actual DTML methods inside Zope or that creates the DTML methods as attributes of the product's class. (See section 15.4.2.2.)

NOTE *When we say ".dtml file" we mean a file created in the product directory; "DTML Method" refers to the corresponding Zope object.*

15.2.3 User Structure

Let's have a look at the user structure, the major function of our sample product. We want to allow a specific group of visitors to our website to create new users and prevent users not in this group from doing so.

To accomplish the latter, we need to include Zope's security features in our product (see Chapter 6 for more information on the Zope security structure).

To accomplish the former, we'll use Zope's built-in Python methods to create a role (which we'll call "WebsiteUser") to which our authenticated users will belong. We'll then assign the appropriate permissions to this role to allow its members to create, edit, and delete users.

To differentiate between these two groups of visitors, we'll use Zope's password authentication. Our example requires a security system that distinguishes among visitors to the website and determines whether each has permission to create users. Visitors with this permission are considered authenticated users, but are prevented from accessing the Zope management screen.

15.2.4 Roles/Permissions Structure

We'll set the security settings in the Python module where we create the necessary role/permissions structure (see section 15.4.4, "The Constructor Methods of the Main Module") so that visitors to the website with permission to create users (that is, all visitors with the role WebsiteUser) cannot access the Zope management screen.

Although it is very easy to create users from the management screen, we want to restrict visitors to creating, editing, and deleting users in the third tier view (that is, via the website). They must not be allowed to access the management screen of Zope—which would allow them to do much more than just create users.

15.3 Product Construction at a Glance

To create a new Zope product and then a new product instance using the management screen, follow these general steps:

1. Create a directory in lib/python/Products of your Zope installation (see section 15.4.1).

2. Code the necessary files for the product and save them to the product directory. (See section 15.4.)

3. Restart the Zope server so that Zope will recognize the new product.

4. Select the product metatype from the folder's add list to access the form for creating a product instance (addWebsiteForm.dtml).

5. Complete and submit the form using the Add button to create an instance of the product.

15.3.1 Major Components

A Zope product's main components are as follows:

__init__.py, the product constructor, identifies the product and registers and initializes it in Zope's product list.

product.py, the product's main module, contains the Python code that instantiates your product in Zope (the constructor method), the product's class definition(s), and ancillary methods and functions. You can replace the name "Product" with any name you choose, but you must keep the file extension .py.

icon.gif is used as an icon for product instances. It appears to the left of the id of a product instance in the Zope management screen. (Zope icons measure 16×16 pixels.) Icons and other static product content are generally placed in a www subdirectory of the main product directory.

metatype is the unique identifier for your product's class(es). Each class added via the folder's add menu in the management interface must be assigned a unique metatype.

add.dtml contains the form used for creating a product instance. This form appears when you select the product from the folder's add menu. DTML files like this are generally placed in a DTML subdirectory of the product.

Python constructor methods create the instance and store it in Zope. (They are generally coded in the main module.)

Product classes define the data elements (properties) and methods available in the product's instances.

Additional .dtml files or image files, if necessary, including support files (discussed in section 15.4.1) to provide additional information on the product or on your own support methods (discussed in section 15.4.1.3).

15.3.2 Support Files

Add support files to a product to document it or to modularize its code, thus making it more readable and easier to maintain. You may include the following common product support files to enhance your product.

15.3.2.1   README.txt

This file can contain a description of your product, product license, or similar item. To see an example, go to the Zope folder Control_Panel/ Product_Management, click on the installed product, then highlight the README.txt file in the corresponding product directory; a README tab appears in the tab bar. When you click on this tab, the text in the README.txt file is displayed, as shown in Figure 15-1.

| Contents | Properties | Define Permissions | Undo | Find | README |

Figure 15-1: The README tab in the tab bar for a product

15.3.2.2   version.txt

The version number in this file appears after the product name in the Control Panel/Product Management screen in Zope, as shown in Figure 15-2.

| ☐ 🗄 beehivecal (Installed product beehivecal (Version 0.3.1)) | 2001-05-20 22:46 |

Figure 15-2: The version number appears after the product in the Product_Management screen

15.3.2.3   support.py

It is a good idea to create a file containing frequently needed Python methods so that you will not have to repeatedly create them in your product; you will be able to import them instead into your product's main module from the Python methods in the support.py file in your product directory. If your product automatically creates non-folderish objects (such as DTML documents/DTML methods, images, and so on) when you create an instance, the relevant files (file1.dtml, file2.dtml, image1.gif, and such) must also be located in the product's directory. If they are in a subdirectory of the product directory instead, make sure in your product that you enter the full paths to the files in Python commands used for creating the objects.

15.3.3 Putting It All Together

Figure 15-3 shows all of the components that make up a complete Zope product.

15.4   Creating the Website Product

We're now ready to build the Website product. In the following sections we will build and assemble all of the necessary components we've described, and when we've finished, we'll have a completed Zope product.

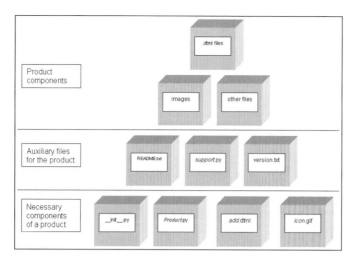

Figure 15-3: The individual components of a complete product

15.4.1 Create the Product Directory

To begin creating Website, you'll first create a new directory in the Zope product directory lib/python/Products/ called "Website." You'll then create in it a Python file called "Website.py," the product's main module (the full code for which you will find in Appendix C). This directory (and the subdirectories "dtml", "public", and "www") will contain the files listed in Table 15-1; the relationship between them is shown in Figure 15-4.

Table 15.1: The components of the sample product 'Website'

Filename	File Contents
__init__.py	The code for registering the product with Zope
icon.gif	The product's image/icon
addWebsiteForm.dtml	The add.dtml form for creating a product instance
Website.py	The main module containing the product's class definition and constructor method
index_html.dtml	Website's homepage
login_html.dtml	The password authentication page
addUserForm.dtml	A form for creating a new user
WebsiteUsers_list.dtml	A page for listing all existing users
edit_WebsiteUser.dtml	A form for modifying an existing user
new_WebsiteUser.dtml	A form for creating a new user
product_html.dtml	A sample page for a product description
standard_html_footer.dtml	A special standard_html_footer for Website
standard_html_header.dtml	A special standard_html_header for Website
about_us_html	A sample page that contains information about our company

NOTE *For a more detailed explanation of the individual files and the roles they play in the product, please see Appendix C.*

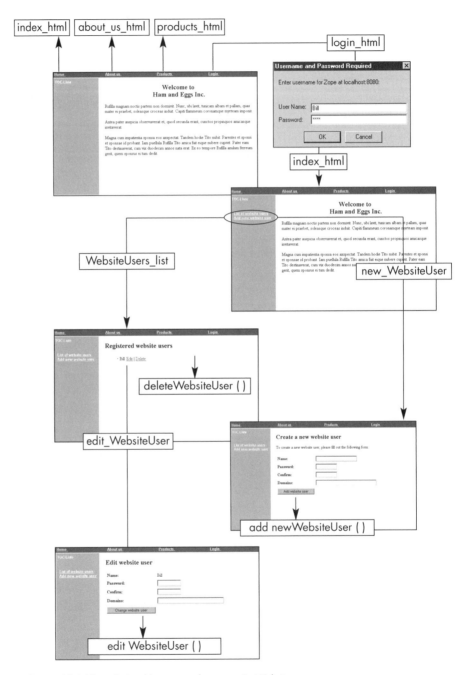

Figure 15-4: The relationship among the pages in Website

15.4.2 The Main Module: Website.py

The main module file of the product Website can be divided into five parts:

1. The various imports from other modules necessary to use specific methods and classes from these modules.

2. Utility methods used only to support and/or simplify certain actions.

3. The class definitions needed for the product.

4. The instance methods in the class and their security assertions.

5. The constructor method of the main module with which product instances can later be created in Zope.

The following section describes each section of the code in detail.

15.4.2.1   Imports

A product's main module contains the methods that create an instance, as well as all of the classes and methods that define the Website product.

In order to access the necessary Zope classes and Python modules needed by our product, we need to import them using the following code:

```
import Globals
from Globals import MessageDialog, DTMLFile
from AccessControl import ClassSecurityInfo
from AccessControl.Permission import Permission
from AccessControl.User import UserFolder
from OFS.Folder import Folder
import StringIO
```

Below is a description of the modules being imported:

The **DTMLFile** class allows us to create DTML method objects from DTML stored in files.

The **Permission** class assigns the necessary permissions to the new role called "WebsiteUser."

MessageDialog generates messages to the user in Zope.

AccessControl is a folder in the directory lib/python containing several modules (such as Permission.py, Role.py, User.py). These modules, in turn, contain methods (used for creating and editing User folders, users, roles, permissions, and so on) for managing security in Zope.

OFS is another folder in the lib/python directory. It contains modules that define most of the standard Zope objects, such as folders, DTML methods, and images.

The **StringIO** module is a standard Python module that allows you to work with text strings as though they are files. It will be used later in a method called "addDocsToFolder" that creates DTML methods in Zope.

15.4.2.2 Utility Functions

The sample product also needs the following utility functions:

- GetDTML(name)
- addDocsToFolder(theFolder, theDocs)

The method GetDTML(name) is a simplification of the method called "DTMLFile(name, globals())." It saves you having to write globals() over and over again. The code for this method is as follows:

```
def GetDTML(name):
    return DTMLFile(name, globals())
```

The method addDocsToFolder(theFolder, theDocs) adds the .dtml files in the product directory as DTML methods in the Zope folder specified by the argument theFolder. In our example, theFolder represents a new instance of our product. When an instance is created, DTML methods are added to it corresponding to .dtml files stored in a subdirectory of the Website product. These DTML methods can then be customized in Zope to suit the needs of the particular Website instance.

The code for the method addDocsToFolder is shown in Listing 15.1.

Listing 15.1: The addDocsToFolder() method

```
def addDocsToFolder(theFolder, theDocs):
    """ Adding several DTML Methods in Zope """
    errs=StringIO.StringIO()
    for key in theDocs.keys():
        id=key
        dtml,title=theDocs[key]
        try:
            thedtml=open(dtml.raw).read()
        except:
            raise RuntimeError, "Can't find " + dtml.raw
        try:
            theFolder.manage_addDTMLMethod(id, title=title, file=thedtml)
        except:
            traceback.print_exc(file=errs)
    errs.seek(0)
    return errs.read()
```

This method requires as arguments a folderish object (theFolder) and a dictionary (theDocs) listing the individual .dtml documents to be created. (See Table 15-2 for a list and descriptions of the .dtml files required for the sample product.) The dictionary must be created outside the class subsequently defined for the product (in section 15.4.2.3) and can be located at the start of the main module, as shown in Listing 15.1. (See Appendix C for the main module's source text.)

In Line 4 ("for key in theDocs.keys()") in Listing 15-1, the terms "key" and "keys" play two different roles: "key" is the for loop variable (which can have any permissible variable name you choose), whereas "keys" used in "theDocs.keys()" is a method of the dictionary that returns the keys as a list; you must use this method name for the loop to function correctly.

The dictionary's individual keys indicate the desired ids for the DTML methods (for example, standard_html_header), which are passed to the method addDocsToFolder using the "key" variable.

In our case, the values for each key are tuples. The first element of a tuple is the DTML object created from the appropriate .dtml file in the public subdirectory of the product directory (created by calling the method GetDTML() defined in Listing 15-2). The second element of each tuple indicates the title to be given to the DTML method in Zope (for example, "Website Standard Header").

To use the method addDocsToFolder() to create the desired DTML methods in an instance of our product, we need to pass the instance as the value for the argument theFolder, as you'll see when we actually call the method in the Website product. (See section 15.4.4.)

Listing 15.2: Dictionary of one object to be created in a product instance

```
Website_pages={
    'standard_html_header':
    (GetDTML('public/standard_html_header'),"Website Standard Header"),
    'standard_html_footer':
    (GetDTML('public/standard_html_footer'),"Website Standard Footer"),
    'index_html':
    (GetDTML('public/index_html'),"Website Index Page"),
    'login_html':
    (GetDTML('public/login_html'),"Password-Check"),
    'new_WebsiteUser':
    (GetDTML('public/new_WebsiteUser'),"Create new WebsiteUser"),
    'WebsiteUsers_list':
    (GetDTML('public/WebsiteUsers_list'),"List of WebsiteUsers"),
    'edit_WebsiteUser':
    (GetDTML('public/edit_WebsiteUser'),"Edit a WebsiteUser"),
    'products_html':
    (GetDTML('public/products_html'),"About our products"),
    'about_us_html':
    (GetDTML('public/about_us_html'),"About the company"),
    }
```

In general, the method addDocsToFolder() does the following:

• For each individual dictionary key passed in the dictionary theDocs, addDocsToFolder() attempts to read the corresponding .dtml file. If the file cannot be read, addDocsToFolder() assumes that the file does not exist at the specified location, and an error message appears ("Can't find ...").

- If the file is found, addDocsToFolder() attempts to create a DTML method using the file's data and the id and title specified in the dictionary by calling the built-in Zope constructor method for DTML method objects: manage_addDTMLMethod. If an error occurs during this process (say, if the id is illegal), then the corresponding error message is displayed.

15.4.2.3 Class Definitions

A *class* is a template used to create objects (instances). We use classes to define all of an instances' attributes, which may contain variable data (such as strings, lists, and dictionaries) or other objects (such as DTMLFile objects) or which may define methods that act on the instance and its data.

The main elements of the Website class are as follows (these will differ from other products):

- A definition of the class as a folderish object, specifying Folder as the base class.
- A definition of the properties for all instances of the product (accessed via the Properties tab in the management screen) that allow the webmaster to make certain changes to the instance. (In our case, only the title property is common to all instances.)
- A definition of new tabs to appear in the management screen tab bar of each instance of the product. These new tabs can be added to existing tabs or may appear on their own.
- The assignment of permissions to be associated with specific instance methods of the product in Zope (accessed via the Securities tab in the management screen). These expand the security model of the instance relative to other objects in Zope.
- The definition of methods available to authenticated users logged in to an instance of the product, including methods for creating, editing, and deleting users.

We'll call the Website product's class "Website." In a Python class definition, you can specify base classes (separated by commas) in parentheses following the class name. All attributes defined in the base classes become attributes of the new class you are defining (called a subclass). The Website class acts like an extended Zope folder, and we can therefore use the built-in Zope Folder class as a base class for Website. By using Folder as a base class, we get all of the capabilities of the Folder class in the Website class. As a result, instances of the Website can contain other objects, just as folders do; this is an example of inheritance.

NOTE *The Folder class has other functionality, such as a property sheet, and it contains many of the standard management screens. If you do not need all of these capabilities in your class, but you still need it to act folderish, you can use ObjectManager as a base class instead (OFS.ObjectManager.ObjectManager).*

Listing 15.3: Class declaration for the Website class

```
class Website(Folder):
    """This product was created by Katrin Kirchner"""
    name='Website'
    id='Website'
    meta_type='Website'
```

Once you have named the class you should include a doc string to describe it. The use of a triple-quoted string as shown in Listing 15.3 is standard practice so that the doc string can span several lines if needed.

15.4.2.4   name, id, icon, meta_type

Now we need to add some information relating to the class, including name, id, and meta_type. The items name and id indicate the name and id of the product.

Use meta_type to specify how your product or class (you may have more than one class in a product) will appear in the folder's add menu. Metatypes must be unique for each object class in Zope; an error will occur when loading the product if another product's class uses the same metatype.

15.4.2.5   Defining Security Info

To be able to properly secure access to a Website's methods, we need to create a *ClassSecurityInfo object*. We can use this object to make the appropriate security assertions for our class and its methods to prevent unauthorized access. In the website class, we create a ClassSecurityInfo object stored in the attribute "security" using this code:

```
security = ClassSecurityInfo()
```

We imported the ClassSecurityInfo class from AccessControl earlier in the module's code (see section 15.4.2.1).

NOTE *This security assertion mechanism first became available in Zope 2.3. Previously, security assertions were made by setting an attribute named __ac_permissions__ on your class. If you read product code developed by others, you are likely to see this method of access control. Although __ac_permissions__ is still supported, it is deprecated in favor of using ClassSecurityInfo.*

Next we will use the security object to make a class-wide security assertion. The declareObjectProtected method of ClassSecurityInfo is used to declare a permission that a user needs in order to access objects created from the class. We use the following code to require the user to have the View permission in order to access a Website instance:

```
security.declareObjectProtected('View')
```

We can make three security assertion on objects as a whole as described in the following table:

ClassSecurityInfo Method	Description
declareObjectPublic()	This, the default security setting, allows access to the object regardless of a user's permissions. This assertion applies only to the object itself; subobjects and methods are still private by default (see section 15.4.6.1 for details).
declareObjectPrivate()	Restricts access to the object from a browser and through-the-web code such as DTML or Python scripts. Use this setting for classes that are only used internally in a product, and which should not be accessible from the web.
declareObjectProtected (permissionName)	Restricts access to the object to users with the specified permission. Use this setting to allow Zope managers to control access to the object with the Security management tab.

15.4.2.6 Declaring Properties

Next we define the properties for the product, which are used for each instance of the class. In this case we only need the property title, which can be used to label the instances.

NOTE *Defining title as a property allows users to modify it through the Zope management screen. If you click the Property tab in an instance, you will see the properties defined for each instance.*

The _properties variable is a tuple, as shown in the following code. Each element of the tuple is a dictionary that describes a single property.

```
properties=(
        {'id': 'title', 'type': 'string', 'mode': 'w'},
        )
```

The individual key/value pairs represent the following:

Key Name	Value Description
id	This is the name of the property. Each property name must be unique for a given class or object.
type	Individual properties can be of different types, such as string, float, and integer.
mode	A property's mode indicates whether the property can be changed ('w' = writeable) or deleted ('d' = deletable) by a user. If the mode key is omitted, the default value 'wd' is used.

15.4.2.7 Adding Management Tabs

The Website.py file (shown in Appendix C) contains the manage_options variable, used to create additional tabs in the Zope management tab bar of instances of your product. Its code looks like this:

```
manage_options=OFS.Folder.Folder.manage_options+(
        #{'label': 'README', 'icon': icon, 'action': 'my_action', 'target': 'manage_main'},
        )
```

To make sure that you do not delete existing tabs from the Folder base class, open them using OFS.Folder.Folder.manage_options and then add your own tabs using +(...).

In this example, the line

```
#{'label':'README','icon':icon,'action':'README.txt','target':'manage_main'},
```

is commented using the hash, or pound, symbol (#) because we do not need new tabs for our product. (This line also appears in the product code with a hash symbol.) To add your own tabs, you must define each in a dictionary, as described in the following table:

Key Name	Value Description
label	Enter the text to appear on your tab.
icon	This assigns a special icon for your tab (optional).
action	Enter the page to be called up when you click on the tab.
target	The value manage_main indicates that the action is to be displayed in the frame on the right of the Zope screen—this is standard when you click on a tab (optional).

15.4.2.8 The Instance Methods in the Class

The instance methods in our class define the behavior and functionality of our class. The individual methods for the Website class can appear in any sequence. For example, Method A, called by Method B, need not appear first in the source text.

15.4.2.9 Securing the Instance Methods

When declaring an instance method for a class used in Zope, we must create the security assertion that controls access to the method. Instance methods in Zope have three modes of access control: public, private and protected. Public methods are available to all users (including anonymous ones), and can be called through the web by URL or from DTML or Python scripts. Private methods are restricted and may only be accessed from external Python code, such as that found in products or external methods. Protected methods can only be called by users with a specific permission and, like public methods, they are web accessible.

Three ClassSecurityInfo methods allow you to make security assertions on methods (and subobjects) of an object, as shown in the following table:

ClassSecurityInfo Method	Description
declarePublic(methodName)	Makes the specified method publicly accessible by all users, through the Web. Use this for innocuous methods that do not need to be secured, and which must be available to everyone including anonymous users.
declarePrivate(methodName)	This is the default. Methods declared as private cannot be directly accessed through the Web, so use this for methods that should not be exposed or published directly through Zope.
declareProtected (PermissionName, methodName)	Methods declared as protected are published only to users with the specified permission assigned to their role(s). Use this assertion to allow Zope managers to control access to the method via the Security management tab.

NOTE *Each of the above methods will also take multiple methodName arguments.*

NOTE *In order for Zope to properly recognize the security assertions of a class, you must call the InitializeClass function of the Zope Globals module (see section 15.5.2.13).*

15.4.2.10 The addNewWebsiteUser Method

The method addNewWebsiteUser() (shown in Listing 15.4) creates a new user, once it determines that no such user exists in the specified User folder. If a user with the same name exists, the method displays an error message (using Message-Dialog) then returns you to the new_user page.

As you can see in the listing, a security assertion is made for this method (using the ClassSecurityInfo object "security" defined in Section 15.4.2.5) before it is defined.

Listing 15-4: The addNewWebsiteUser() method for the Website product

```
# Allow users with the "Manage users" permission access to this method
security.declareProtected('Manage users', 'addNewWebsiteUser')

def addNewWebsiteUser(self, name, pwd, confirm, roles, domains, REQUEST, RESPONSE):
    """ Creates a new WebsiteUser if the user name does not exist already"""
    if self.acl_users.getUser(name):
        return MessageDialog(
            title   ='User already exists',
            message='There is already a user with this name.',
             action ='new_WebsiteUser'
        )
```

```
    else:
        self.acl_users._addUser(name, pwd, confirm, roles, domains, REQUEST)
        RESPONSE.redirect('index_html')
```

The addNewWebsiteUser() method uses a built-in private method, _addUser, of the user.py module to create a new user (see Chapter 8 for more information on this). The method's arguments are shown in Table 15-3.

Table 15-3: Data for creating a new user

Argument	Description
self	Instance of the product
name	The user's name
pwd	The user's password
confirm	Confirm password
roles	Roles for the user, as a list
domains	Internet domains from which the user can log in (as a list)
REQUEST	The REQUEST object (provided by Zope)
RESPONSE	The RESPONSE object (provided by Zope)

The addNewWebsiteUser() method is coded to first see whether the user name already exists in the User folder (acl_users) of the folder indicated with self. It does so using the method getUser(name), which returns a user object if one with that name exists and None if not. Because all user object values are considered a true value in Python and None is considered false, we can check the results of getUser(name) directly with an if statement to see if the user exists.

If the user exists, use MessageDialog to generate an HTML page that contains a message and an OK button. Clicking OK opens the URL specified by the action argument. The title argument indicates what should appear in the <HEAD> element of the HTML page for use as the title of the page.

If the user does not exist, a call is made to the _addUser method of the User folder in the instance of the product (a built-in private method that you can use to directly add a new user in Zope from Python). We pass to this method all information about the user to be created (username, password, and so on). Once this call is completed, we redirect the user to the home page of the WebSite instance (index_html).

The method addNewWebsiteUser() is now finished. If you have already created an instance of the product, any users already logged in to the website can use it to create new users.

NOTE *This method on its own is not enough to allow visitors to create new users. DTML methods must be created to build the website interface and, as mentioned above, to create the security model that authenticates users.*

15.4.2.11 The editWebsiteUser Method

The editWebsiteUser method (shown in Listing 15-5) is very short, because we do not initially need to check whether the user to be modified already exists in the User folder acl_users. The method editWebsiteUser() is called in the DTML method WebsiteUsers_List, which generates a list of users present in the User folder.

Listing 15-5: The method editWebsiteUser() for the Website product

```
# Allow users with the "Manage users" permission access to this method
    security.declareProtected('Manage users', 'editWebsiteUser')

    def editWebsiteUser(self, name, pwd, confirm, domains, roles, REQUEST, RESPONSE):
        """Changes existing WebsiteUser"""
        self.acl_users._changeUser(name,pwd,confirm,roles,domains)
        return MessageDialog(
            title   ='User changed',
            message='The user has been changed.',
            action ='index_html'
            )
```

The links Edit and Delete appear after the usernames when the user views the user list in the product. If you click on Edit, a form appears allowing you to edit the details for that user. If you click the Change User button on the edit form, this method is called and the data is changed.

The editWebsiteUser method takes the same arguments as addNewWebsiteUser().

The User folder has the method _changeUser() for changing a user; this method is used with the User folder acl_users, as follows:

```
self.acl_users._changeUser(name,pwd,confirm,roles,domains)
```

15.4.2.12 The deleteWebsiteUser Method

Now all we need is another method that allows authenticated users to delete users. As you know, authenticated users have access to a list of users in acl_users and, by clicking on a link, they can edit or delete that user. The link for deleting a user calls the method deleteWebsiteUser() (shown in Listing 15.14) and transfers the user's name to be deleted as a string. When you click Delete, the user is deleted immediately.

Listing 15-6: The method deleteWebsiteUser() for the Website product

```
# Allow users with the "Manage users" permission access to this method
    security.declareProtected('Manage users', 'deleteWebsiteUser')

    def deleteWebsiteUser(self, name):
```

```
"""Deletes a WebsiteUser"""
self.acl_users._delUsers([name])
return MessageDialog(
    title   ='User deleted',
    message='The user has been deleted.',
    action ='index_html'
    )
```

Because the method for deleting a user—_delUsers() (defined in User.py)—expects a list of user names as its argument, we must pass our single name in a list by putting square brackets around it. Although _delUsers() can delete more than one user at a time, we do not use this feature in our product.

```
self.acl_users._delUsers([names])
```

15.4.2.13 Initalizing the Class

We have now coded the entire Website class definition. In order for our security assertions to be properly recognized by Zope, we must add a line after the class definition that calls the InitializeClass function of the Globals module, passing our class as its argument:

```
Globals.InitializeClass(Website)
```

15.4.3 Defining the Constructor Form

In order for users to create instances of the Website class, we must provide a form that allows them to specify the necessary values for the new instance, such as its id and title. To do so, we define a DTML file in the Website product that contains the form's template. We then need to make this file into a DTML object that can be accessed from Zope.

15.4.3.1   addWebsiteForm.dtml

DTML files used with products are generally stored in a "dtml" subdirectory of the main product directory. Below is the listing for the addWebsiteForm.dtml file stored in the Website product's dtml directory:

```
<dtml-var standard_html_header>
<form action="manage_addWebsite" method=post>
<h2>Add a new Website</h2>
<p>The product Website is a folderish object with several DTML Methods
as well as a User Folder containing a user already created.</p>
<table>
<tr>
<th>Id:</th>
<td><input type=text name=id size=20></td>
<tr>
```

(continued on next page)

```
<th><em>Title:</em></th>
<td><input type=text name=title size=20></td>
<tr>
<td></td>
<td><input type=submit value=Add></td>
</table>
</form>
<dtml-var standard_html_footer>
```

As you can see, the only difference between this code and other DTML methods and documents we have created inside Zope is that this code is stored as a separate file.

15.4.3.2 Creating the Constructor Form Object

It is not enough to simply write the constructor form's DTML code into a file in the product's dtml directory. In order to make this form accessible by Zope, we must use this file to create a DTMLFile object, which is analogous to the DTML method objects made inside Zope. Zope will be able to access this DTMLFile once we have defined it as an attribute of the Website product. To do so, we add the following line of code to the Website.py module:

```
manage_addWebsiteForm=DTMLFile('dtml/addWebsiteForm', globals())
```

15.4.4 The Constructor Method of the Main Module

The constructor method creates an instance of a class, properly initializes it, and stores it in Zope. The principal steps we use to code the Website class's constructor method are:

1. Define the constructor method and its necessary arguments, such as id and title, which will be passed from the constructor form (manage_addWebsiteForm for Wesite).

2. Create an instance of the class (Website) and store it in a variable. (Our example uses the variable named instance.)*

3. Assign the id and title as attributes of the new instance.*

4. Define a User folder in the instance.

5. Establish a role for the instance (which, in our example, has the role named "authenticated users" with the permission for creating new users via the website).

6. Assign permissions to the roles.

7. Create the necessary DTML methods for the product instance in Zope using addDocsToFolder().

8. Change the permissions for one of the DTML methods so that visitors to the website who have the role User can create new users.

(See Appendix C for the entire constructor method code.)

Items marked with an (*) above are not specific to this product and would be performed by nearly all product constructors.

When you want to create an instance of the product, the constructor method of that product is called by the constructor form in the Zope management screen. (This is the form you see when you select the product (in our case, Website) from the add object menu of a folder.)

In our case, the form, located in the file addWebsiteForm.dtml, is called using manage_addWebsiteForm in the main module Website.py (see section 15.4.2.7). Once the id and title of the instance are entered in this form, they are passed to the addWebsite constructor method when you click Add; thus, id and title must be included in the declaration in addWebsite. Zope automatically passes the values from the form fields into these two arguments.

The following is the method definition for our product's constructor:

```
def manage_addWebsite(self, id, title, REQUEST=None):
    """Add a new Website"""
```

First, it creates an instance of the Website class and store it in a variable named "instance:"

```
instance=Website()
```

Next it assigns the instance an id and title from the argument values passed to the constructor.

```
instance.id=id
    instance.title=title
```

Because we want to create a User folder when the product instance is created, we create it by calling the UserFolder class and storing the resulting User Folder instance in the new variable named user_folder (UserFolder is a class defined in User.py). The following code does this:

```
user_folder=UserFolder()
```

Next we put the new user folder into our Website instance (instance) using the built-in method _setObject(), available for all folderish Zope objects. To indicate that _setObject is to be called on our Website instance, we use the Python dot notation as follows:

```
instance._setObject('acl_users', user_folder)
```

_setObject takes two arguments: The object's id (in this case, acl_users) and the object itself (which we stored in the user_folder variable).

We next create a new role called 'User' in the new Website instance. The relevant method, _addRole(), requires only the name of the role as its argument.

```
instance._addRole('WebsiteUser')
```

Now, we can set the permissions for the WebsiteUser role on the new Website instance. To set several permissions for the role, we create a list of the desired permission names, making sure they match exactly those shown in the Zope management screen's security tab.

```
p_list = ['Access contents information',
          'Manage users', 'View']
```

We can now run through this list step-by-step (for...in... loop) and assign each of these permissions to the WebsiteUser role.

```
for permission in p_list:
    p=Permission(permission,'',instance)
    p.setRole('WebsiteUser', permission in p_list)
```

Permissions are assigned to roles using the method setRole, which is called up via the permission p.setRole(...). As a result, the role is assigned to the permission and not the other way around.

To do so, we first assign the Permission class to a variable (in this case, p). This class requires the name of the permission ("permission"), the value (in this case, a blank string) and the object in which it will be used (in this case, instance).

Now that we have properly initialized the instance, we can put the new instance of our product into Zope with the following line:

```
self._setObject(id, instance)
```

NOTE *In this case, _setObject() is called on self. Zope passes the self argument to the constructor, it contains a reference to the folder where the user is creating the product instance.*

In section 15.6.2 we examined the method addDocsToFolder along with the pregenerated .dtml files as DTML methods in the instance of a product. The argument for addDocsToFolder that contains the DTML files to be created must be stored as a dictionary. Using the following call for the method addDocsToFolder, all of the DTML methods contained in the dictionary (called "Website_pages") are placed in the instance:

```
addDocsToFolder(instance, Website_pages)
```

15.4.4.1 Changing the Assignment of Permissions for login_html

Finally, we need to change the assignment of permissions for one of the DTML methods we have just created (namely login_html, which is used to authenticate visitors to our website) so that only those visitors who enter a valid username and password will be authenticated.

To use login_html for this purpose, we first deactivate acquisition (Acquire permission settings?) for its View permission, so that anonymous users will be forced to authenticate. We then activate the permission for the WebsiteUser role that is allowed to view the method. (For a more detailed explanation of Zope authentication, please refer to Chapter 6.)

This way to set permissions (other than using setRole()), although a bit complicated, is a good example of how to manipulate permissions programmatically:

```
old_permissions = self.permission_settings()
    new_permissions = []
    permissions_for_WebsiteUsers = []
    for item in old_permissions:
        if item['name']=='View':
            permissions_for_ WebsiteUsers.append(item['name'])
        else:
            new_permissions.append(item['name'])
    instance.login_html.manage_acquiredPermissions(new_permissions)
    instance.login_html.manage_role('WebsiteUser', permissions_for_ WebsiteUsers)
```

For the permission assignments on the Website instance, we use the assignment of permissions for the folder in which the instance is created. We get these assignments by calling the method permission_settings(). (See the end of Chapter 8 for a detailed description of this method.)

The permission_settings() provides a dictionary with all permissions and indicates the roles assigned these permissions. (Remember here that we receive a list of all available permissions.) Each dictionary element is processed, and we use the name keyword to obtain the names of the corresponding permissions. Within the loop that processes the dictionary, we determine which of two lists the permission belongs to and append its name to the appropriate one. (One list is later used to activate the permissions for the WebsiteUser role; the other list is needed to deactivate Acquire permission settings? for the appropriate permissions.)

To decide whether a permission belongs in the Activated or Deactivated list, you must know that the method responsible for activating and deactivating Acquire permission settings? (manage_acquiredPermissions()) expects a list of the permissions for which the corresponding checkbox is deactivated, because activated is the default setting for Acquire permission settings? in Zope. In contrast, the method that manages the permissions for a specific role (manage_role()) awaits a list of the permissions to be activated.

Once the loop has finished and both lists have been created, we can start setting the permissions. Because the permissions must be set specially for the DTML method login_html, the two methods manage_acquiredPermissions() and manage_role() must, of course, be called for this object.

If you see the Security screen for this DTML method after you create the instance, the permissions assignments should look like the one shown in Figure 15-5. In login_html in our example, we only need to change the View permission.

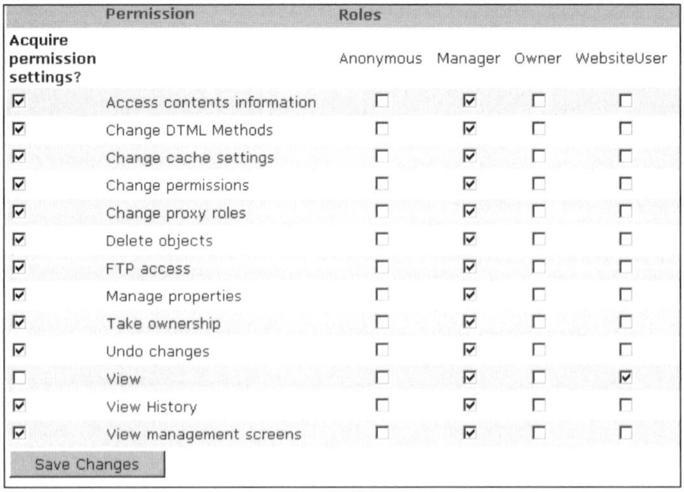

Acquire permission settings?	Permission	Anonymous	Manager	Owner	WebsiteUser
✓	Access contents information	☐	✓	☐	☐
✓	Change DTML Methods	☐	✓	☐	☐
✓	Change cache settings	☐	✓	☐	☐
✓	Change permissions	☐	✓	☐	☐
✓	Change proxy roles	☐	✓	☐	☐
✓	Delete objects	☐	✓	☐	☐
✓	FTP access	☐	✓	☐	☐
✓	Manage properties	☐	✓	☐	☐
✓	Take ownership	☐	✓	☐	☐
✓	Undo changes	☐	✓	☐	☐
☐	View	☐	✓	☐	✓
✓	View History	☐	✓	☐	☐
✓	View management screens	☐	✓	☐	☐

Save Changes

Figure 15-5: Permissions assignments for the DTML document login_html

To be sure that, after we submit the form (addWebsiteForm), the browser returns to the contents screen of the folder in which the instance was created, add the following lines:

```
if REQUEST is not None:
    return self.manage_main(self, REQUEST)
```

15.4.4.2   Completed addWebsite Constructor Method
Here is the complete method code listing at a glance:

```
def manage_addWebsite(self, id, title, REQUEST=None):
    """Add a new Website"""

    instance=Website()
    instance.id=id
    instance.title=title
    user_folder=UserFolder()
    instance._setObject('acl_users', user_folder)
    instance._addRole('WebsiteUser')
    p_list = ['Access contents information',
             'Manage users', 'View']
    for permission in p_list:
        p=Permission(permission,'',instance)
        p.setRole('WebsiteUser', permission in p_list)
    self._setObject(id, instance)
    addDocsToFolder(instance, Website_pages)
    old_permissions = self.permission_settings()
    new_permissions = []
```

```
permissions_for_WebsiteUsers = []
for item in old_permissions:
    if item['name']=='View':
        permissions_for_WebsiteUsers.append(item['name'])
    else:
        new_permissions.append(item['name'])
instance.login_html.manage_acquiredPermissions(new_permissions)
instance.login_html.manage_role('WebsiteUser', permissions_for_WebsiteUsers)

if REQUEST is not None:
    return self.manage_main(self, REQUEST)
```

15.4.5 Writing the __init__.py File

Zope uses the __init__.py file to recognize a product, and executes the __init__.py files for each product whenever the Zope server is started. If a product's directory contains a bytecode-compiled version of __init__.py (recognizable from the file extension .pyc), Zope checks at startup to see whether the modification date of the compiled version is more recent than that of a non-compiled version located in the product directory. If the modifiation date of the non-compiled __init__.py file is more recent, a new __init__.pyc file is compiled from it. Thus, if you change the code in __init__.py, a new __init__.pyc will be generated automatically when you restart Zope; the same holds true for all of the Python module files in your product.

Because compiling occurs only when you start the Zope server, the Zope server must always be restarted whenever you make changes to a product's Python files, such as the __init__.py file, the main module, and so on. If you notice that Zope has installed the incorrect version of a product, you must delete your product from the Product_Management list in the Zope Control_Panel and restart the Zope server to install the new version of your product.

NOTE *The product Refresh (http://www.zope.org/Members/hathawsh/Refresh) allows you to recompile and reload a single product without restarting the entire Zope server. This feature is included in Zope 2.4.0 and later.*

15.4.5.1 __init__.py Overview
Once you've created Website.py, do the following in the file __init__.py:

* Import the product's main module: Website.

* Define the initialize function, called by Zope to register your product.

* In the initialize function, call the built-in registerClass method and supply the class, constructors, add permission name, and icon path.

15.4.5.2 Import Main Module
In order to access the functions and class defined in the Website module we created in section 15.4.2.3, we must import it using the following code statement:

```
import Website
```

15.4.5.3 Define the Initialize Function

When Zope starts, it will import our product directory, which in turn will execute the __init__.py file we are creating. Once Zope imports the product, it checks to see if it defines a function named Initialize. If it does, Zope calls this function for the product, and passes the registration context object to it. This object contains the method registerClass which is used to register the product's classes with Zope.

Website __init__.py uses the following code to open the Initialize function definition:

```
def initialize(context):
    """Register the Website class"""
```

A product's Initialize function will generally contain one or more calls to the registerClass method of the context object (passed by Zope in the context argument). One call to registerClass must be made for each class in the product that defines a distinct object metatype.

Table 15-4 describes the arguments that can be passed to registerClass:

Table 15-4: registerClass arguments

registerClass Argument	Description
instance_class	The product class to be registered.
meta_type	Specifies the class's Zope metatype, which will appear in the add object menu of folderish objects. If omitted, the class's meta_type attribute is used. It is generally preferable to specify the metatype directly in the class (omitting this argument) for better code readability and maintenance. (Optional.)
permission	The name of the security permission needed to create instances of the class in Zope. If omitted, Zope creates one based on the metatype. It is preferable to specify the permission name explicitly, however. (Optional.)
constructors	A list of the callable constructor objects and methods used to create instances of the class in Zope. The first constructor given is the method or object called when the class's metatype is selected from a folder's add menu. All constructor methods specified are automatically protected by the permission name specified (above).
icon	The relative path within the product to the image file to be used with the product. When specified, Zope automatically adds the appropriate icon attribute value to the class based on this path. (Optional.)
permissions	A list of additional security permissions used by the class. If omitted, these names are taken from any security assertions made in the class definition (see section 15.6.4). (Optional.)

The following code shows the call to registerClass in the Initialize function, used to register the Website class for use in Zope. (We've placed the arguments on multiple lines for readability):

```
context.registerClass(
        Website.Website,
        constructors = (
            Website.manage_addWebsiteForm,
            Website.manage_addWebsite
        ),
        permission = 'Add Website',
        icon = 'www/icon.gif'
    )
```

Let's look at the specific arguments we pass to register the Website class.

- For the first argument (instance_class), we pass the Website class from the Website module using the Python dot notation (Website.Website).

- Next, we pass the two constructors for the class, the DTMLFile object manage_addWebsiteForm (the form presented to the user when creating a Website as discussed in section 15.5.3) and manage_addWebsite (the method that actually creates the Website instance and stores it in Zope, as discussed in section 15.5.4). Since the constructor form is first in the tuple being passed, it will be called when a user chooses "Website" from the folder's add menu.

- Next, a permission name is provided to protect the constructors: Add Website. Only users with this permission will be able to create instances of our Website object in Zope. (This permission will appear in the security management tab in Zope.)

- In the last argument, icon, we pass the relative file path to the image file that we want to use as the icon for Website objects in Zope.

NOTE *Notice that we did not explicitly pass a value for meta_type here. Because we defined this attribute in the Website class (see section 15.5.2.4), we can safely omit this argument and Zope will simply use the class's attribute value.*

15.4.5.4 Completed __init__.py
The listing below shows the completed code for the __init__.py module:

```
import Website

def initialize(context):
    """Register the Website class"""

    context.registerClass(
        Website.Website,
        constructors = (
```

(continued on next page)

```
                Website.manage_addWebsiteForm,
                Website.manage_addWebsite
        ),
        permission = 'Add Website',
        icon = 'www/icon.gif'
)
```

Summary

Our simple example product has introduced us to the components we need to create when developing a product. (You'll find complete source-code listings and further explanation of the Website product's files in Appendix C.)

Now that you have created a working Zope product and know the fundamentals of writing one, you can develop products to help you create your own Web applications.

Of course, once you begin writing your own programs, you will sooner or later encounter error messages. Chapter 16 explains the error messages you are likely to receive and describes techniques for debugging your Zope code.

16

DEBUGGING

Debugging is often a programmer's least favorite task. However, because everybody makes mistakes, the process of debugging is unavoidable for all programmers.

This chapter explores the general concept of debugging and then looks at two debugging topics specific to Zope.

16.1 Errors When Starting the Zope Server

When you start a Zope server, a number of errors may cause the Zope process to terminate or run incorrectly, as follows:

```
Error Value: Invalid python version
```

Explanation: The Zope server is incompatible with the Python version you are using. This error is specific to UNIX because, under UNIX or UNIX-like operating systems, Python is not integrated into Zope, and, in this case, you are using a version of Python that is invalid for use with Zope.

Solution: Update your version of Python. (Windows versions of Zope are supplied with Python.)

NOTE *Different errors may occur depending on your operating system. See the relevant product documentation.*

```
ErrorValue: Invalid argument
```

Explanation: You tried to start the Zope server with an illegal command-line option.

Solution: See the file z2.py in the Zope directory for information on how to use the options correctly.

```
ErrorValue: Invalid number of threads
```

Explanation: There are too many threads running.

Solution: Limit the number of threads by changing the options in the start script, then restart.

```
Error Value: Invalid Value for "x" option
```

Explanation: An invalid value was given to the command-line option x.

Solution: See the file z2.py in the Zope directory for information on how to use the options correctly.

16.2   Python and DTML Errors

When your program displays an error message, you know that something is behaving unexpectedly somewhere in your code. The art of debugging lies primarily in your ability to locate the cause of errors. Once you have located the error, correcting the problem is generally routine.

Error messages sometimes result from variable data in an inconsistent or unexpected state. For example, although you may think that at a specific time, a variable has a specific value or a function is called and the correct parameters are passed, this may not be the case. This condition may lead to an error message, or worse, unexpected and inexplicable behavior by the program. To find the error, check all of the variable values when the bug appears.

Because a program in a large project can have over a thousand lines of code, it is not practical to check every line. However, you can use several time-saving techniques to avoid such a "brute force" approach to problem solving.

16.2.1 Binary Searching

Zope allows you to perform binary searches to help you isolate the source of errors. In binary searches, the code is broken into halves, which are then searched to locate the error. The half that contains the error is then subdivided into halves, and so on, until the line that contains the error is found.

For example, suppose you have tracked an error to a specific function in your program. You know that this function produces an incorrect value, but you do not know where the incorrect assignment takes place. Using binary searching (and assuming your function is 300 lines long) you can output the value of the variable in line 150 by artificially creating an error.

The following Python line produces a run-time error that returns the value of a variable:

```
raise RuntimeError, "The value of the variable xyz here is: " + str(xyz)
```

In DTML, you would write the following code to create the same run-time error:

```
<dtml-raise RuntimeError>
    The value of the variable xyz here is: <dtml-var name="xyz">
</dtml-raise>
```

If this variable has the correct value, the error must be in the second half of the function; otherwise, the error must be in the first half of the function. If the error is in the second half of the function, you would output the variable in line 225; if the error were in the first half, you would run line 75.

Using method, you can quickly isolate errors by halving sections until you locate the line in which the incorrect call occurs. If this line involves a method call, you must repeat this process on the method in question until you find the incorrect assignment of the calculation. (Don't forget to remove the error messages you inserted when you finish debugging!)

NOTE *When debugging external Python code, as in an external method or product, you can use the Python print statement to output variable values at run time without stopping the execution of the code. The printed values are output to the console window where the Zope server was started.*

16.2.2 Defensive Coding

No large project is without errors in its first version, so you may as well count on errors occurring from the outset and write your program to make debugging easier using these guidelines:

- Use informative names for variables, objects, and functions and comment your code so that you (and others) can understand it later. Be consistent in your naming conventions and coding style.

- Always write your code as if another person will be debugging it, even if that person will be you.

- Code your programs in the simplest and most straightforward way possible. Avoid clever tricks and shortcuts that merely save typing.

- Never write more than one instruction per line so that you can output your variable assignments in each line.

- Modularize your code. Write short code blocks and keep the code in a single object or file manageable in size. It is much easier to debug small, logical parts of a program than one written as a single huge file.

- Proofread your code and test it in your mind before running it to make sure you have not skipped any steps or misspelled or misplaced any names.

- Write "sanity checks" into your code that test argument values to make sure they make sense. A simple way to do this in Python is to convert arguments explicitly to the desired type before acting on them (use the float(), int(), str(), and list() functions for this purpose).

These basic principles of good programming style will serve you well when it comes to debugging.

16.2.3 Intermittent Errors

The most difficult errors to find and fix are intermittent ones. Intermittent errors are often ignored because they happen only rarely and are therefore more difficult to notice or reproduce. But not fixing intermittent errors immediately will only cause you more problems, because as a program ages it becomes more difficult for the programmer to understand the code. So fix all errors as soon as you learn about them.

To find intermittent errors, first try to reproduce it by creating a situation in which it occurred. Once you can create the error at will, you will probably have discovered the cause of the error—or at least found a solid clue.

In Zope, both the standard Python error messages and Zope-specific error messages may occur, as discussed in the following sections.

16.2.4 Standard Python Error Messages

Table 16-1 lists the standard Python error messages that may also occur when you are working with Zope.

16.2.5 DTML Error Messages

To debug DTML code, you will often need to use a different procedure to find the error. Each time you create or modify an object, Zope performs a syntax check. If an error is found during this check, the object is neither created nor modified, and you will need to click the Back button to return to edit mode for the object. You must resolve all syntax errors before you can create, modify, or test an object.

With few exceptions, Zope error messages all have the same format (see Figure 16-1). They begin with a general description of the error ("No closing tag") followed by the name of the tag that caused the error ("for tag <dtml-in>") and the location of the error ("on line 4 of index_html").

Table 16-1: Standard Python Error Messages

Error	Explanation
AttributeError	An object attribute could not be found.
EOFError	A read operation tried to read past the end of a file.
IOError	An input or output error occurred, usually involving a filesystem or possibly the network.
ImportError	An error occurred importing a Python module.
IndexError	The sequence index value is outside the permitted range.
KeyError	The key was not found in a dictionary or dictionary-like (mapping) object.
KeyboardInterrupt	The program was interrupted by the user.
MemoryError	Too much memory has been consumed to continue.
NameError	The name could not be found in the namespace.
OverflowError	The range of a data type was exceeded.
RuntimeError	A generic, uncategorized error occurred.
SyntaxError	The syntax of the Python program is incorrect.
SystemError	An internal system error occurred; the program will continue working.
SystemExit	The system stopped.
TypeError	The wrong data type was used for a parameter or operator.
ValueError	The parameter has an illegal value.
ZeroDivisionError	Division by zero was attempted.

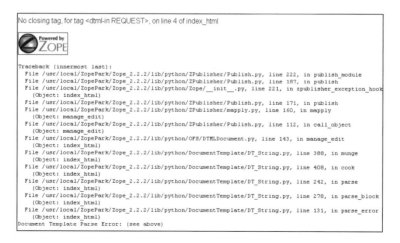

Figure 16-1: A Zope error message with traceback

However, these error messages can be misleading, because often a missing quote on an attribute or missing right angle bracket at the end of a dtml tag can cause the rest of the dtml code to be ignored. In this case, the tag with the actual error is not the one specified in the error message. For example, look at this incorrect DTML code:

```
<dtml-if name="today">
    Yesterday was <dtml-var expr="(today-1).day()>
</dtml-if>
```

In Line 2, the quote is missing at the end of the expr attribute. However, the error Zope returns when you try to save this is

```
No closing tag, for tag <dtml-if name="today">, in line 1
```

As you can see, line 3 does in fact contain a closing tag for the dtml-if in line 1. The problem is that Zope thinks this line is part of the value of the expression attribute from line 2 because there is no closing quote after day(), so Zope doesn't recognize line 3 as a dtml tag at all.

16.2.6 Debug Mode

When debug mode is activated in Zope (which it is if you use the default Zope start script) you will see a *traceback* of the error after the text of the error page. Otherwise, the traceback is displayed in the HTML source text of the page, and you can view it by choosing View Page Source or View Frame Source after right-clicking on the error page.

The traceback shows the route of execution from the module that caused the exception (always the bottom file in the traceback) to the module that controls Zope output, as well as the objects or expressions executing in each module at the time of the error. (A more detailed description of exceptions is given in section 16.3.1 below.)

In the case of DTML errors, the final module is always

```
File /usr/local/Zope-x.x.x-src/lib/python/DocumentTemplate/DT_String.py,
```

as should be apparent in Figure 16-1. Unfortunately, this also makes the traceback less useful for debugging DTML. The error message and the objects shown in the traceback must be sufficient to locate the error.

NOTE *You can greatly enhance the information provided by Zope error messages by installing the ZDebug product. Although still in development at this writing, it is still a highly useful tool for debugging. Download it from http://www.zope.org/Members/hathawsh/ZDebug.*

16.3 Errors Specific to Zope

The error messages listed in Table 16-2 are specific to Zope.

Table 16-2: Error Messages Specific to Zope

Error	Explanation
Bad Request	An invalid request was entered.
CopyError	The object cannot be copied.
DateTimeError	There is an error in the date or time format.
Forbidden	This action is forbidden.
HistorySelectionError	An error occurred when working with a history function.
InError	An error occurred when working with the In-tag.
Invalid Object Name	The object was not found in the module.
Invalid Permission	The permission is invalid.
MailHostError	A mail-host-specific error occurred.
ModuleError	The module cannot be accessed.
ParseError	A syntax error in a DTML object occurred.
SuperCannotOwn	A superuser cannot own objects.
Time Error	An invalid time was specified.
Type Exists	This type already exists.
Unauthorized	Unauthorized use or access to an object was attempted.
UndoError	An error occurred during an undo action.
ValidationError	A parameter is invalid.
VersionError	An error occurred when using a version function.

16.3.1 Zope Error Messages

Following are some examples of Zope error messages as they occur in practice:

AttributeError

An object attribute cannot be accessed.

```
Error Type  : AttributeError
Error Value : 'string' object has no attribute x
```

Explanation: An attempt was made to call the attribute x in a string, but there is no attribute by that name. This error can also occur if the attribute exists, but it is private to the object and not published through Zope.

NOTE *The AttributeError and SystemError errors occur more frequently when you are working with Zope but actually belong to the standard Python errors.*

Bad Request

This type of error indicates that an HTTP request is not valid, For example,

```
Error Value: The id __ contains characters illegal in URLs.
```

Explanation: The specified id contains illegal characters.

```
Error Value: The id index_html is invalid - it is already in use.
```

Explanation: An attempt was made to assign an existing id name (in this case: index_html).

CopyError

You cannot copy an object. This may be because copying is not permitted by the object you want to copy, or the object to which you want to copy the object cannot accept the new object.

```
The object __ does not support this operation.
```

Explanation: The selected object does not support copying.

```
Cannot paste into this object.
```

Explanation: You cannot paste this object into this folderish object because it cannot contain the type of object(s) you have in the clipboard.

DateTimeError:

A specified time zone does not exist, or a time was specified in the wrong format.

```
Unrecognized timezone
```

Explanation: The time zone used is not recognized.

```
Unknown time zone in date
```

Explanation: The specified date contains a time format that does not exist or that is not supported.

```
Invalid date
```

Explanation: The specified date format is not valid.

Forbidden

An action is forbidden. This may be because the user does not have the appropriate permissions.

```
Zope Error


Error Type:  Forbidden
Error Value:  You are not authorized to change index_html because you do not have
proxy roles.
```

HistorySelectionError

The selected action cannot be carried out (see section 3.1.5 on the history management tab).

```
No historical revision was selected.
```

Explanation: No element in the history list was selected.

```
Only one historical revision can be copied to the present.
```

Explanation: More than one element in the history list was selected to serve as the most recent version.

```
Only two historical revisions can be compared.
```

Explanation: An attempt was made to compare more than two elements in the history list.

InError

Problems occurred when processing an In tag. See section 4.3.10, "The In tag."

```
Error Value: Strings are not allowed as input to the in tag.
```

Explanation: An attempt was made to use the In tag in a string, which is forbidden.

Invalid Object Name

An object or a method cannot be found in the specified Python module. For example, assume you create an external method, and the specified test_obj method is not contained in the module called "test." The following message would appear:

```
The specified object, test_obj, was not found in module, test.
```

Explanation: The test_obj method is not located in the module called test.

KeyError

This can occur when you attempt to access an object from the namespace variable using the _[...] notation and the name is not found. This error also occurs in any dictionary lookup attempted with a key that is not in the dictionary or mapping (dictionary-like) object (such as a Zope folder or the REQUEST object).

```
A key was not found in the namespace. Either it was entered incorrectly or it does
not exist.
```

HINT *Check the spelling of the variables listed in the error message. Remember that Zope and Python names are case sensitive.*

MailHostError

An error occurred when sending electronic mail via a MailHost object. For more information, see section 4.3.12, "The Sendmail tag."

```
No mailhost was specified in tag
```

Explanation: The mail host was not specified in the Sendmail tag.

```
An unsupported encoding was specified in tag
```

Explanation: An incorrect or unsupported value was set for the encode parameter.

Module Error

You cannot access a module.

```
The specified module, TestModule, couldn't be found.
The specified module, TestModule, couldn't be opened.
```

Explanation: This error occurs when you try to create an external method and either write the name of the Python module incorrectly or are not currently in the Extensions directory.

ParseError

Parse errors occur when you try to save an object (a DTML method or DTML document) that contains errors. You cannot save objects before any parse errors have been resolved, such as the following:

```
unexpected end tag
```

Explanation: An end tag exists that is not needed or is in the wrong location.

```
Explanation:more than one else tag for a single if tag
No more than one else block is allowed
Explanation: Two or more else tags were used in an if block.
The __ attribute was used but neither of the start, end, or size
```

Explanation: An attribute was used that must be used with the start, end, or size attribute of a dtml-in tag, but none of the attributes are contained in the tag.

```
Expression (Python) Syntax error
```

Explanation: The wrong Python syntax was used in an expression.

```
invalid parameter
```

Explanation: An invalid parameter was specified.

```
A try..finally combination cannot contain any other else, except or finally blocks.
```

Explanation: Two or more else, except, or finally tags were used in a try...finally block.

```
The else block should be the last block in a try
```

Explanation: Additional tags were used after an else tag within an if-else block.

```
two exprs given
```

Explanation: Two expressions were used in a tag.

```
branches and branches_expr given tree
```

Explanation: Both the branches and the branches_expr attributes were used in a tree tag.

SuperCannotOwn

The superuser cannot own or create any objects.

```
Error Type: SuperCannotOwn
Error Value: Objects cannot be owned by the superuser
```

HINT *Create a new user with the manager role or log on as another user if you want to create objects.*

SystemError

An internal system error occurred.

```
Error Value: infinite recursion in document template
```

Explanation: A circular call of methods exceeded Zope's recursion threshold. This error helps prevent an infinite chain of DTML calls that would hang the Zope server.

The AttributeError and SystemError errors occur more frequently when you are working with Zope but actually belong to the standard Python errors.

TimeError

A specified time is outside the time span implemented in the current version of Python.

```
The time __ is beyond the range of this Python implementation.
```

TypeError

A type error occurred. For example, too many arguments were passed to a method

```
too many arguments; expected 1, got 2
```

or an invalid name was used in an expression.

```
illegal name used in expression
```

Remember that the first argument of instance methods, self, is often passed implicitly by Python, so often you need only explicitly pass the remaining arguments.

Type Exists

A specified meta type or a specified permission already exists and cannot be used twice.

```
The type __ is already defined.
The permission __ is already defined.
```

Unauthorized

Access to an object is denied. An incorrect username or password may have been entered. When this error occurs, the user will be asked to enter a username and password for a user with sufficient rights.

```
Zope Error
Zope has encountered an error while publishing this resource.
Unauthorized
Sorry, a Zope error occurred.
You are not authorized to add DTML Documents.
```

UndoError

This error occurs in the Undo screen if an action cannot be undone because it conflicts with a subsequent action. (See section 3.1.7 for a detailed description of the Undo function.)

```
non-undoable transaction
```

Explanation: The selected action cannot be undone.

```
Invalid undo transaction id
```

Explanation: The id of an action you want to undo is not valid.

```
Undoable transaction
```

Explanation: This error occurs if you try to undo a different action from the last action you carried out.

ValidationError

A parameter passed to a function is not valid. A number range may be too large or too small.

```
 Error Value: range() too large
```

Explanation: The parameter passed to the range() method was too large or too small.

```
Error Value: pow(x, y, z) with z=0
```

Explanation: The pow method was called with z = 0, which is not permitted.

ValueError

An invalid value was passed.

```
The prefix, __, should be a relative path.
The file name, __, should be a simple file name.
unknown tag testtag
```

Version Error

An error occurred while working with Zope versions. An attempt may have been made to delete a non-empty version or an object locked by a version. (For more information, see Chapter 5, "Working with Zope Versions.")

```
Error Value: Attempt to delete a non-empty version.
```

Explanation: An attempt was made to delete a non-empty version.

```
Error Value: You may not change the database cache size
zope/server/lib/python/App/CacheManager.py while working in a version
```

Explanation: The cache size cannot be changed while you are working in a version.

Summary

As a rule, the debugging process follows these steps:

1. Determine the type of error that occurred (syntactic error, semantic error, and so on) and the circumstances that triggered it.

2. Find the source of the error (DTML document, DTML method, ZClass, Python file, and so on).

3. Locate the error (which line, expression, variable, and so on).

4. Correct the error and test.

You have now learned about the different types of errors you may encounter in your work with Zope. These include errors that can occur when you start the Zope server that are the result of errors in the Python source code as well as errors that can occur when you work directly in the Zope management screen.

17

EXTERNAL DATA ACCESS

You can choose from a number of ways to place data on the Zope server and take data from it to store on a different storage device. This chapter will look at three of these ways and their associated programs.

17.1 FTP

File Transfer Protocol (FTP) is one way in which you can transfer data onto the Zope server. To access your Zope server via FTP, you will need an FTP client program. A simple one (that is included with both Windows and Unix) is the command-line FTP program. Here is a quick example of how to connect to a Zope server from the command line using Linux:

```
% ftp localhost 8021
```

Begin by executing the FTP command as above, supplying it with the hostname (in this case the local machine) and the port number (8021 by default for Zope). If you do not specify a port number, the FTP program uses port 21 (the standard FTP port).

Once the FTP program connects to your Zope server, the following message should appear:

```
Connected to localhost.localdomain.
------
2001-06-18T04:22:59 INFO(0) ZServer Incoming connection from 127.0.0.1:3160
220 mycomputer.mydomain.com FTP server (Medusa Async V1.13 [experimental]) ready.
Name (localhost:username):
At the prompt above, enter the Zope username to log in as and press enter. Then
enter the password.
331 Password required.
Password:
230 Login successful.
------
2001-08-18T04:23:21 INFO(0) ZServer Successful login.
Remote system type is UNIX.
Using binary mode to transfer files.
ftp>
```

If you have successfully logged in, you can execute standard FTP commands, such as ls, cd, get, and put.

For example, to get a listing of objects in the current folder, use the ls command:

```
ftp> ls
227 Entering Passive Mode (127,0,0,1,12,92)
150 Opening ASCII mode data connection for file list
drwxrwx--- 1 Zope      Zope         0 Jan 20 21:39 Control_Panel
drwxrwx--- 1 Zope      Zope         0 May 31 04:36 QuickStart
---------- 1 Zope      Zope         0 Dec 30  1998 acl_users
-rw-rw---- 1 Zope      Zope        92 Jan 20 21:39 index_html
-rw-rw---- 1 Zope      Zope      1365 Jan 20 21:39 standard_error_message
-rw-rw---- 1 Zope      Zope        53 Jan 20 21:39 standard_html_footer
-rw-rw---- 1 Zope      Zope       128 May 21 17:32 standard_html_header
226 Transfer complete
```

To download an object (such as a DTML document) from Zope to your local computer, use the get command:

```
ftp> get index_html
local: index_html remote: index_html
227 Entering Passive Mode (127,0,0,1,12,94)
150 Opening Binary mode data connection for file 'index_html'
226 Transfer complete
92 bytes received in 0.00787 secs (11 Kbytes/sec)
```

This creates a file on your local computer containing the DTML source of the index_html DTML document.

FTP can also be a convenient way to upload many objects into Zope (such as images, or Web pages) that reside as files on your computer. You can use the **mput** command, for example, to upload an entire directory of files into Zope at once, rather than uploading them one at a time through the Zope management screen.

NOTE   *For more information on the available FTP commands, use the help command or see the Unix FTP manual page (type* man ftp *at the command prompt).*

17.1.1 Using Graphical FTP Clients

There are also many graphical FTP clients that you can use to connect to Zope (one is included with Internet Explorer 5 for Windows), but one Windows program that we like in particular is WS_FTP from Ipswitch. (You can download an evaluation copy from their website: www.ipswitch.com.) The following sections will use WS_FTP to describe the transfer of data by FTP.

Once you have installed WS_FTP, start it up. You should see a screen similar to the one shown in Figure 17-1.

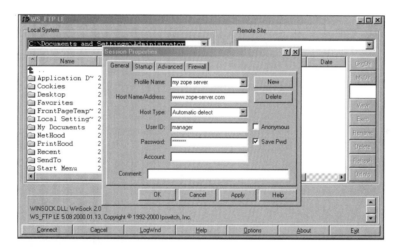

Figure 17-1: Window for establishing a connection in WS_FTP

Complete the fields as follows:

Profile Name   Enter a name for the connection.

Host Name/Address   Enter the host name or the IP address of your Zope server
                            (for example: localhost, www.mycompany.com).

User ID   Enter your Zope username here.

Password   Enter your password here.

You can leave the remaining fields blank or unchanged. You will, however, need to make a number of changes in the Advanced tab. Click on the tab and change the Remote Port number to 8021, as shown in Figure 17-2.

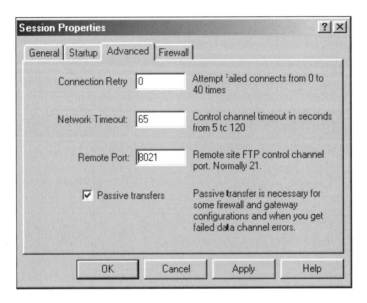

Figure 17-2: Configuring the port in the Advanced tab

Now click OK to connect to the Zope server.

17.1.1.1 Local System/Remote System

A window divided into two panes appears on your screen as shown in Figure 17-3. On the left-hand side, you can browse through your hard drive—the local system. On the right-hand side, you see the contents of your Zope server—the remote system.

17.1.1.2 Drag and Drop

To move files between the two systems, click on the desired file or files, then click on the top or bottom arrow button. You can also drag and drop files to move them.

NOTE *Zope tries to create an object appropriate for the contents of a file that you drag from the local system into Zope. For example, a text document will create a DTML document, an image file will create an image object, any other file type will create a file object.*

17.2 WebDAV

WebDAV offers a second option for accessing data on your Zope server. By default, the standard ZServer configuration in Zope supports WebDAV, there is not additional configuration to enable it. WebDAV uses the same HTTP protocol as normal web requests, but is simliar in operation to FTP. This can be advantageous when accessing a Zope server from behind a firewall where FTP access has been blocked.

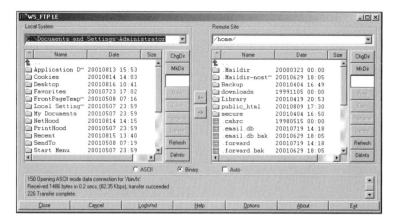

Figure 17-3: The working window in WS_FTP showing the remote and local systems

Windows Internet Explorer 5.0 or higher comes with a WebDAV client (called Web Folders) that allows you to graphically navigate your Zope server.

To use WebDAV on Windows:

1. Open Internet Explorer.

2. Open the File menu and select Open. In the dialog box that appears, enter the URL for the server you want to access, as shown in Figure 17-4. Click on the checkbox Open as Web Folder.

Figure 17-4: The Open dialog to use WebDAV

3. Click on OK.

The objects on the Zope server are displayed in a window similar in layout to Windows Explorer, as shown in Figure 17-5.

You can now use the objects as you would files in Windows Explorer, meaning you can move, delete, and copy objects. You cannot, however, edit or modify any objects directly from this window.

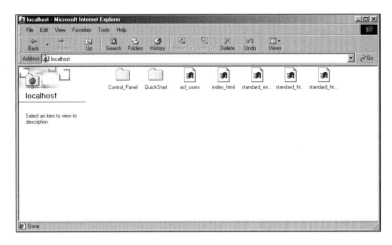

Figure 17-5: Working window with WebDAV

Another way to enable access to Zope's WebDAV functionality from both DOS and Windows is to use WebDrive from RiverFront Software, which allows you to create a new drive letter corresponding to your Zope server. To learn more about this program, visit http://www.riverfrontsoftware.com/webdrive.htm.

NOTE *You can also use the Web Folders support found in Microsoft Office 2000, which allows users to open and save files from Excel and Word, for example, directly into Zope using WebDAV.*

17.2.1 WebDAV for Linux and Unix

Users of Linux or other Unix-type operating systems can use an open-source command line WebDAV client called "cadaver," which operates much like the command-line FTP program, except that it connects to WebDAV servers. The program and source code can be downloaded for free from: http://www.webdav.org/cadaver/.

You'll find an exhaustive list of software supporting WebDAV along with technical documentation about it at http://www.ics.uci.edu/pub/ietf/webdav/.

17.3 XML-RPC

A third way to access external data in Zope is with XML-RPC. For this purpose, we'll introduce the Zope Management System (ZMS) program (an enhanced version of the Radio Userland program by David Brown), which uses the XML-RPC protocol.

A similar program for the GNOME desktop environment for Linux/Unix is called "gnope." Gnope allows you to use a separate graphical interface to manage Zope outside of a web browser. Gnope is free and can be downloaded at http://sourceforge.net/projects/gnope/.

To use ZMS, you must install a server component (ru_utils.tgz) as you would a normal Zope product. This component is available for download from the ZMS homepage at http://zopefish.weblogs.com/DownloadZMS. Once this is installed, install Radio Userland as you would any other Windows application (http://radio.userland.com). When you complete these two steps, you will need to return to the ZMS homepage to download and install the Manage Zope Suite.

Once your installation is complete:

1. Start Radio Userland and open the file suites.manageZope.fttb via the File menu, as shown in Figure 17-6.

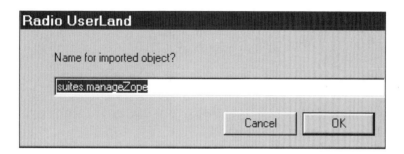

Figure 17-6: Window for opening the file suites.manageZope.fttb

2. Click OK and a window opens.

3. To install the ZMS Client components for Radio Userland, double-click the arrow in front of the init object. You will then see a new window as shown in Figure 17-7.

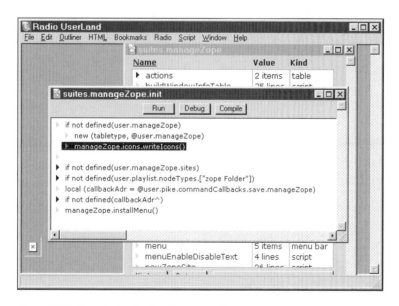

Figure 17-7: The window for the file manageZope

4. Click Run.

5. Radio Userland now has a menu option called "Zope." If you do not see this menu option, close Radio Userland and restart it. If you still cannot see the menu option or if error messages are displayed, read the official ZMS documentation at the following site: http://zopefish.weblogs.com/manageZopeDocs.

6. If everything worked, open the File menu and select New.

7. Now open the Zope menu and select Add Zope Site for Management. You are asked to enter the following information relating to the Zope site (see Figure 17-8):

host   The name of the Zope server you want to access.

port   The port number on the Zope server.

site path   The path, if the user only has access to a specific folder (for example: www.beehive.de/PR/) or a slash (/) for the root folder.

username   Your username.

password   Your password.

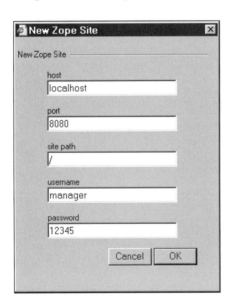

Figure 17-8: Create a connection to the Zope server

8. Switch to the window that opened when you clicked New as shown in Figure 17-9. Click the gray arrow.

Figure 17-9: New window with connection to the Zope server

9. Double-click the folder symbol. The folder on your Zope server appears as shown in Figure 17-10.

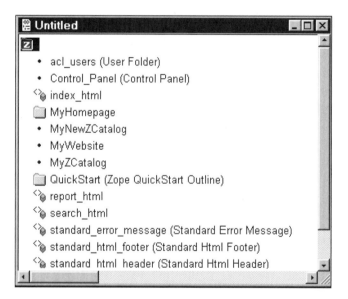

Figure 17-10: Outline of the Zope server

To create new DTML documents, method, or folders, click the right mouse button. The context menu shown in Figure 17-11 appears, from which you can select the action you want to carry out or the object you want to create.

Expand
View in Browser...
Get Properties...
New DTML Document
New DTML Method
New XML Document
New Folder
Delete...
Collapse
Expand All Subheads
Cut
Copy
Paste
Get Info
Debug

Figure 17-11: Context menu

A particular advantage of ZMS is its ability to edit DTML documents and methods. Because Zope's DTML syntax is compatible with XML and Radio Userland is designed to work with XML, you can expand and collapse individual segments of the DTML code. This will make it easier to work with long source texts, such as tables and comments, which can simply be expanded.

When you have finished making your changes, save the file to apply the changes to your Zope server.

Summary

This chapter has shown you different ways to access data, such as DTML Documents or Image objects, in your Zope server so that you can work with them more like normal files.

Using these services: FTP, WebDAV, and XML-RPC, you can work with Zope outside of the confines of a web browser. Combined with development tools on your local machine, this can be a convenient way to perform development and content management tasks in Zope.

DTML AND BUILT-IN ATTRIBUTES

A.1 The var Tag

The following table lists all var attributes along with examples and corresponding screen output. Attributes marked with an asterisk (*) require at least one argument. This is a more complete version of information presented in Table 4.1.

Attributes for the var Tag

Attribute	Function	Example	Output
name*	See "The name Attribute" in Table 4.1.		
expr*	See "The expr Attribute" in Table 4.1.		
fmt*	See "The fmt Attribute" in Table 4.1.		
null	Defines a string that will be output instead of the value "null." If the value for null is omitted, no text is inserted.	`null="The result returns an empty list."`	The result returns an empty list.

(continued on next page)

Attributes for the var Tag (continued)

Attribute	Function	Example	Output
missing	Defines a string to be inserted if the variable referred to by name is not in the namespace. If the value for missing is omitted, no text is inserted.	`missing="Not found"`	Not found
lower	Changes all letters to lowercase.	`title_or_id lower`	testpage
upper	Converts all letters to uppercase.	`title_or_id upper`	TESTPAGE
capitalize	Capitalizes the first letter.	`AUTHENTICATED_USER capitalize`	Manager
spacify	Converts the underscore character (_) into white space.	`id spacify (id="index_html")`	index html
thousands_commas	Inserts commas into character strings that consist solely of numbers at the thousand position.	`teststring thousands_commas (teststring="12000")`	12,000
html_quote	Characters significant in HTML are replaced with appropriate HTML entities.	`teststring html_quote (teststring="<")`	&lt;
url_quote	Characters not legal in URLs are properly escaped for insertion into href values.	`teststring url_quote (teststring="<")`	%3c
url_quote_plus	Functions like url_quote, but spaces are converted to plus signs (+) for insertion into href URL CGI query values.	`teststring url_quote_plus teststring="two words"`	two+words
sql_quote	Characters significant to SQL, such as single quotes, are properly escaped (important for SQL methods).	`Teststring sql_quote (teststring="How're you?")`	How're you

(continued on next page)

Attributes for the var Tag (continued)

Attribute	Function	Example	Output
newline_to_br	Inserts an HTML line break tag ( ) in the source code at each new line in the string value.	teststring newline_to_br (teststring= "Hello\nYou")	Hello You
size	Displays only the specified number of characters from a string.	teststring size=6 (teststring="How're you?")	How're...
etc	Specifies a string that is inserted instead of the omitted characters (used with size).	teststring size=6 etc="---" (teststring="How're you?")	How're —

Standard fmt Attribute Formats

Name	Description
AMPM	Returns the time including seconds.
AMPMMinutes	Returns the time without seconds.
aCommon	The time is displayed in the format Mar 1, 2002 1:45 pm.
aCommonZ	The time is displayed in the format Mar 1, 2002 1:45 pm US/Eastern.
aDay	Returns the abbreviated name of the day of the week.
aMonth	Returns the abbreviated name of the month.
ampm	Returns the suffix am or pm.
Date	Returns the date string for an object.
Day	Returns the full name of the day of the week.
DayOfWeek	Same as Day: Returns the full name of the day of the week.
day	Returns the day as a number.
dayOfYear	Returns the day of the year in the context of the time zone display for the object.
dd	Returns the day as a two-digit string.
fCommon	The time is displayed as March 1, 1997 1:45 pm.
fCommonZ	The time is displayed as March 1, 1997 1:45 pm US/Eastern.
h_12	Returns the time in 12-hour mode.
h_24	Returns the time in 24-hour mode.

(continued on next page)

Standard fmt Attribute Formats (continued)

Name	Description
hour	Returns the time in 24-hour mode.
isCurrentHour	Returns as True if the object Date/Time is the same as the current time (in the context of the time zone display of the object).
isCurrentMonth	Returns as True if the object Date/Time is in the current month (in the context of the time zone display of the object).
isFuture	Returns as True if the object Date/Time is in the future.
isLeapYear	Returns as True if the current year (in the context of the time zone of the object) is a leap year.
isPast	Returns as True if the object Date/Time is in the past.
Mon_	Returns the full name of the month.
Mon	Same as aMonth: Returns the abbreviated name of the month.
Month	Returns the full name of the month.
minute	Returns the minutes.
mm	Returns the month as a two-digit string.
month	Returns the month as a number.
notEqualTo(t)	Compares the DateTime object with another DateTime object OR with a decimal number, such as those returned by the Python time module. Returns as True if the object Date/Time is not equal to the specified DateTime time or the time in the time module.
PreciseAMPM	Returns the timestring for the object.
PreciseTime	Returns the timestring for the object.
pCommon	The time is displayed as Mar. 1, 2002 1:45 pm.
pCommonZ	The time is displayed as Mar. 1, 2002 1:45 pm US/Eastern.
pDay	Returns the name of the day abbreviated with a period.
pMonth	Returns the name of the month abbreviated with a period.
rfc822	Returns the date in RFC 822 format (the format used in HTTP headers).
second	Returns the seconds.
TimeMinutes	Returns the timestring for the object without seconds.
Time	Returns the timestring for the object with seconds.
timezone	Returns the time zone in which the object is displayed.
year	Returns the object's calendar year.
yy	Returns the calendar year as a two-digit number.

A.1.1 Special Formats

These special formats can be used with the fmt attribute on other data types.

Special Format	Description
whole-dollars	Displays a numeric value with the dollar sign.
dollars-and-cents	Displays a numeric value with the dollar sign and two decimal places.
collection-length	Returns the length of a collection of objects.
structured-text	Renders the value as structured text, which generates HTML from Zope structured text data.

The examples in the table below all format the value -20. See section 4.3.1.2.

C-Style Formats for the fmt Attribute

Code	Description	Example	Result
d	Decimal numbers with preceding sign	fmt="%.3d"	-020
e	Scientific notation	fmt="%.3e"	-2.000e+001
E	Scientific notation	fmt="%.3E"	-2.000E+001
f	Real decimal numbers	fmt="%.3f"	-20.000
g	e or f abbreviated	fmt="%.3g"	-20
G	E or F abbreviated	fmt="%.3G"	-20
i	Decimal numbers with preceding sign	fmt="%.3i"	-020
o	Octals without preceding sign	fmt="%.3o"	37777777754
s	Character string	fmt="%.2s"	-2
u	Decimal numbers without preceding sign	fmt="%.3u"	4294967276
x	Hexadecimal numbers with lowercase letters and without preceding sign	fmt="%.3x"	ffffffec
X	Hexadecimal numbers with uppercase letters and without preceding sign	fmt="%.3X"	FFFFFFEC

A.2   The Namespace Variable

Namespace Attribute Variables

Attribute	Function	Example	Output
abs(number)	Calculates the amount of a number.	"_.abs(-3)"	3
chr(number)	Returns the character associated with a numeric ASCII value.	"_.chr(97)"	a
divmod(number 1, number 2)	Calculates the whole proportion and the whole remainder when dividing two numbers.	"_.divmod(20, 3)" "_.divmod(12, 3)"	(6, 2) (4, 0)
float(number)	Converts a value to a floating point (decimal) number.	"_.float(4)"	4.0
getitem(name[,call])	Looks up a name in the namespace (for instance, _[...]), but also takes an optional second argument that determines if the returned object should be called. If the argument is omitted, the object is not called, which is the opposite of the behavior of _[...].	"_.getitem('some_name')"	Content of some_name
hash(object)	Returns the hash value of an object.	"_.hash(index_html)"	504824376
hex(number)	Converts a number into hexadecimal.	"_.hex(5)" "_.hex(8)"	0x5 0x10
int(number)	Converts a value to an integer. Any decimal values are truncated, and no rounding occurs.	"_.int(4.25)" "_.int('4.85')"	4 4
len(seq)	Calculates the number of elements in a sequence.	"_.len('Hello')" "_.len(['I', 'You'])"	5 2
max(seq)	Outputs the largest element in a list.	"_.max(,1', ,3', ,4', ,5')" "_.max(['Ah','You'])"	5 You

(continued on next page)

Namespace Attribute Variables (continued)

Attribute	Function	Example	Output
namespace (name1= Value1, name2=Value2, etc.)	Returns a new namespace containing the name and value pairs specified as arguments. See also section 4.3.8, "The with Tag," and section 4.3.9, "The let Tag."		
oct(number)	Presents a number as an octal number.	"_.oct(5)" "_.oct(8)"	0x5 0x10
ord(letter)	Returns the ASCII number of a character.	"_.ord('a')"	97
math	See "The Math Module" under section 4.3.2.2; attributes are shown below.		
whrandom	See "The Whrandom Module" under section 4.3.2.2; attributes are shown below.		
string	See "The String Module" under section 4.3.2.2; attributes are shown below.		
range(count[, start][, step])	Returns a list of count integers (generally used for looping) starting at start (default 0) and incrementing by step (default 1).	_.range(4)	[0,1,2,3]
round(number, decimal places)	Rounds a number off to a specified number of decimal places.	"_.round(2.1234, 2)"	2.12
str(Object)	Converts a value into a character string.	"_.str(AUTHENITCATED _USER)"	manager

A.2.1 Modules

Math Module Attributes

Attribute	Function	Example	Output
acos(X)	Calculates the arc cosine of a number.	"_.math.acos(0.5)">	1.0471975512
asin(X)	Calculates the arc sine of a number.	"_.math.asin(0.5)">	0.523598775598
atan(X)	Calculates the arc tangent of a number.	"_.math.atan(0.5)">	0.463647609001
atan2(X,Y)	Calculates the arc tangent of the quotients of X and Y.	"_.math.atan2(0.5, 2)">	0.244978663127
ceil(X)	Returns the smallest whole number larger than X.	"_.math.ceil(4.33)">	5.0
cos(X)	Calculates the cosine of a number.	"_.math.cos(45)">	0.525321988818
cosh(X)	Calculates the hyperbolic cosine for a number.	"_.math.cosh(45)">	1.74671355287e +019
e	The Euler number.	"_.math.e">	2.71828182846
exp(X)	Calculates the exponential X of the base e.	"_.math.exp(5)">	148.413159103
fabs(X)	Calculates the absolute value of a floating point number.	"_.math.fabs(-5.5)">	5.5
floor(X)	Returns the largest decimal value smaller than X.	"_.math.floor(-5.5)">	-6.0
fmod(X,Y)	Calculates the real remainder when dividing real numbers.	"_.math.fmod(-5.5, 2.0)">	1.5
frexp(X)	Calculates the mantissa and exponent to the base 2 of a decimal number.	"_.math.frexp(5)">	(0.625, 3)
hypot(X,Y)	Calculates the hypotenuse of a right triangle given the length of its two bases using the formula: $X^2 + Y^2 = Z^2$.	"_.math.hypot(3, 2)">	3.60555127546
ldexp(X,Y)	Calculates the product of X and the exponential of Y to the base 2.	"_.math.ldexp(3, 2)">	12.0

(continued on next page)

Math Module Attributes (continued)

Attribute	Function	Example	Output
log(X)	Calculates the natural logarithm (to the base e) of a number.	"_.math.log(8)">	2.07944154168
log10(X)	Calculates the logarithm of a number to the base 10.	"_.math.log10(8)">	0.903089986992
modf(X)	Returns the fractional and the whole portion of a number as a tuple.	"_.math.modf(8.75)">	(0.75, 8)
pi	The mathematical constant Pi.	"_.math.pi">	3.14159265359
pow(X,Y)	Raises X to the power of Y.	"_.math.pow(2, 4)">	16.0
sin(X)	Calculates the sine of a number.	"_.math.sin(45)">	0.850903524534
sinh(X)	Calculates the hyperbolic sine of a number.	"_.math.sinh(45)">	1.74671355287e +019
sqrt(X)	Calculates the square root of a number.	"_.math.sqrt(16)">	4.0
tan(X)	Calculates the tangent of a number.	"_.math.tan(45)">	1.61977519054
tanh(X)	Calculates the hyperbolic tangent of a number.	"_.math.tanh(45)">	1.0

A.2.1.1 The String Module

String Constants

Attribute	Constants
digits	The string 0123456789
hexdigits	The string 0123456789abcdefABCDEF
lowercase	Produces a string that contains all lowercase letters, for example abcdefghijklmnopqrstuvwxyz.
uppercase	Produces a string that contains all uppercase letters, for example ABCDEFGHIJKLMNOPQRSTUVWXYZ.
letters	Produces a string composed of the partial strings lowercase and uppercase.
whitespace	Produces string that contains only characters regarded as white spaces, specifically: space, tab, line feed (line break), return, form feed (page break), and vertical tab.

String Module Methods

Attribute Name	Explanation	Example	Screen Output
atof(S)	Converts a string into a floating point number.	"_.string.atof('12')"	12.0
atoi(S, [BASE])	Converts a string into an integer (to an optional base).	"_.string.atoi('8')" "_.string.atoi('-256', 16)"	8 (as integer) -598 (to the base 16)
capitalize(W)	Capitalizes the first letter of a string.	"_.string. capitalize ('hello')"	Hello
capwords(S)	Capitalizes the first letter of all words in a string.	"_.string.capwords('hello, how're you?)"	Hello How're You?
find(S, SUB[, START])	Returns the offset of the substring in the string S. If the substring is not found in the string, -1 is returned.	"_.string.find('Hello ', 'e')" "_.string.find('Hello ', 'a')"	1 -1
rfind(S, SUB[, START])	Similar to find, except that it searches the string from right to left.	"_.string.rfind('Home sweet Home', 'o')"	12
index(S, SUB[, START])	Similar to find, except that it returns an error message if the substring is not found.	"_.string.index ('Hello', 'a')"	Error Type: ValueError Error Value: substring not found in string.index
count(S, SUB[, START])	The number of non-overlapping occurrences of a string in another string.	"_.string.count('aaabb b', 'aa')" "_.string.count('aaaab bb', 'aa')"	1 2
lower(S)	Converts all uppercase letters into lowercase.	"_.string.lower('Hell o, How're you? ')"	hello, how're you?
maketrans (FROM, TO) und translate(S, TABLE[, DELS])	Defines a translation table that can be used by translate.	<dtml-call "REQUEST. set('transtab', _.string.maketrans('a bcdef', 'fedcba'))"> "_.string.translate(' hallo du', _['transtab'])"	hfllo cu
split(S[, SEP[, MAX]])	Splits a string into a list; with the space character as the default separator.	"_.string.split('one two three')"	['one','two','three']

(continued on next page)

String Module Methods (continued)

Attribute Name	Explanation	Example	Screen Output
join(WORDS[, SEP])	Joins elements; the default value placed between elements is the space character.	`"_.string.join(['one','two','three'])"`	'one two three'
lstrip(S)	Removes all spaces at the start of a string; spaces at the end of strings are not changed.	`"_.string.lstrip(' Hello ')"`	'Hello '
rstrip(S)	Removes all spaces at the end of a string; spaces at the start of a string are not changed.	`"_.string.rstrip(' Hello ')"`	' Hello'
strip(S)	Removes spaces at the start and end of a string.	`"_.string.strip(' Hello ')"`	'Hello'
swapcase(S)	Swaps upper- and lowercase letters.	`"_.string.swapcase('Hello ')"`	hELLO
upper(S)	Converts all characters to uppercase.	`"_.string.upper('Hello')"`	HELLO
zfill(S, WIDTH)	Adds zeros to a string until it reaches the specified length.	`"_.string.zfill('12', 5)"`	00012

A.2.1.2 The whrandom Module

Attribute Name	Explanation	Example	Screen Output
choice(SEQ)	Selects a random element from a list.	`"_.whrandom.choice(['1', '2', '3'])"`	1 or 2 or 3
randint(a, b)	Selects a random integer from a to b.	`"_.whrandom.randint(1, 5)"`	1 or 2 or 3 or 4 or 5
random()	Selects a real number between 0 and 1.	`"_.whrandom.random()"`	0.5
uniform(a, b)	Selects a real number between the specified numbers.	`"_.whrandom.uniform(1, 5)"`	1.25

A.2.2 Client-Server Communication

REQUEST Object Attributes

Attribute Name	Explanation	Example	Screen Output
AUTHENTICATED _USER	Displays the user object of the user currently logged in. Displays the user "Anonymous User" if no user is logged in.	AUTHENTICATED_USER	manager
AUTHENTICATION _PATH	Displays the path of the acl_users folder in which the current user is defined.	AUTHENTICATION_PATH	/Test/Folder1 (if the current user is defined in the acl_users-folder in /Test/Folder)
PARENTS	Returns highest folder-like object in the object hierarchy starting from the current document backward. PARENTS[-1] always refers to the root folder.	"PARENTS[0]['id']" "PARENTS[1] ['title']"	GWS_Training Zope
PUBLISHED	The actual object being published to the client by Zope.	PUBLISHED	<DTMLMethod instance at 96eddb8>
URL URL0	Returns the full URL of the object requested by the client's web browser.	URL	http://localhost:80 80/Order1/Test/in dex_html
URL1 - URLn	The URL path to the object up to the nth object above it in the path; used to create links to objects higher in the Zope hierarchy.	URL1 URL2	http://localhost:80 80/Order1/Test http://localhost:80 80/Order1
BASE BASE0	Returns the base of the URL requested.	BASE	http://localhost:80 80
BASE1 - BASEn	The URL path with n objects is added to the BASE.	BASE1	http://localhost:80 80/Order1
HTTP_REFERER	The URL of the previous page on which the user clicked a link or a submit button to arrive at this page; useful for creating links to go back to the previous page.	http_REFERER	URL of page that linked to this one.

(continued on next page)

REQUEST Object Attributes (continued)

Attribute Name	Explanation	Example	Screen Output
cookies	Displays the values set as cookies in the form of a dictionary.	`"REQUEST.cookies"`	{'tree-s': 'eJzTiFZ3hANPW/ VYHU0ALlYElA', 'dtpref_rows': '10', 'dtpref_cols': '65'}
form	The result is the values set by a form in dictionary format.	`"REQUEST.form"` `"REQUEST.form ['field1']"`	{'field1': 'hello', 'myfield': 'you'} hello
has_key(name)	Returns 1 if the specified variable name is contained in the REQUEST; returns 0 if the specified variable name is not contained in the REQUEST.	`"REQUEST.has_key('U RL0)">` `"REQUEST.has_key('U RL9')"`	1 (because URL0 is contained in the REQUEST) 0 (because URL9 is not contained in the REQUEST)
set(name, value)	Sets a variable in REQUEST with the specified name and value.	`"REQUEST.set('myvar ', 'Content of myvar')"`	None (has no result that can be evaluated)
get(name[,default])	Retrieves a variable by name from REQUEST and optionally allows you to specify a default value if the variable is not set.	`"REQUEST.get('myvar ','')"`	The value stored in myvar or an empty string if myvar is not set

RESPONSE Object Attributes

Name	Explanation
setStatus(status)	Sets the HTTP status code of a query; the argument can be either an integer or a string from {OK, Created, Accepted, NoContent, MovedPermanently, MovedTemporarily, NotModified, BadRequest, Unauthorized, Forbidden, NotFound, InternalError, NotImplemented, BadGateway, ServiceUnavailable}; this will be converted into an integer value. (See "HTTP Status Codes" below.)
setHeader(name, value)	Sets a HTTP-Return-Header-Name with a value and deletes any previous value set for the header.
getStatus()	Gives the current HTTP-Status-Code an integer. (See "HTTP Status Codes" below.)
setBase(base)	Sets the base URL for the returned document.
expireCookie(name)	Removes an http cookie from the browser. The response contains a HTTP-Header that removes the cookie called "name" if it exists by sending a new cookie with an elapsed expiration date.

(continued on next page)

RESPONSE Object Attributes (continued)

Name	Explanation
setCookie(name, value,...)	Causes the response to contain an HTTP-Header that sets up a cookie with the key name and the value "value" on browsers in which cookies are activated, thus overwriting all previously set values for the cookie in the response object. Additional cookie parameters can be inserted by specifying the keyword parameters expires, domain, path, max_age, comment, and secure.
getHeader(name)	Returns the value associated with a HTTP-Return-Header or None if no such header was set in the response.
appendHeader (name, value)	Adds value to the http response header, name. If a header by the specified name already exists, the value is appended to the existing header, preceded by a comma.
redirect(location)	Redirects to another URL without resulting in an error.

HTTP Status Codes

Status as String	Status as Integer
OK	200
Accepted	202
MovedPermanently	301
MovedTemporarily	302
NotModified	304
BadRequest	400
Unauthorized	401
Forbidden	403
NotFound	404
InternalError	500
NotImplemented	501
BadGateway	502
ServiceUnavailable	503

CGI-Defined Web Query Variables Defined in the REQUEST Object

Name	Description
SERVER_SOFTWARE	The name and version of the information server software that responds to the query, using the format Name/Version.
SERVER_NAME	The hostname, the DNS Alias, or the IP address of the server as it appears in the URL.
GATEWAY_INTERFACE	The version of a CGI specification that the server is using. Format is CGI/Version.
SERVER_PROTOCOL	The name and version of the information protocol from which the query originates. Format is Protocol/Version.
SERVER_PORT	The port number to which the query was sent.
REQUEST_METHOD	The method that was used to create the query. For HTTP: GET, HEAD, POST, and so on.
PATH_INFO	The part of the queried URL (without the start string) that follows the name of the Zope installation or module published by ZPublisher.
PATH_TRANSLATED	The server returns a translated version of PATH_INFO, which takes the path and maps it from a virtual to a physical one.
SCRIPT_NAME	Returns a virtual path to the executed script; used with self-referring URLs.
QUERY_STRING	The information that follows the ? in the URL, which refers to this script. This is the query information.
REMOTE_HOST	Returns the name of the host that created the query. If the server does not have this information, it should call REMOTE_ADDR and leave REMOTE_HOST blank.
REMOTE_ADDR	Returns the IP address of the remote host that placed the request.
AUTH_TYPE	If the server supports user authentication and the script is protected, this log-specific authentication method is used to confirm the validity of the user.
REMOTE_USER	If the server supports user authentication and the script is protected, the user is authenticated under this name.
REMOTE_IDENT	If the HTTP Server supports RFC 931 identification, this variable is set to the username obtained from the sever. Restrict use of this variable to login only.
CONTENT_TYPE	In the case of queries that have information attached, for example HTTP POST and PUT, this is the content type for the data.
CONTENT_LENGTH	Returns the length of the specified content as entered by the client.

A.2.2.1 The in Tag

Attributes for the in Tag

Name	Explanation
name	The name of the variable that returns the sequence to be iterated.
expr	An expression that returns the sequence to be iterated.
mapping	The items of the sequence should be treated as mapping objects, such as dictionaries. Each key of each item is mapped to the namespace inside the in block.
sort	The sort attribute is used to sort a sequence of objects before the sequence is iterated. The value attribute is the name of the attribute (or key if the mapping attribute is specified) according to which the items are to be sorted.
sort_expr	Like sort, but allows the sequence to be sorted by the attribute or key name returned in an expression. This allows the sort order to be chosen at run time.
start	The name of a variable that specifies the starting sequence item of the current batch. If omitted, iteration starts at the first item.
size	The size of each batch of sequence items to iterate. If omitted, the entire sequence is iterated at once.
skip_unauthorized	Using this attribute results in sequence items being omitted if access to this item is not permitted. If this attribute is not used, an Unauthorized error occurs if unauthorized items are iterated over.
orphan	The number of items needed to expand the last batch to keep it from being too small. If this is omitted, this value defaults to 3.
overlap	The number of items that overlap between batches. If this is omitted, there is no overlap.
previous	If this attribute is used, the iterative addition is not carried out. If there is a previous batch, the text inside the in tag is inserted and batch processing variables that are associated with an earlier batch are accessible.
next	Has the same meaning and use as the previous attribute, with the exception that variables are prepared with the next batch.

Variables Defined Inside the in Body

Name	Explanation
sequence-item	The current element being iterated.
sequence-key	The key associated with the sequence of an item; defined if an element is a two item tuple. Its value is set to the first item and its sequence-item to the second item.
sequence-index	The index (where the first number is 0) of the current item being iterated.
sequence-number	The number of the current item being iterated, where the first item is number 1.
sequence-start	The variable is true if the current element is the first item of the current batch; if not, it is false. This is useful if text must be inserted at the start of an in tag, particularly if the text refers to a batch variable defined by the in tag.
sequence-end	The variable is true if the current element is the last one of the current batch; if not, it is false. This is useful if the text must be inserted at the end of an in tag, particularly if the text refers to a batch variable defined by the in tag.
sequence-even	Set to true if sequence-index is an even number. Can be used to alternately shade rows in a table.
sequence-odd	Set to true if sequence-index is an odd number.

A.2.2.2 More Variables Defined by the in Tag

In the tables below, replace nnn with the name of an attribute in your sequence items.

Summary and Statistics Variables

Name	Explanation
total-nnn	The sum of numeric values
count-nnn	The total number of existing values
min-nnn	The minimum value of an attribute in the sequence
max-nnn	The maximum value of an attribute in the sequence
median-nnn	The average of the existing values
mean-nnn	The average value of the numeric values
variance-nnn	The variance of the numeric values calculated with a degree of freedom that comes after the (count −1)
variance-n-nnn	The variance of the numeric values calculated with a degree of freedom that comes after the count

(continued on next page)

Summary and Statistics Variables (continued)

Name	Explanation
standard-deviation-nnn	The standard deviation of the numeric values calculated with a degree of freedom that comes after the (count −1)
standard-deviation-n-nnn	The standard deviation of the numeric values calculated with a degree of freedom that comes straight after the count

Special Element Grouping Variables

Name	Explanation
first-nnn	Returns true if the current item is the first of the displayed items with the current value for the variable nnn; if not, it returns false. Used for grouping.
last-nnn	Returns true if the current item is the last of the displayed items with the current value for the variable nnn; if not it returns false. Used for grouping.

Batch Processing Variables

Name	Explanation
batch-start-index	The index (starting with 0) of the start of the current batch.
batch-end-index	The index (starting with 0) of the end of the current batch.
batch-size	The size of the current batch.
previous-sequence	Set to true on the first element of the batch if a batch precedes it.
previous-sequence-size	If previous-sequence is true, this is set to the number of elements in the previous batch.
previous-sequence-start-index	If previous-sequence is true, this is set to the start index of the previous batch. Used to construct previous-batch links.
next-sequence	Set to true on the last element of a batch if there is another batch after it.
next-sequence-size	If next-sequence is true, this is set to the number of elements in the next batch.
next-sequence-start-index	If next-sequence is true, this is set to the start index of the next batch. Used to construct links to the next batch.
sequence-query	The query string passed in the web request. Can be inserted into a link href to replay the query for a different batch.

A.2.2.3 The tree Tag

Attributes for the tree Tag

Name	Explanation
name	See "The name Attribute" in Table 4.1.
expr	See "The expr Attribute" in Table 4.1.
branches	The name of the method used to find subobjects. The default is tpValues, a method that finds folderish objects. The method objectValues finds all objects and subobjects beneath another object. The value must be a method name.
branches_expr	An expression that is evaluated to find subobjects. This attribute performs the same function as the branches attribute, and the value it receives is an expression instead of the name of the method.
id	The name of the method or attribute used to determine the Id of an object in order to calculate a tree status. The default method is tpId.
url	The name of the method or attribute used to determine the URL of an object. The default method is tpURL.
leaves	The name of a document that uses "leaves" to expand subjects that do not have subobjects.
header	The name of a document to be displayed above any branch expansion. This allows you to "mark" a branch in a hierarchy.
footer	The name of the document displayed beneath each expansion.
nowrap	Either 0 or 1. If 0, the branch content can wrap if it is too wide to fit in the browser window. The default value is 0.
sort	Sorts the branches before text is inserted. The attribute value is the name of the attribute by which the elements are to be sorted.
assume_children	Either 0 or 1. If 1, it is automatically assumed that all objects have subobjects and consequently are always displayed with a "+" sign in front of them when they are not expanded. Only when an item is expanded will a search be carried out among subobjects. This can be useful for avoiding time-consuming searches.
single*	Either 0 or 1. If 1, only one branch of the tree can be expanded. Each expanded branch is collapsed if a new branch is expanded.
skip_unauthorized	Either 0 or 1. If 1, no errors are generated if an attempt is made to display subobjects for which the user does not have authorization.

Variables in the tree Tag Body

Name	Explanation
tree-item-expand	True if the current element is expanded.
tree-item-url	The relative URL of the current element.
tree-root-url	The URL of the DTML document in which the tree tag appears.
tree-level	The depth of the current element.
tree-colspan	The number of tree nestings called.
tree-state	The tree status; output as a list of ids and sublists of sub-ids.

Attributes for the sendmail Tag

Name	Function	Example
mailhost	The Zope MailHost object that manages data required to send electronic mail. If this attribute is used, the smtphost is unnecessary.	`<dtml-sendmail mailhost="MailHost1">`
smtphost	The address of the SMTP server to be used. If this attribute is used, the Mailhost attribute is unnecessary.	`<dtml-sendmail smtphost= "mail.mycompany.com">`
port	This attribute can be used only with the smtphost attribute, and the port number for a connection must be specified. If the smtphost attribute is used without the port attribute, the port number is set to 25 by default.	`<dtml-sendmail smtphost= "mail.mycompany.com" port="20">`
mailto	The recipient's address. Multiple addresses are separated by commas.	`<dtml-sendmail mailhost=Mailhost1`
mailfrom	The sender's address.	`mailto="abc@beehive.com"`
subject	The subject of the message.	`mailfrom="xyz@mycompany.com"`
		`subject="Meeting today">`

Attributes for the MIME Tag and the Boundary Tag

Attribute	Function	Example
type	Indicates the type and format of the data. The default value is application/octet stream.	Type="image/bmp"
disposition	Sets the content disposition of the following data. If the disposition is not specified in a MIME or boundary tag, the content disposition MIME header is not inserted into the message.	disposition="attachment"
name	Indicates the name of the file object to be attached. If the name attribute is used in the MIME tag, the message is sent as an attachment and not as standard text.	name="wordfile"
encode	Sets the encoding method for the files to be sent. The default value is base64, which is suitable for sending binary files to most mail clients. The following options are available: base64, uuencode, x-uuencode, quote-printable, uue, x-uue and 7bit. If encode is set to 7bit, no encoding is applied. This is appropriate for textual document formats such as HTML.	encode=uuencode

THE REQUEST OBJECT

REQUEST

The DTML command <dtml-var name="REQUEST"> generates output like the following on screen. The REQUEST contains a list of existing Zope variables from the variable space in a Zope installation, at a given time.

form

cookies

    tree-s   eJzTiFZ3hANPW/VYHUOALlYElA

other

```
AUTHENTICATION_PATH
TraversalRequestNameStack    []
    tree-s    eJzTiFZ3hANPW/VYHUOALlYElA
    URL    http://localhost:8080/My_Homepage/index_html
    AUTHENTICATED_USER    katrin
    roles    ['Manager', 'Owner']
```

(continued on next page)

```
SERVER_URL      http://dev4.dmz.beehive.de
name       Egon
URL0       http://localhost:8080/My_Homepage/index_html
URL1       http://localhost:8080/My_Homepage
URL2       http://localhost:8080
BASE0      http://localhost:8080
BASE1      http://localhost:8080
BASE2      http://localhost:8080/My_Homepage
BASE3      http://localhost:8080/My_Homepage/index_html
```

environ

```
HTTP_ACCEPT_ENCODING      gzip
GATEWAY_INTERFACE      CGI/1.1
SERVER_PORT      8080
PATH_TRANSLATED      /My_Homepage/index_html
                              HTTP_VIA      1.0  (Squid/2.2.STABLE5)
HTTP_COOKIE      tree-s="eJzTiFZ3hANPW/VYHUOAL1YElA"
HTTP_ACCEPT_LANGUAGE      en
PROFILE_PUBLISHER      /usr/local/Zope_2.2.2/var/profile.txt
HTTP_X_FORWARDED_FOR      unknown
REMOTE_ADDR      192.168.1.1
SERVER_NAME      localhost
HTTP_USER_AGENT      Mozilla/4.7 [en] (WinNT; I)
HTTP_ACCEPT_CHARSET      iso-8859-1,*,utf-8
HTTP_ACCEPT      image/gif, image/x-xbitmap, image/jpeg, image/pjpeg, image/png, */*
channel.creation_time      971686366
SERVER_PROTOCOL      1.0
PATH_INFO      /My_Homepage/index_html
HTTP_HOST      localhost:8080
REQUEST_METHOD      GET
SCRIPT_NAME
SERVER_SOFTWARE      Zope/Zope 2.2.2 (source release, python 1.5.2, linux2) ZServer/1.1b1
HTTP_CACHE_CONTROL      max-age=259200
CONNECTION_TYPE      keep-alive
HTTP_REFERER      http://localhost:8080/My_Homepage/index_html/manage_edit
```

The variables *name* and *roles* (under other) were previously set as follows using REQUEST.set:

```
<dtml-call expr="REQUEST.set('name', 'Egon')">
<dtml-call expr="REQUEST.set('roles', ['Manager', 'Owner'])">
```

As you can see, the REQUEST is divided into four sections: form, cookies, other, and environ, and each section contains variables. This sample REQUEST does not contain any variables in the *form* section because there was no HTML form with which variables were set at the time the REQUEST was made.

The following are probably the most commonly used variables:

```
AUTHENTICATED_USER       manager
URL0      http://localhost:8080/My_Homepage/index_html

   .            .
   .            .
   .            .

BASE0      http://localhost:8080

   .            .
   .            .
   .            .

PATH_INFO      /My_Homepage/index_html
HTTP_ REFERER      http://localhost:8080/My_Homepage/test_html
```

AUTHENTICATED_USER returns the users (with password) currently logged on or 'Anonymous User.'

URL0 returns the complete path of the current object whereas URL1 returns the path of the folder in which the current object is located. Accordingly, URL2, URL3, and so on return the path of each superordinate folder.

BASE0, BASE1, BASE2, ... also return the corresponding path although these start at the root folder and work downwards until the current object is reached.

PATH_INFO returns the path of the current object without the base (for example http://localhost:8080/ =Base; /My_Homepage/index_html =PATH_INFO).

HTTP_REFERER indicates the URL from which the current object was called.

You can directly access the data stored in the REQUEST:

```
<dtml-var name="URL0">
<dtml-var name="HTTP_REFERER">
```

The following is another method for outputting data:

```
<dtml-var expr="REQUEST['URL0']">
<dtml-var expr="REQUEST.HTTP_REFERER">
```

SOURCE CODE FOR THE WEBSITE PRODUCT

C.1 Source Text for _ _init_ _.py_ for the Website Product

```python
__version__='Version 0.1'
__doc__='Website'

import Website

def initialize(context):
    """Register the Website class"""

    context.registerClass(
        Website.Website,
        constructors = (
            Website.manage_addWebsiteForm,
            Website.manage_addWebsite
        ),
        permission = 'Add Website',
        icon = 'www/icon.gif'
    )
```

C.2 Source Text for *Website.py* for the Website Product

```
############################################################
##   Import of the necessary modules, classes and methods   ##
############################################################

import Globals
from Globals import MessageDialog, DTMLFile
from AccessControl import ClassSecurityInfo
from AccessControl.Permission import Permission
from AccessControl.User import UserFolder
from OFS.Folder import Folder
import StringIO


############################################################
##   Supporting methods to create DTML Methods in Zope     ##
############################################################

def GetDTML(name):
    return DTMLFile(name, globals())

def addDocsToFolder(theFolder, theDocs):
    """ Adding several DTML Methods in Zope """
    errs=StringIO.StringIO()
    for key in theDocs.keys():
        id=key
        dtml,title=theDocs[key]
        try:
            thedtml=open(dtml.raw).read()
        except:
            raise RuntimeError, "Can't find " + dtml.raw
        try:
            theFolder.manage_addDocument(id, title=title, file=thedtml)
        except:
            traceback.print_exc(file=errs)
    errs.seek(0)
    return errs.read()


############################################################
##   Dictionary with .dtml-files that have to be           ##
##   converted to DTML Methods                             ##
############################################################

Website_pages={
    'standard_html_header':
    (GetDTML('public/standard_html_header'),"Website Standard Header"),
```

```
        'standard_html_footer':
        (GetDTML('public/standard_html_footer'),"Website Standard Footer"),
        'index_html':
        (GetDTML('public/index_html'),"Website Index Page"),
        'login_html':
        (GetDTML('public/login_html'),"Password-Check"),
        'new_WebsiteUser':
        (GetDTML('public/new_WebsiteUser'),"Create new WebsiteUser"),
        'WebsiteUsers_list':
        (GetDTML('public/WebsiteUsers_list'),"List of WebsiteUsers"),
        'edit_WebsiteUser':
        (GetDTML('public/edit_WebsiteUser'),"Edit a WebsiteUser"),
        'products_html':
        (GetDTML('public/products_html'),"About our products"),
        'about_us_html':
        (GetDTML('public/about_us_html'),"About the company"),
        }


##########################################################
##    Class definition of the product Website           ##
##########################################################

class Website(Folder):
    """This product was created by Katrin Kirchner"""

    name='Website'
    id='Website'
    meta_type='Website'

    ##########################################################
    ##  Create a ClassSecurityInfo object for our class     ##
    ##  so that we can make security assertions for the     ##
    ##  attributes defined in the class                     ##
    ##########################################################

    security = ClassSecurityInfo()

    ##########################################################
    ##  Set default security for instances of the class     ##
    ##  Users must have the "View" permission to have any   ##
    ##  access to the Website instance.                     ##
    ##########################################################

    security.declareObjectProtected('View')
```

(continued on next page)

```
#######################################################
## Define the default properties for the class      ##
#######################################################


_properties=(
    {'id': 'title', 'type': 'string', 'mode': 'w'},
    )


#######################################################
##  Example for adding your own tab to the Tab-bar of  ##
##  instances of the product (commented out with #)     ##
#######################################################


manage_options=Folder.manage_options+(
    #{'label':'my_label','icon':icon,'action':'my_action','target':'manage_main'},
    )


#######################################################
##  Method for creating a new WebsiteUser            ##
#######################################################


# Allow users with the "Manage users" permission access to this method
security.declareProtected('Manage users', 'addNewWebsiteUser')

def addNewWebsiteUser(self, name, pwd, confirm, roles, domains, REQUEST, RESPONSE):
    """ Creates a new WebsiteUser if the user name does not exist already"""
    if self.acl_users.getUser(name):
        return MessageDialog(
            title   ='User already exists',
            message='There is already a user with this name.',
            action ='new_WebsiteUser'
            )
    else:
        self.acl_users._addUser(name, pwd, confirm, roles, domains, REQUEST)
        RESPONSE.redirect('index_html')


#######################################################
##  Method for changing the password, the            ##
##  Internet-Domains and maybe the role of an         ##
##  existing WebsiteUser                              ##
#######################################################


# Allow users with the "Manage users" permission access to this method
security.declareProtected('Manage users', 'editWebsiteUser')

def editWebsiteUser(self, name, pwd, confirm, domains, roles, REQUEST, RESPONSE):
    """Changes existing WebsiteUser"""
    self.acl_users._changeUser(name,pwd,confirm,roles,domains)
```

```
        return MessageDialog(
            title  ='User changed',
            message='The user has been changed.',
            action ='index_html'
            )


    ########################################################
    ##  Method for deleting an existing WebsiteUser        ##
    ########################################################

    # Allow users with the "Manage users" permission access to this method
    security.declareProtected('Manage users', 'deleteWebsiteUser')

    def deleteWebsiteUser(self, name):
        """Deletes a WebsiteUser"""
        self.acl_users._delUsers([name])
        return MessageDialog(
            title  ='User deleted',
            message='The user has been deleted.',
            action ='index_html'
            )


############################################################
##     Properly initialize the class in Zope              ##
############################################################


Globals.InitializeClass(Website)


############################################################
##     Showing the form to create a new instance of       ##
##     the product Website                                ##
############################################################


manage_addWebsiteForm=DTMLFile('dtml/addWebsiteForm', globals())


############################################################
##     Method for creating an instance of the product     ##
##     Website, including the DTML Methods and the        ##
##     User Folder                                        ##
############################################################


def manage_addWebsite(self, id, title, REQUEST=None):
    """Add a new Website"""
```

(continued on next page)

```
######################################################
##  Assigning the class Website to a                ##
##  variable instance                               ##
######################################################

instance=Website()
instance.id=id
instance.title=title

######################################################
##  Creating the User Folder                        ##
######################################################

user_folder=UserFolder()
instance._setObject('acl_users', user_folder)


######################################################
##  Creating the role 'WebsiteUser'                 ##
######################################################

instance._addRole('WebsiteUser')

######################################################
##  Setting the permissions for the role            ##
##  'WebsiteUser'                                    ##
######################################################

p_list = ['Access contents information',
          'Manage users', 'View']
for permission in p_list:
    p=Permission(permission,'',instance)
    p.setRole('WebsiteUser', permission in p_list)

######################################################
##  Creating an instance of the product within      ##
##  the current folder                              ##
######################################################

self._setObject(id, instance)

######################################################
##  Creating the DTML Methods                       ##
######################################################

addDocsToFolder(instance, Website_pages)
```

```
#####################################################
##  Changing the permission setting of login_html  ##
##  for the password check                         ##
#####################################################

old_permissions = self.permission_settings()
new_permissions = []
permissions_for_WebsiteUsers = []
for item in old_permissions:
    if item['name']=='View':
        permissions_for_WebsiteUsers.append(item['name'])
    else:
        new_permissions.append(item['name'])
instance.login_html.manage_acquiredPermissions(new_permissions)
instance.login_html.manage_role('WebsiteUser', permissions_for_WebsiteUsers)

if REQUEST is not None:
    return self.manage_main(self, REQUEST)
```

C.2.1 addWebsiteForm.dtml

```
<dtml-var standard_html_header>
<form action="manage_addWebsite" method=post>
<h2>Add a new Website</h2>
<p>The product Website is a folderish object with several DTML Methods
as well as a User Folder containing a user already created.</p>
<table>
<tr>
<th>Id:</th>
<td><input type=text name=id size=20></td>
<tr>
<th><em>Title:</em></th>
<td><input type=text name=title size=20></td>
<tr>
<td></td>
<td><input type=submit value=Add></td>
</table>
</form>
<dtml-var standard_html_footer>
```

addWebsiteForm.dtml is the constructor form for the Website class. It loaded and stored as a DTMLFile object in the Website class. When submitted, it calls the manage_addWebsite constructor method of the main Website module.

C.3 The DTML Methods for the Website Product

The following section contains the source text of the DTML files which create the Website product for each instance as well as brief descriptions of the methods. These files are stored in the public directory of the product.

C.3.1 WebsiteUsers_list.dtml

```
<dtml-var standard_html_header>
<h2>Registered website users</h2>
<p>
<dtml-call "REQUEST.set('UL', acl_users.getUserNames())">
<ul>
<table>
<dtml-in UL>
<tr>
<td><li><dtml-var sequence-item></li></td>
<td>
<a href="edit_WebsiteUser?uname=<dtml-var sequence-item>"><font color="#0068a0">Edit</font></a> |
<a href="deleteWebsiteUser?name=<dtml-var sequence-item>"><font color="#0068a0">Delete</font></a>
</td>
</dtml-in>
</tr>
</table>
</ul>
</p>
<dtml-var standard_html_footer>
```

This DTML method is used to list the users which exist in the acl_users of an instance of the product. Using acl_users.getUserNames() you obtain a lost of existing users. This list is then processed with <dtml-in>. Each username is then displayed on the website with links for editing and deleting the user after each name. These links pass on the relevant username to the DTML method (edit_WebsiteUser) or the Python method (Delete_WebsiteUser()).

C.3.2 edit_WebsiteUser.dtml

```
<dtml-var standard_html_header>
<h2>Edit website user</h2>
<p>
<dtml-call "REQUEST.set('uname', acl_users.getUser(_['uname']))">

<form action="editWebsiteUser" method=post>
<table>
<tr>
  <th align=left>Name:</th>
  <td><dtml-var uname><input type="hidden" name=name value="<dtml-var uname>"></td>
```

```
  </tr>
<tr>
  <th align=left>Password:</th>
  <td><input type=password name=pwd size=10></td>
</tr>
<tr>
  <th align=left>Confirm:</th>
  <td><input type=password name=confirm size=10></td>
</tr>
<tr>
  <th align=left>Domains:</th>
  <td><input type="text" name="domains:tokens" size=30 value="<dtml-in "uname.getDomains()"><dtml-var
sequence-item> </dtml-in>"></td>
</tr>
<dtml-if "AUTHENTICATED_USER.has_role('Manager')">
<tr>
  <th align=left valign=top>Roles:</th>
  <td><select name="roles:list" size=5 multiple>
        <dtml-in valid_roles>
        <dtml-if expr="_vars['sequence-item'] != 'Anonymous'">
        <dtml-if expr="_vars['sequence-item'] != 'Shared'">
          <OPTION <dtml-if "_['sequence-item'] in _['uname'].getRoles()">SELECTED</dtml-if>
VALUE="<dtml-var sequence-item html_quote>"><dtml-var sequence-item>
        </dtml-if>
        </dtml-if>
        </dtml-in valid_roles>
     </select>
  </td>
</tr>
<dtml-else>
  <tr><input type="hidden" name="roles:list" value="WebsiteUser"></tr>
</dtml-if>
<tr>
  <td><input type=submit value="Change website user"></td>
</tr>
</table>
</form>
</p>
<dtml-var standard_html_footer>
```

When this DTML method is called up, the username to be modified must be passed on. This is achieved by clicking on the Edit link on user list page. The DTML method edit_WebsiteUser generates a form in which you can change the password and Internet domains of the user in question. As a Manager you have the permissions necessary to assign a user to another role.

C.3.3 index_html.dtml

This DTML method is merely used to generate a simple welcome screen. This is a static page containing any content you wish.

C.3.4 login_html.dtml

```
<dtml-call "RESPONSE.redirect('index_html')">
```

The DTML method login_html causes a password query to be generated if the user has not yet logged in (if the user has already logged in, nothing happens when the [Login] button is pressed). This is achieved via the Security settings for this DTML method. The View permission is explicitly set for just the roles 'Manager' and 'User'; 'Anonymous' is not given this permission.

If the user has been authenticated with the correct username and password, this DTML method returns the browser to the welcome screen.

C.3.5 new_WebsiteUser.dtml

```
<dtml-var standard_html_header>
<h2>Create a new website user</h2>
<p>
To create a new website user, please fill out the following form:
</p>

<form action="addNewWebsiteUser" method=post>
<table>
<tr>
  <th align=left>Name:</th>
  <td><input type=text name=name size=20></td>
</tr>
<tr>
  <th align=left>Password:</th>
  <td><input type=password name=pwd size=10></td>
</tr>
<tr>
  <th align=left>Confirm:</th>
  <td><input type=password name=confirm size=10></td>
</tr>
<tr>
  <th align=left>Domains:</th>
  <td><input type="text" name="domains:tokens" size=30></td>
</tr>
<dtml-if "AUTHENTICATED_USER.has_role('Manager')">
<tr>
  <th align=left valign=top>Roles:</th>
  <td><select name="roles:list" size=5 multiple>
```

```
        <dtml-in valid_roles>
        <dtml-if expr="_vars['sequence-item'] != 'Anonymous'">
        <dtml-if expr="_vars['sequence-item'] != 'Shared'">
            <OPTION VALUE="<dtml-var sequence-item html_quote>"><dtml-var sequence-item>
        </dtml-if>
        </dtml-if>
        </dtml-in valid_roles>
      </select>
  </td>
</tr>
<dtml-else>
  <tr><input type="hidden" name="roles:list" value="WebsiteUser"></tr>
</dtml-if>
<tr>
  <td><input type=submit value="Add website user"></td>
</tr>
</table>
</form>
<dtml-var standard_html_footer>
```

This DTML method generates a form with which you can create a new user. You can freely enter the username, password, and Internet domain; the 'User' role is added automatically (<input type="hidden" name="roles:list" value="User">). This means that newly created users have all of the permissions of other users (as well as those which allows them to edit and delete).

C.3.6 products_html.dtml

The DMTL method products_html generates a product description page as an example. This is a static page containing any desired content.

C.3.7 standard_html_footer.dtml

```
      </td>
    </tr>
    </table>
  </td>
  </tr>
  </table>
</body>
</html>
```

The standard_html_footer closes the table and HTML document opened in the standard_html_header (see above).

C.3.8 standard_html_header.dtml

```
<html>
  <head><title></title></head>

  <body link="white" vlink="white" alink="white" bgcolor="white">
  <font face="Arial">
  <table width="100%" bgcolor="#0068a0" cellpadding="4" cellspacing="0" border="0">
  <tr>
    <td width="25%">
      <a href="index_html"><font face="Arial" size="2">
        <b>Home</b>
      </font></a>
    </td>
    <td width="25%">
      <a href="about_us_html"><font face="Arial" size="2">
        <b>About us</b>
      </font></a>
    </td>
    <td width="25%">
      <a href="products_html"><font face="Arial" size="2">
        <b>Products</b>
      </font></a>
    </td>
    <td width="25%">
      <a href="login_html"><font face="Arial" size="2">
        <b>Login</b>
      </font></a>
    </td>
  </tr>
  </table>

  <table width="100%" cellpadding="4" border="0" height="100%">
  <tr>
    <td width="22%" bgcolor="#b9b9b9" valign="top">
      <font color="white" size="2" face="Arial "><b>TOC-Liste</b></font>
      <p><font color="white" size="2" face="Arial"><b><br>
      <dtml-if "AUTHENTICATED_USER.has_permission('Manage users', acl_users)">
      <a href="new_WebsiteUser">Add new website user</a><br>
      <a href="WebsiteUsers_list">List of website users</a><br>
      </dtml-if></b></font>
    </td>
    <td valign="top"  width="80%" >
    </font>
      <table width="100%" cellpadding="15" border="0" height="100%">
      <tr><td valign="top">
```

The standard_html_header generates a navigation bar which appears at the top of the website ('Home', 'About Us', 'Products', 'Login').

In addition, it also creates the TOC list at the left of the screen. This TOC list only appears for users who have logged in and have the 'Manage users' permission.

C.3.9 about_us_html.dtml

about_us_html generates a static page which can contain information about the company.

SOME ZCATALOG
MODULE METHODS

Following are definitions of and comments about common ZCatalog module methods. When using many of them, remember to call them in DTML first, because once they are edited, the browser is redirected to a page of the management screen, which is not usually desired in the third view.

getVocabulary()

If you have created a new vocabulary (with Create one for me) and you want to use this method, you must modify the module ZCatalog.py slightly. (If you are using an existing vocabulary, you do not need to make this change.)

To make the needed change, in the method __init__(), replace the line

```
self.vocab_id=vocab_id
```

with the following:

```
if vocab_id=='create_one_for_me_' or vocab_id==None:
self.vocab_id = 'Vocabulary'
else:
    self.vocab_id
```

The method getVocabulary() gets the vocabulary for the relevant ZCatalog as an object.

manage_edit(self, RESPONSE, URL1, threshold=1000, REQUEST=None)

This method is used only to change the threshold (see section 11.2.6, "The Advanced Screen"). If you do not enter a value for the threshold, the threshold will be set by default to 1,000 subtransactions.

RESPONSE and URL1 must be passed when calling the method, but the other parameters are not essential. For example, the following entry can be used:

```
<dtml-call "manage_edit(RESPONSE, URL1, threshold=50000)">
```

manage_subbingToggle(self, REQUEST, RESPONSE, URL1):

This method is used to switch subtransactions on and off. After the method has been processed, Zope displays the Status screen.

manage_catalogObject(self, REQUEST, RESPONSE, URL1, urls=None)

This method is called when you click the Update button on the Cataloged_Items screen for specific objects whose check boxes have been activated. It reindexes the selected objects. The urls parameter specifies a list in which the path to the relevant object is saved.

manage_uncatalogObject(self, REQUEST, RESPONSE, URL1, urls=None)

The manage_uncatalogObject() method is called when you click the Remove button on the Cataloged_Items screen. As with manage_catalogObject(), urls specifies a list of paths for selected objects. Using this method, you can delete all selected objects from the ZCatalog.

manage_catalogReindex(self, REQUEST, RESPONSE, URL1)

Using this method, you can reindex the entire ZCatalog. This method is called when you click the Update Catalog button on the Cataloged_Items screen.

manage_catalogClear(self, REQUEST=None, RESPONSE=None, URL1=None)

This method is called using the Clear Catalog button on the Cataloged_Items screen. It deletes all references to the indexed objects from the ZCatalog. The objects themselves are not deleted.

manage_addColumn(self, name, REQUEST=None, RESPONSE=None, URL1=None)

This method is called using the Add button on the MetaData_Table screen. You can use it create a new column in the metadata table or on the search results page.

manage_delColumns(self, names, REQUEST=None, RESPONSE=None, URL1=None)

Using this method, you can delete columns from the table of metadata; the relative metadata is no longer displayed on a search results page. The method is called when you click the Delete button on the MetaData_Table screen. The names parameter specifies a list of the names of the metadata to be deleted.

manage_addIndex(self, name, type, REQUEST=None, RESPONSE=None, URL1=None)

This method is called when you click the Add button on the Indexes screen. The name parameter specifies the title of the new index, and type specifies the type of index (KeywordIndex, TextIndex, or FieldIndex).

manage_delIndexes(self, names, REQUEST=None, RESPONSE=None, URL1=None)

Using this method, you can delete existing indexes. The method is called when you click the Delete button on the Indexes screen. The names parameter specifies a list of the indexes to be deleted.

catalog_object(self, obj, uid)

This method is called by the manage_catalogObjects() method and causes a single object to be indexed. It can be called in DTML, because it does not redirect the browser to a specific page after execution.

uncatalog_object(self, uid)

This method is called by the manage_uncatalogObjects() method and causes a single object to be deleted from the ZCatalog. The uid parameter specifies the object path: for example,

```
<dtml-call "uncatalog_object('/MyZCatalog/index_html')">
```

This method can be called in DTML, because it does not redirect the browser to a specific page after execution.

uniqueValuesFor(self, name)

This method returns all of the objects in the ZCatalog that have been indexed in the categories listed in name, the title of the metadata column.

getpath(self, rid)

The transfer argument, rid, is the integer of the object being searched for in the catalog. This method returns the path for this object.

getobject(self, rid, REQUEST=None)

This method requires only the transfer argument, rid (data_record_id). The rid value is the integer identifying the indexed object you are searching for.

schema(self)

This method lists all metadata present in the ZCatalog.

indexes(self)

This method lists all indexes contained in the ZCatalog.

index_objects(self)

This method lists all indexed objects in the ZCatalog.

_searchable_arguments(self)

This method can be used only in Python, in products, or in external methods. It returns a dictionary with all searchable indexes: for example,

```
{'title': {'optional': 1},
 'meta_type': {'optional': 1},
 'id': {'optional': 1},
 'summary': {'optional': 1},
 'bobobase_modification_time': {'optional': 1}}
```

_searchable_result_columns(self)

This method, which can be used only in Python, creates a list of dictionaries. The dictionaries describe the columns on the results page—for example

```
[{'name': 'title', 'type': 's', 'parser': , 'width': 8},
 {'name': 'id', 'type': 's', 'parser': , 'width': 8},
 {'name': 'summary', 'type': 's', 'parser': , 'width': 8},
 {'name': 'meta_type', 'type': 's', 'parser': , 'width': 8},
 {'name': 'bobobase_modification_time', 'type': 's', 'parser': ,
  'width': 8},
 {'name': 'data_record_id_', 'type': 's', 'parser': ,
  'width': 8}]
```

The values of the key parser are only visible in the Source Code screen of a HTML page and can be as follows, for example:

```
<built-in function str>
```

searchResults(self, REQUEST=None, used=None, query_map= { type(regex.compile("")): Query.Regex, type([]): orify, type(()): orify, type(""): Query.String, }, **kw)

This method can be called without a transfer argument. It creates a list of all cataloged objects in the relevant ZCatalog. You can go through this list and make the objects visible by displaying their IDs, as shown here:

```
<dtml-in "searchResults()">
<a href="<dtml-var
      "getpath(data_record_id_)" url_quote>">
<dtml-var id></a><br>
</dtml-in>
```

To access individual objects using this list, use the method getpath(). The record ID of the current object is passed to this method.

If you do not want to see the third view of an object when you click the link, expand the link in the in-loop with /manage_workspace, as follows:

```
<a href="
<dtml-var "getpath(data_record_id_)" url_quote>
/manage_workspace">
```

all_meta_types(self)

This method lists all metatypes, all entries from the Available Objects menu, in the form of a tuple. The individual tuple entries are dictionaries with the following form:

```
{'permission': 'Add External Methods',
'name': 'External Method',
'product': 'ExternalMethod',
'action': 'manage_addProduct/ExternalMethod/methodAdd'}
```

valid_roles(self)

This method returns all valid roles contained in the ZCatalog and the opposite folders.

E

GLOSSARY

.dtml File A .dtml file is a file in a Zope product created as a DTML method or document when a product instance is created.

_-Variable See *Underscore Variable.*

Acquisition Acquisition is the Zope mechanism by which object properties are inherited, thus creating the Zope object hierarchy.

Anonymous Anonymous is a standard role in Zope, initially assigned to all users until they log in with a username and password.

Authenticated User An Authenticated User is one who is currently logged into the system. If no user is currently logged in, 'Anonymous' users are considered the Authenticated User.

Authentication Authentication is the process by which Zope identifies its users. See *Login.*

Available-Objects menu The Available-Objects menu indicates which objects can be created at the current location in Zope. To create an object, select the metatype for the object from the 'Available Objects' menu.

Base Class/Top Class A base or top class is a class which passes its properties and methods to its subclass, which then "inherits" those properties and methods.

Case Sensitivity Python is "case sensitive" which means that it differentiates between upper and lowercase letters.

Class A class is the scheme by which objects are derived. The methods and attributes of the derived objects are implemented in a class.

Constructor Method A class's constructor method is used to allow certain actions to be carried out as soon as class instance is created. One example of such an action would be setting standard attributes.

Container Tag A Container tag is a non-empty tag containing a start and an end tag. Its two body tags contain additional source code.

Debugging Debugging describes the process of searching for errors in program code.

DTML Tag As with HTML tags, DTML tags represent instructions or commands. You can only use DTML commands in DTML tags; HTML tags will not be understood.

External Method An external method is a Zope object which links Zope and a Python module in the file system.

First View The first view displays the source code which Zope implements.

Folderish Object A folderish object is a Zope object which can contain other objects. Folderish objects include folders or ZCatalogs.

Globbing Globbing is a ZCatalog option. When you create a ZCatalog with globbing, you can search it using wildcards, like an asterisk (*). You can also perform partial word searches.

Header Line Form The Header lines form, which only exists for the sendmail tag, is an alternative to providing a DTML tag with attributes and values.

Instance Another name for an object.

Local Role All Zope users can be assigned one or more local roles for an object, which determine the user's permissions with regard to that object. Set local roles to restrict or expand a user's permissions relative to the object.

Login Users enter usernames and passwords in the login screen to log on and identify themselves to Zope.

Management Screen The Management Screen's interface lets you work with the objects in a Zope server. See also *Second View*.

Manager Manager is a standard role in Zope, which initially has all permissions except for 'Take Ownership'.

Meta-Type A product's meta-type appears in the Available Objects menu in the Zope Management screen. Product instances are created using this meta-type.

Namespace   The namespace contains the names of all valid variables for an object. This means that a defined variable can be referred to there and its value then determined.

Non-folderish Object A non-folderish object is a Zope object which cannot contain other objects. Non-folderish objects include DTML methods, DTML documents, and files.

Object   An object is derived from a class and has methods and attributes. All objects in a class have the same methods.

Owner   Owner is a standard role in Zope, which by default has the 'Take Ownership' permission.

Ownership   Each Zope object has an "Owner" except for objects created when you install Zope. The user who creates a Zope object is automatically that object's owner.

Permissions   Permissions or rights specify which actions a user can carry out in Zope. Permissions can only be assigned to roles, and cannot be assigned directly to users.

Product Directory   The Product directory is a subdirectory of /lib/python/ Products/ that contains all files needed for a particular product.

Properties   Properties are an object's characteristics or attributes.

Python   Python is a programming language. Zope is mostly written in Python.

Reserved Words   Reserved words are words which cannot be used as names for objects because they are already used in Python or Zope.

Second View   The second view incorporates the entire Management screen. When you are working in the Management screen, you are working in the 'second view'.

Subclass   Subclasses "inherit" and expand on the properties of their base class. Instances of different subclasses have the same basic properties because they inherit them from the same base class.

Tab Bar   The tab bar, at the top right of the frame on the the Zope Management screen, is used to access an object's individual views.

Third View   When you are viewing a Zope object with a web browser, you are in the 'third view'.

Tuple   A tuple is a list of elements whose sequence cannot be changed. For example, `'hello'`, `'you'` is a two-tuple with strings.

Underscore Variable   The underscore variable accepts a wide range of useful attributes which allow you to perform, among other things, mathematical calculations and string manipulations. Most importantly, you can use these variables to refer to objects in expr- expressions whose names do not comply with Python syntax.

User Folder Individual users are created and managed in Zope's User Folder (acl_users).

Use A User is someone who uses Zope and who has a username, password, domain and role(s).

Versions See *Zope Versions.*

Vocabulary A Vocabulary contains words in the cataloged objects of a ZCatalog, which can be stored and searched.

ZClasses Use ZClasses to quickly create your own Zope products without a lot of programming.

Zope Products Zope Products are distributions programmed in Python which can be installed on a Zope server. When a product is installed, objects can be created on the Zope server with the functionality implemented in the product.

Zope Versions Zope Versions allow you to work on different versions of a project without affecting a functioning version of that product during the development process.

INDEX

email messages, sending with Zope,
93–*95*, 131
    customer orders, 202
    permissions needed for, 137, 140,
    141
emergency user, 112
empty DTML tags, 65
empty lists, 122
end tag, 65, 66
equal-sign assignment (=) operator,
    258
error messages. *See also* permissions
    bypassing, 99
    deliberately causing, 100
    during login, 154, *155*
    method used to display Zope, 37
    with misleading information, 314
    resulting from variable data,
    310–312
    specific DTML, 312, 314
    specific Python, 312, *313,* 315
    specific Zope, *315*–321
    Unauthorized user, 114, *155*
    when calling a Python method,
    259
    when creating User folders, 279
    when deleting a version, 106
    when specifying names, 80
    when starting the Zope server,
    309–310
    when viewing DTML methods,
    184
errors
    authentication bug in Internet
    Explorer 5.0+, 18
    finding the source of, 310–312
    intermittent, 312
    runtime, 311
etc attribute, 69
except tag, 99
expr attribute, 68

abbreviating, 67
Extensions directory, 270
external method objects, 273–274
    permission to add, 136–137
external methods
    creating, 270–271, 272–274
    debugging, 311
    definition of, 250
    permission to change, 139
    using, to change roles and
    permissions, 274–280

F

Field index, 213
    queries, 222–224
file extensions
    .dtml, 282
    .py, 137, 270
    .zexp, 49
file objects, 97
files. *See also* DTML files
    associating with proper
    applications, 97
    creating, 25–27
    linking to, with DTML, 29–30
    permission to change, 139
    saving Microsoft Office 2000, 328
    sending, as email attachments,
    96–98
File Transfer Protocol (FTP),
    323–326
finally tag, 100
Find, advanced search feature, 48
Find Objects screen, 208–210, *211*
Find tab, 46–48
first tier of Zope, 61
Floating Point Numbers, 251–252
    operators for, *257*
float (property type), 44, 170, 173

HTML files, linking to, with DTML, 29–30

html_quote attribute, 69

http request and response, 75

I

icons, creating custom, 165

identification numbers (OID), 160

if tag, 66, 79–81

image archive, creating, 24–25

image files, permission to change, 139

image objects

    changing the size of, 27

    creating, 25–27

    displaying inside instances, 199

imported objects, ownership of, 118

Import/Export button, 48, 140

Import/Export objects, 140

Import/Export screen, *49*

Import/Export tab, 48–50

import statement in Python code, 267

indexed objects

    displaying all, in the ZCatalog, 217

    indexing and searching for, 205

    location of, 207

    modifying, 208

indexes, types of ZCatalog, 212–213

Indexes screen, 212–213

index_html, 24, 37

    creating, for e-commerce site, 197–199

    sample code for, 151

    two views of, 151–*152*

indicators, 63

indirection, 71–72

inheritance, 260

example of, 292

init(), 259

Initialize(), 306–307

InitializeClass(), 296, 299

init.py, 305–308

in loops, 189, 199

insert(), 227, 253

installation of Zope, 8–16

instance methods for classes, 295–296

instances, 159. *See also* ZClass objects

    creating, constructor method for, 300–*305*

    creating, with Python, 249, 261–262

    creating custom icons for, 165

    creating folderish, 168

    displaying images within, 199

    of products, 283

    property sheets, 167

    types of objects contained in, 167–168

in tag, 86–89

Integer Values, 251

    operators for, *257*

Internet, client-server

    communication over, 75–*78*

Internet Explorer

    authentication bug in versions 5.0+, 18

    FTP clients, 325, 327

int (property type), 44, 170

IP addresses, assigning on Linux systems, 14

J

Join/Leave screen, 104, 105

Join/Leave Versions (permission), 140

K

L

M

Manage Vocabulary (permission), 140

Manage ZCatalog Entries (permission), 140

Math module, 72

messages with date variables, 72

Metadata screen, 210–212

meta_type attribute
    of objects, 92
    of products and classes, 293, 307

meta types
    definition of, 163
    specifying only one, 189

method marshaling, 238

methods, 22. *See also* DTML methods; external methods; functions; Z SQL methods
    instance, 295–296
    private, 272, 295
    Python, 259–262
    views, *175*
    ZCatalog brain, *221*

Methods tab, 165

Microsoft Internet Explorer. *See* Internet Explorer

Microsoft Office 2000 files, saving to Zope, 328

middleware, Zope as, 6–7

MIME tag, 96–98

missing attribute, 69

moveObject(), 272

mput (Linux command), 325

multiple selection (property type), 45, 171, 172–173, *174*

MySQL, using with Zope, 231–236

MySQL monitor, 231
    bypassing, when submitting queries, 236

N

name attribute, 65, 68
    abbreviating, 67

names, 63–64
    rules for creating, 68
    that are stored as variable data, 71–72
    that do not begin with a letter, 71

namespaces, 36. *See also* with tag
    DTML, 63–64
    errors, 80

namespace stack, 64, *65*
    avoiding searches of, 76
    importance of, 199

namespace variable, 71–*75*, 266

navigation in Zope
    in left frame of management screen, 20
    returning to Edit screen, 41
    through search results, 218

newProduct, 51

Next (link), 218, 219

none (data type), 255

non-empty DTML tags, 65

non-folderish objects
    permissions for, 132–134
    place in acquisition chain, 116

null attribute, 69

numbers
    beginning with zero, 251
    generating random, *74*

numeric information, formatting, 70–*71*

numeric types supported by Python, 251–252

numeric values in DTML code, 76

O

Z

ZCatalog. *See also* vocabularies; Z
Search Interface
brain methods, 221
creating, 205–206
indexes, *222*
index types, 212–213
metadata, 210–212, 220
permissions for, 139, 140
queries, 219–225
query limitations, 225
screens, 206–214
using with Z SQL methods, 214
ZCatalog:CatalogAware, 168
ZClasses. See also instances
adding, to a product, 162–164
assigning help topics to views,
177
changing the information for,
165–168
creating, 160
creating objects with, 184–185
uses for, 157–158
ZClasses:ObjectManager, 168
ZClass objects
editing, 186–197
id field, 169
interface for working with,
187–190
title field, 169, 171
ZDebug, 314
zero, numbers beginning with, 251
.zexp file extension, 49
Z Gadfly Database Connections,
permission for, 138
Z MySQL connection, establishing,
234–235
ZMySQLDA, 234

Zope. *See also* welcome screen; Zope
server
as a content management server,
7–8
full name of, 3
hardware requirements, 8
history of, 2–3
as an independent webserver, 12
installation, 8–16
log-in window, *13*
platforms it runs on, 8
tiers, 61–62
versions covered by this book,
1–2
DTML syntax from 1.x, 66
installing, earlier than 2.2.0,
12
Undo screen before and after
2.2.0, 135
virtual hosting in 2.3 and later,
138
ZopeTutorial since 2.2.0, 139
Versions feature, 103–110
web application programming
with, 5–6
as a web application server, 6–7
where to get, 8
Zope, The Book of, website with
updates to, 2
Zope Corporation web support, 18
Zope Help, 51
Zope Management System (ZMS),
328–332
Zope Object Database (ZODB), 53,
54. *See also* Gadfly
pros and cons of using, 229–230
Zope objects. *See* objects
Zope products. *See* products
Zope Public License (ZPL), 8
Zope Python scripts, 263–269

Does this look familiar?

Zope Error

Zope has encountered an error while publishing this resource.

Error Type: **Insufficient Training**
Error Value: **Time**

Troubleshooting Suggestions

Is your Zope knowledge limited?
Is your time limited?
Are your financial resources limited?

Training information to solve your Zope challenge(s) is available from **beehive**.
beehive is the only recognized Zope training provider in both Europe and North America.

beehive provides Zope training courses at regular intervals for businesses,
individuals and groups of all sizes.

Detailed course overviews and registration forms can be found at:
    `http://www.beehive.de/zope/training/index.html`.

beehive would be happy to help you solve your Zope challenge(s).

THE LINUX COOKBOOK

Tips & Techniques for Everyday Use

by MICHAEL STUTZ

The Linux Cookbook shows Linux users of all levels how to perform a variety of everyday computer tasks such as: editing and formatting text; working with digital audio; and creating and manipulating graphics. The quick-reference, "cookbook"-style format includes step-by-step "recipes."

2001, 400 PP., $29.95 ($44.95 CDN)
ISBN 1-886411-48-4

THE BOOK OF VMWARE

The Complete Guide to the VMware Workstation

by BRIAN WARD

This guide to VMware software, which allows users to run multiple OSs simultaneously on a single computer, was developed with VMware, Inc. and covers device emulation; guest OS configuration; networking and file transfers; and more. The CD-ROM includes a demo verson of VMware for Linux and Windows, and copies of all discussed utilities.

DECEMBER 2001, 350 PP. W/CD-ROM, $39.95 ($55.95 CDN)
ISBN 1-886411-72-7

THE BOOK OF JAVASCRIPT

A Practical Guide to Interactive Web Pages

by THAU!

Rather than offer cut-and-paste solutions, this tutorial/reference focuses on understanding JavaScript and shows web designers how to customize and implement JavaScript on their sites. The CD-ROM includes code for each example in the book, script libraries, and relevant software.

2000, 424 PP. W/CD-ROM, $29.95 ($44.95 CDN)
ISBN 1-886411-36-0

PROGRAMMING LINUX GAMES
Learn to Write the Linux Games People Play

by LOKI SOFTWARE, INC. WITH JOHN R. HALL

Programming Linux Games discusses important multimedia toolkits (including a very thorough discussion of the Simple DirectMedia Layer) and teaches the basics of game programming. Understand the state of the Linux gaming world and learn to write and distribute games to the Linux community.

2001, 432 PP., $39.95 ($59.95 CDN)

ISBN 1-886411-49-2

THE LINUX PROBLEM SOLVER
Hands-on Solutions for Systems Administrators

by BRIAN WARD

This book is a must-have for solving technical problems related to printing, networking, back-up, crash recovery, and compiling or upgrading a kernel. The CD-ROM supports the book with configuration files and numerous programs not included in many Linux distributions.

2000, 283 PP. W/CD-ROM, $34.95 ($53.95 CDN)

ISBN 1-886411-35-2

Phone:

1 (800) 420-7240 OR
(415) 863-9900
MONDAY THROUGH FRIDAY,
9 A.M. TO 5 P.M. (PST)

Fax:

(415) 863-9950
24 HOURS A DAY,
7 DAYS A WEEK

Email:

SALES@NOSTARCH.COM

Web:

HTTP://WWW.NOSTARCH.COM

Mail:

NO STARCH PRESS
555 DE HARO STREET, SUITE 250
SAN FRANCISCO, CA 94107
USA

Distributed in the U.S. by Publishers Group West

Linux Journal's team of industry experts has put together a complete line of reference materials designed for Linux operating system users, programmers, and IT professionals. Visit your local bookstore or the Linux Journal Web site for other Linux Journal Press products. You may also request a free issue of the monthly magazine, Linux Journal, online at **http://www.linuxjournal.com.**

UPDATES

The book was carefully reviewed for technical accuracy, but it's inevitable that some things will change after the book goes to press. Visit the Web site for this book at **http://www.nostarch.com/zope_updates.htm** for updates, errata, and other information.